THE PENGUIN CLASSICS

FOUNDER EDITOR (1944–64): E. V. RIEU

Editor: Betty Radice

LUCIUS ANNAEUS SENECA (*c.* 4 B.C.–A.D. 65) was born in
Corduba, Spain, the second son of Annaeus Seneca the elder.
His father had a great respect for the traditional virtues of
republican Roman life, and brought his three sons up accord-
ingly. As a young adult, Seneca studied intensively the Stoic
and Pythagorean philosophies and resided in Egypt for a
period because of ill health. By A.D. 33 he was married to his
first wife, had held the office of quaestor, and was achieving
success as an advocate and teacher of rhetoric; he was also
attracting attention by his incisive style of writing. He was
forced to retire into private life at one point because of the
suspicions of the emperor Caligula. He returned on the accession of Claudius, but was exiled in A.D. 41 to Corsica, accused
of adultery with Claudius' niece. He wrote several works
during the eight years in Corsica, including *De Ira*. He was
recalled to Rome in A.D. 48 to act as tutor to the future emperor Nero, and became his principal civil adviser when he
took power. The first five years of the reign were peaceful
and moderate, for which much credit must be given to Seneca.
However the feud between the emperor and his mother,
Agrippina, weakened his position and he asked to retire in
A.D.62. Nero and Seneca parted on seemingly amicable terms,
but the various political conspiracies which followed implicated Seneca, though probably on very flimsy evidence, so
that his death was ordered in A.D. 65. Seneca anticipated the
emperor's decree by committing suicide after several painful attempts; his second wife, Paulina, who tried to share her
husband's fate, survived him by a few years.

E. F. WATLING was educated at Christ's Hospital and University College, Oxford. His translations of Greek and Roman
plays for the Penguin Classics include the seven plays of
Sophocles, nine plays of Plautus, and this selection of the
tragedies of Seneca.

SENECA

THYESTES
PHAEDRA
THE TROJAN WOMEN
OEDIPUS
WITH
OCTAVIA

TRANSLATED
WITH AN INTRODUCTION
BY E. F. WATLING

PENGUIN BOOKS

Penguin Books Ltd, Harmondsworth, Middlesex, England
Penguin Books, 40 West 23rd Street, New York, New York 10010, U.S.A.
Penguin Books Australia Ltd, Ringwood, Victoria, Australia
Penguin Books Canada Ltd, 2801 John Street, Markham, Ontario, Canada L3R 1B4
Penguin Books (N.Z.) Ltd, 182–190 Wairau Road, Auckland 10, New Zealand

—

First published 1966
Reprinted 1970, 1972, 1974, 1976, 1978, 1980, 1982, 1984

—

—

Made and printed in Great Britain
by Richard Clay (The Chaucer Press) Ltd,
Bungay, Suffolk
Set in Monotype Bembo

CONTENTS

INTRODUCTION

FOR want of convincing evidence to the contrary, scholars have on the whole accepted the tradition that the dramatic works ascribed to SENECA were written by the same Lucius Annaeus Seneca (c. 4 B.C.–A.D. 65) who was the author of a large collection of philosophical essays and letters, and whose life, more particularly the later part of it, as a minister closely and at last fatally involved in the turbulent affairs of the reign of Nero, is known in some detail from the pages of Tacitus and Suetonius. Dissent from this identification is prompted not so much by any ascertainable facts as by the sense which all readers feel of an astonishing incongruity between the humanity and dignity of the prose works and the bombastic extravagance, the passionate yet artificial rhetoric, of the tragedies. And not less has been noticed, and frequently commented on, the discordance between the high moral principles professed by the philosopher and the cynical time-serving behaviour of the emperor's adviser. A trace of the disgust which this paradox could arouse even in the seventeenth century, when Seneca's reputation in England stood higher than at any other time, appears in a line spoken by a character in Marston's play *The Malcontent*, who replies to the mention of Seneca's name: 'Out upon him! He writ of temperance and fortitude, yet lived like a voluptuous epicure, and died like an effeminate coward' – not an entirely true statement but a typical plain man's summary judgement of an enigmatical personality.

The extant prose works[1] include treatises on philosophical

1. See Appendix II for some translated extracts, chosen mainly for comparison with passages in the plays.

subjects, personal addresses of consolation or advice to friends and relatives, and works on natural science, and are concluded by a series of letters to one friend, Lucilius, written in a few last years of precarious and disillusioned retirement. It is these letters, with their flashes of humorous self-revelation, their tolerance of human weakness though not of human viciousness, their zealous inquiry into all departments of thought and action, that have most retained the affection of modern readers and secured some sympathy for the ageing philosopher defeated by worldly wickedness. In the earlier works, prolixity and repetition even of the most unexceptionable sentiments can cloy the appetite and dull the effect of the occasional passages of true eloquence and epigrammatic brilliance. The Roman critic Quintilian[1] pronounced the verdict from which few readers would dissent: 'There is in Seneca much with which one can agree, much even to admire; but his work requires selection; one could wish that he had done the selecting himself.' Of the tragedies, with which we are here primarily concerned, the literary fate has been a peculiar one. Their reputation in the author's own lifetime, or immediately afterwards, can only be guessed, in the absence of any evidence of their actually having been performed; but at least their preservation is a reasonable ground for assuming them to have commanded some respect. Among scholars of the last two centuries, few have done anything but condemn the Senecan tragedies as horrible examples of literary and dramatic incompetence, travesties of the noble Greek drama, the last wretched remnants of declining Roman taste. The following extract from Schlegel's lectures on drama (published in English in 1815) is representative of the view which all but excluded Seneca the tragedian from the serious consideration of classical students:

1. *Inst. Or.*, x. 1. 125.

The state of constant outrage in which Rome was kept by a series of blood-thirsty tyrants led to similar outrages upon nature in rhetoric and poetry ... [the Senecan tragedies] are beyond all description bombastic and frigid, utterly devoid of nature in character and action, full of the most revolting violations of propriety, and so barren of all theatrical effect, that I verily believe they were never meant to leave the schools of the rhetoricians for the stage. With the old Tragedies, those highest of the creations of Grecian poetical genius, these have nothing in common but the name, the exterior form, and the mythological matter: and yet they set themselves up beside them in the evident intention of surpassing them, in which attempt they come off like a hollow hyperbole contrasted with a most heartfelt truth. Every commonplace of tragedy is worried out to the last gasp; all is phrase, among which even the simplest is forced and stilted. An utter poverty of mind is tricked out with wit and acuteness. ... Their persons are neither ideal nor real men, but misshapen giants of puppets; and the wire that sets them a-going is at one time an unnatural heroism, at another a passion alike unnatural, which no atrocity of guilt can appal.

By this and similar pronouncements the modern student will easily have been brought to the conclusion that to read the Senecan tragedies in the original language is an unrewarding task, and to read them in translation, *a fortiori*, a waste of time! They are, of all the Latin 'classics' from Plautus to Pliny, probably the least familiar to the averagely well-informed student. Yet between the Seneca of the Roman Empire and the Seneca of today stands the Seneca of the Renaissance, a sage admired and venerated as an oracle of moral, even of Christian, edification; a master of literary style and a model of the purest principles of dramatic art. The well-known dictum of Francis Meres in his *Palladis Tamia* (1598) is a typical compliment to both the Roman and the English master-dramatist: 'As Plautus and Seneca are accounted the best for Comedy and Tragedy among the Latins, so Shakespeare among the English is the most excellent in both kinds for the stage.' (The writer was not troubled by the fact that there was no other known Roman tragedian for comparison with Seneca, and only one rival to Plautus.) The prestige of Seneca, in the moral sphere at least, was owed primarily to his prose writings, and especially to those passages[1] in which he expressed his ideas about religion, worship, and man's attitude to the gods (or often 'god') in terms acceptable to Christian minds.[2] But the tragedies, too, were valued for their moral lessons, and were put forward by their Elizabethan translators as works calculated to edify their readers or audiences:

And whereas it is by some squeymish Areopagites surmyzed, that the readinge of these Tragedies, being enterlarded with many Phrases and sentences literally tending (at first sight) sometime to the prayse of Ambition, sometime to the mayntenaunce of cruelty, now and then to the ratification of tyranny, cannot be digested without great daunger of infection; to omit all other reasons, if it might please them with no forestalled judgment, to mark and consider the circumstaunces, why, where, and by what manner of persons such sentences are pronounced, they cannot in any equity otherwise choose but find good cause ynough to leade them to a more favourable and milde resolution. For it may not at any hand be thought and deemed the direct meaning of Seneca himselfe, whose whole wrytinges (penned with a peerless sublimity and loftiness of style) are so farre from countenancing vice, that I doubt whether there bee any amonge all the Catalogue of Heathen wryters, that with more gravity of Philosophicall sentences, more waightyness of sappy words, or greater authority of sound matter beateth down sinne, loose lyfe, dissolute dealinge, and unbrydled sensuality: or that more sensibly, pithily, and

1. Cf. Appendix II, 8.
2. The legend of Seneca's acquaintance and correspondence with St Paul, and the possibility of his having been directly influenced by Christian teaching, are discussed in C. T. Crutwell's *A History of Roman Literature* (Griffin, 1877).

bytingly layeth downe the guedon of filthy lust, cloaked dissimu-
lation, and odious treachery: which is the dryft, whereunto he
leveleth the whole yssue of ech one of his Tragedies.[1]

... the most lamentable Tragedy of that most Infortunate
Prince Oedipus, for thy profit rudely translated. Wonder not at
the grossenesse of the Style ... mark thou rather what is ment by
the whole course of the History: and frame thy lyfe free from such
mischiefes, wherewith the world at this present is universally over-
whelmed, the wrathfull vengeaunce of God provoked, the Body
plagued, the mynde and Conscience in midst of deepe devouring
daungers most terribly assaulted, in such sorte that I abhorre to
write: and even at the thought thereof I tremble and quake for
very inward griefe and feare of minde: assuredly perswading
myselfe that the right high and immortall God will never leave
such horrible and detestable crimes unpunished. . . . For the which
cause, so much the rather have I suffered this my base translated
Tragoedy to be published. . . . Mine only entent was to exhorte
men to embrace Vertue and shun Vyce, according to that of the
right famous and excellent Poet Virgil: *discite justiciam moniti, et
non temnere divos.*[2]

The enthronement of Seneca in one particular century of
European, and especially of English, culture is a phenom-
enon as remarkable as the chance which brought the
humane philosopher himself to a position of dangerous
eminence at the right hand of Rome's most notorious
tyrant.

*

Annaeus Seneca the elder was a native of Corduba in
Spain, born about 54 B.C. His long life of some ninety years
was devoted to the study and profession of rhetoric, and
for this purpose he must have spent some time in residence

1. From Newton's Preface to his edition of *The Tenne Tragedies*,
1581.
2. From Neville's Preface to his translation of *Oedipus*, 1563.

at Rome, whence he took back to his native town a profound knowledge of his subject and a respect for the traditional virtues of republican Roman family life. *Antiqua et severa* are the words used by his son Lucius Annaeus, our tragedian, of the home into which he was born, about 4 B.C.; and he would no doubt have applied the same epithets to his father, who would be in his sixties by the time the boy was old enough to take notice of personal characteristics. The elder Seneca's extant works, known as *Controversiae* and *Suasoriae*, were written for the instruction of his sons and consist of models and exercises in rhetoric – the art which was firmly established in ancient Rome as the indispensable basis of humane education and respectable advancement in public life: the exact equivalent of a classical education in imperial England. From such an upbringing the three sons of Seneca (of whom Lucius Annaeus was the second) proceeded to various degrees of public eminence, and to their deaths all in the same year of terror A.D. 65. The eldest, Annaeus Novatus, had become proconsul of Achaia; he had previously been adopted by, and taken the name of, Junius Gallio, and under this name he is known to history as having preserved an aloof indifference to a petty religious squabble in Athens.[1] The youngest son Annaeus Mela prospered mainly in financial affairs, and was the father of the poet Lucan. Both these brothers were denounced as traitors, and committed suicide, in the purge which followed the anti-Neronian conspiracy of Piso and which ended the life of L. Annaeus Seneca.

The adult education of the young Seneca began with intensive study of the Stoic and Pythagorean philosophies;[2] an early enthusiasm for the vegetarian system of Pythagoras lasted for a while, until his father pointed out the dangers

1. Acts, XVIII. 12 ff.
2. Cf. Appendix II, 3.

of becoming known as a 'crank', especially when such eccentricities were popularly associated with religious heresies of various kinds. His early years also included a period of ill-health (probably tuberculosis) and of residence in Egypt, where his aunt was the wife of the Prefect. By A.D. 33 he was married to his first wife (whose name is not known), had held the office of quaestor, and was achieving success in his profession of advocate and teacher of rhetoric and attracting attention by his incisive style of writing. He attracted also the jealous suspicions of the emperor Caligula, whose threats he was forced to evade by temporary retirement into private life. On the accession of Claudius he was able to return to his career, but a second setback occurred when in A.D. 41 he was accused, at the instigation of the emperor's diabolical wife Messalina, of adultery with Julia the daughter of Germanicus, and was exiled to Corsica, where he spent eight years. He was by now the father of a son and daughter; a second son died on the eve of his exile, and his wife was dead before his return.

Out of the lonely meditations of these eight years came two of the three works known as 'Consolations'. One had already been written 'To Marcia', a bereaved mother,[1] a second was addressed to Polybius, the powerful freedman of Claudius, and combined 'consolation' on the death of a brother with advice on public administration and servile flattery of the emperor and his entourage. The third, to his mother Helvia, on the subject of his own exile, is one of his most sincere and likeable compositions.[2] He was probably also engaged at this time on the treatise *De Ira* (published about A.D. 49), a brilliant and eloquent plea for the stoical control of the baser emotions, and perhaps on some of his work on natural phenomena, which was to appear near

1. Cf. Appendix II, 1.
2. Cf. Appendix II, 2.

the end of his life. It is not unlikely that his experiments in
the composition of tragedy began in this period of unlimited leisure.

In A.D. 48 Messalina was executed for her illegal and
treasonable marriage to Gaius Silius, and the emperor
married Agrippina. The abilities of Seneca had not been
forgotten at Rome during his exile; by Agrippina's influence he was now recalled to be tutor to her twelve-year-old
son Lucius Domitius, the future emperor Nero. He was
also appointed to the office of praetor. By the time Nero
was eighteen years old, his advancement to the position of
heir-apparent had been secured by his adoption into the
Claudian family and his marriage to Octavia, daughter of
Claudius; it only remained for Agrippina to remove her
husband, which she did, by poison, in A.D. 54. From that
date Seneca became the emperor's principal civil adviser,
in association with Burrus who commanded the praetorian
guard. The first five years of the new reign surprised every-
one, and became proverbial among historians as a period
of wise and moderate government; for which credit must
certainly be given to Seneca's ability to combine firmness
and high principle with tactful indulgence in his direction
of the young emperor's tastes and ambitions – an influence
extending, one would imagine, more widely than is grudg-
ingly allowed by Tacitus:[1] 'Burrus's influence lay in
soldierly efficiency and seriousness of character, Seneca's in
amiable high principles and his tuition of Nero in public
speaking.' It is clear, however, that it was from Seneca that
Nero learnt, not only how to speak, but what to say: 'Nero
pledged himself to clemency in numerous speeches; Seneca
put them into his mouth, to display his own talent or
demonstrate his high-minded guidance.' It is uncertain

1. *Annals*, XIII. 2. Grant's translation (Penguin Classics), here and
in other quotations.

whether among Seneca's literary compositions should be included the ribald satire *The Pumpkinification of the Late Claudius*, a farcical fantasy on the reception of the departed emperor into everlasting life. But it is recorded that he wrote for Nero a tongue-in-cheek panegyric on Claudius, the recitation of which reduced the audience to helpless laughter.[1] More to his credit are the works *De Vita Beata* and *De Beneficiis*, and, despite its tendency to offer flattery in the guise of instruction, the *De Clementia* addressed to his royal pupil.

But it was not long before a growing feud between Agrippina and her son disturbed the security of Seneca's position; and the part played by him in Nero's atrocious matricide appears, at the best, ambiguous; he certainly failed, or had no desire, to curb the emperor's violence, and he provided him with the letter of justification which was sent to the senate.[2] There is reason to believe that he condoned, and possibly profited by, many of Nero's attacks on his enemies; and in return his own acquisition of enormous wealth brought him into disrepute. A senator prosecuted for extortion and embezzlement while governor of Asia retorted: 'What branch of learning, what philosophical school, won Seneca three hundred million sesterces during four years of imperial friendship? In Rome, he entices into his snares the childless and their legacies. His huge rates of interest suck Italy and the provinces dry.'[3] With the death of Burrus in A.D. 62, his position became still more precarious, and he himself chose this moment to ask for retirement. In a dignified interview he thanked Nero for his kindness over fourteen years, and offered to surrender all his superfluous property. Nero replied that the

1. Tacitus, *Annals*, XIII. 3.
2. ibid, XIV.3–8.
3. ibid, XIII. 42.

obligations were all on his side – adding, ambiguously, 'Your gifts to me will endure as long as life itself; my gifts to you, gardens and mansions and revenues, are liable to circumstances' – and they parted with ceremonies of mutual affection.[1] Before the year was out – the year of the events concentrated into the tragedy *Octavia* – Nero had removed Burrus's successor, Rufus, retaining the reliable services of his colleague Tigellinus, and had discarded his wife Octavia for his new love Poppaea. At the same time Seneca had been denounced for association with the anti-Neronian conspiracy led by Piso, for in fact Seneca's name had been put forward as a possible successor to the throne. His nominal withdrawal into private life and into the resumption of his literary pursuits could not save him from the consequences of his public career; Nero was not likely to leave for long at large a potential opponent so well acquainted with his own dark secrets. In A.D. 65 (the year after the fire of Rome) the Pisonian conspiracy came to a head, and Seneca was implicated, on the slender evidence of a letter expressing friendly compliments to Piso. His death was ordered, and Seneca made preparations to meet it in the manner which he had often contemplated, and advocated in his letters, as the only one befitting a man of dignity.[2] After painful attempts to end his life by incision of the veins, he had recourse to poison, which still failed to have the desired effect; finally, a hot bath hastened the loss of blood, and a steam bath brought his life to an end by suffocation. His wife Paulina attempted to share his fate, but on Nero's orders her suicide was arrested and she survived her husband by a few years.

Of the earliest assessments of Seneca's character, that of Dio Cassius is perhaps the most uncompromising, which

1. Tacitus, *Annals*, XIV. 53–6.
2. Cf. Appendix II, 9.

describes him as totally unscrupulous and inconsistent, preaching liberty and encouraging a tyrant; condemning flattery and courtship, enjoying luxury and contributing to flattery of the court; and sexually libertine. A modern critic has a more charitable view:[1]

> Seneca, with his high brain-power and the low vitality of prolonged ill-health, with his clever, subtle mind and his lack of solid commonsense, with his amiable but not passionate temperament, is perhaps after all not so hard to understand. He desired more than most to do the right things; but he hated more than most the unpleasant things, especially unpleasantness with other people. In a perfectly desperate position, with only one path before him, he could tread it finely; but it was a desperate position indeed when that agile brain could not find a way round and justify to itself the same. Less clever he would have proved a great deal more edifying.

*

The tragedy of violence and intrigue in the real life about them, as well as in the organized spectacles of butchery in the amphitheatres (against which Seneca made his protest), seems to have blunted the taste of the Roman people for tragedy as a dramatic art. It is generally agreed that the tragedies of Seneca were intended for reading or recital at private gatherings and could never have appeared in what we should call public performance; partly because in many of their scenes the implied condemnation of autocracy would have had too dangerous a topical application; and partly because there were, so far as we know, no public opportunities for such performances. What we do know of the nearest approach to tragic acting in Nero's time suggests something between ballet and opera, with the emphasis on the individual virtuoso's art of evoking, in song and mime,

1. F. L. Lucas, *Seneca and Elizabethan Tragedy*, Cambridge, 1922.

the passions and torments of a Hercules or an Oedipus –
an art of which Nero fancied himself both as connoisseur
and exponent. Of what passed for dramatic performance
some glimpse can be gathered from scattered references
such as this from Suetonius:[1]

> He gave an immense variety of entertainments – coming-of-
> age parties, chariot races in the Circus, stage plays. . . . At the
> Great Festival, as he called the series of plays devoted to the hope
> of his reigning for ever, parts were taken by men and women
> of both Orders; and one well-known knight rode an elephant
> down a sloping tight-rope. When he staged 'The Fire', a Roman
> play by Afranius, the actors were allowed to keep the valuable
> furnishings they rescued from the burning house. . . . In the
> 'Daedalus and Icarus' ballet, the actor who played Icarus, while
> attempting his first flight, fell beside Nero's couch and spattered
> him with blood. . . .

A generally lively programme, with amateur enthusiasm
contributing, and plenty of realistic, preferably dangerous,
and often unseemly, action. Even a hundred years earlier
Cicero, at the festival celebrating the opening of Rome's
first permanent theatre, complained[2] of the pathetic performances of old-fashioned actors past their prime, and of
the spectacular ostentation which had been imposed upon
the old tragedies: 'Who wants to see six hundred mules
in *Clytaemnestra* or three hundred goblets in *The Trojan
Horse*, or a battle between fully equipped armies of horse
and foot?' A rhetorical exaggeration, no doubt, but an
indication of the way things were going. Even so, a tradition persisted for the composition of tragedy on the Greek
pattern, and if such works made little impression on public
audiences they were regarded as worthy employment for
the pens of erudite authors or even of men of business in

1. Suetonius, *Nero*, 11. Graves's translation (Penguin Classics).
2. *Ep.* VII. 1. *Ad M. Marium*, 55 B.C.

their spare time. Knowing little or nothing of the public fate of most of these works, we do at least know that Cicero himself, and his brother Quintus, wrote tragedies; Julius Caesar wrote one, *Oedipus*; Ovid's *Medea* was esteemed as highly as any of the varied works for which he has become known to posterity; and there is record of a performance of a tragedy *Thyestes*, by L. Varius Rufus, at the festival in celebration of the victory of Actium. To have a play performed, for some special occasion, was an accident that none of such authors counted on, or particularly desired – if they were of the same mind as Ovid, who writes from exile:[1] 'You tell me that my poetry is being performed to full houses and winning much applause; as far as I am concerned, I never wrote with the theatre in mind, as you very well know, and my Muse was always indifferent to applause.'

Nor did Seneca, we may be quite sure, have anything like public performance in mind when he wrote his adaptations of Greek tragedies. To appreciate the purpose and achievement of this rather curious branch of Latin literature, so far as we can from the isolated group of specimens available to us, we must first remember that Roman drama, such as it was, grew up in social and artistic conditions far different from those which produced the drama of Athens. The practical, busy cosmopolitanism of the rising republic took kindly to the comic legacy of the declining Greek theatre, but, though tragedies were translated and imitated from the same period onwards, the diffuse Roman society and the increasingly sophisticated Roman mind could never recapture the singleness of spirit which in a Greek city-state found expression in the ritual of tragedy. In its comparatively short season of flowering, Greek tragedy itself had moved from the religious intensity of Aeschylus,

1. *Tristia*, v. 7.

through the more humane art of Sophocles, to the sceptical rationalism of Euripides; and it was here that Roman tragedy began, where the Greek left off. In Euripides the Romans found their example of drama used as a medium for the exercise of the human voice and brain in debate, in the opposition of conflicting interpretations of the mysteries of life, and the art of picturesque and exciting narrative. They found also examples of the creation of types of character corresponding to human experience, the autocrat and his obedient or recalcitrant minister, the poor at the mercy of the rich, the woman rebellious against the mastery of man or pitifully bruised and bereaved by the cruelties of man's world; and they found those useful adjuncts to drama, the ghost arising to threaten or foretell calamity, and the confidant, usually known as 'Nurse', to console or advise the distraught heroine. The Roman devotion to rhetoric found a stimulating example in Euripides; his lines were quotable, and his *sententiae* appealed to the Roman artist in verbal dexterity. Consequently, although Seneca, and presumably others unknown to us, took the subjects of their tragedies widely from the whole field of Greek drama, their adaptations reflect the manner of Euripides more nearly than that of Aeschylus or Sophocles. At the same time, the form of drama was changing; the synthesis of dramatic dialogue and choral song in a single poetic structure was falling apart, until the function of the chorus lingered on only as a conventional ornament contributing nothing to the theme of the play. This development was accompanied by a modification of the form of the theatre itself, when the reduction of the circular *orchestra* to a semi-circle or less, together with the increasing elaboration of the architecture of the stage, transferred the emphasis from the poetic ritual of the chorus to the display of 'acting' on the stage. Some doubt must remain as to what sort of

theatre would accommodate Cicero's 'six hundred mules';
but probably the larger amphitheatres were used for a
debased form of pageant-tragedy.

With these considerations in mind, by what criteria
should we judge the value of the Senecan tragedies as
drama? The historical question as to whether they were in
fact ever 'performed' is not of great importance and in-
volves in any case only a hair's-breadth distinction of terms.
If they were ever 'recited', without the book, in dialogue
form by two or more persons, to however private an audience, and on however simple a stage, then they were 'performed' in all essential meanings of the term and in a sense
which must be perfectly intelligible to a modern playgoer
with experience of the infinitely wide range of technique,
from the most realistic to the most imaginative or 'abstract',
that the theatre can accommodate. It was only the influence
of the realistic theatre of the nineteenth century, and early
twentieth, that drove critics to the conclusion that Senecan
drama not only was never acted but never could be – and
this, oddly enough, despite the example of the equally
'unrealistic' Greek tragedies, not to mention the whole
history of English poetic drama. Thus the stagecraft of
Seneca has been dismissed as impracticable for no better
reason than that he represents persons talking in a way in
which no living person ordinarily talks, and suggests events
which could not literally take place before the eyes of an
audience (such as the sacrifice in *Oedipus*). On such grounds
Professor Beare[1] finds that 'the internal evidence . . . shows
that the author has not visualized the actions of his characters. The usual technique of bringing characters on or
taking them off is ignored' – so it is by many modern
dramatists, if by usual is meant the technique of Pinero or
Shaw – 'We often realize that a person is conceived as

1. W. Beare, *The Roman Stage*.

21

present only by the fact that a speech is put into his mouth; we cannot tell when he leaves the stage except by the fact that no more words are attributed or addressed to him' – of course, there are no stage directions,[1] but a stage-director could supply them; and this surely suggests that the author *did* visualize the presence or absence of his characters, though he may have sometimes omitted to supply clues for the reader.[2] 'A long speech,' Professor Beare continues, 'is attributed to Clytaemnestra (*Agamemnon*, 108–24), yet it appears from the remarks of the other person present[3] that Clytaemnestra has been silent; the speech must therefore represent her thoughts' (why not? 'Look how our partner's rapt!' *Macbeth*, I. 3).

It is not by such an approach that we can appreciate what Seneca was trying to do. 'Action' in the realistic sense is not the mainspring of his technique; it could be described as the illusion of action evoked by words – or, if that is no more than a definition applicable to all drama, let us call it the creation of dramatic tension by words with the

1. And there will be almost none in my translations; there are few places, in fact, where the action is not implicit in the spoken words.

2. J. C. Scaliger, *Poetics*, I. 21, as quoted in English by Malone, *Historical Account of the English Stage:* 'At present in France [*c.* 1556] plays are represented in such a manner that nothing is withdrawn from the view of the spectator. . . . The persons of the scene never depart during the representation; he who ceases to speak, is considered as if he were no longer on the stage. But in truth it is extremely ridiculous that the spectator should see the actor listening, and yet he himself should not hear what one of his fellow-actors says concerning him, though in his own presence and within his hearing; as if he were absent, while he is present.' – Note that Scaliger finds the custom strange and absurd; but it may well have been a method used in the performance of Senecan tragedies, and it illustrates the lengths to which anti-realistic stage technique can go.

3. NURSE: What ponderest thou in secret?

minimum of visual aid. As long ago as 1927, T. S. Eliot[1] noticed that 'Seneca's plays might be practical models for the modern "broadcasted" drama'. Where in other writers action, or activity in the prosecution of the plot, might be looked for, Seneca will cheerfully suspend the action for the recital of a monologue which may be quite inappropriate, on any realistic basis, to the time and situation, but entirely relevant to the character of the speaker or his mood at that moment in the drama. In the application of this technique, Seneca's choice of dramatic speech is confined to a very narrow range; almost the only alternative to monologue (in which the speaker delivers his thoughts with equal freedom either with or without regard to the presence of any other person on the stage) is the formal 'stichomythia' – a line-for-line fencing match between two opponents. Not only do these styles of speech recur persistently but their subject-matter also tends to be repeated, so that certain speeches or dialogues might almost be transposable from one play to another. There is the 'simple life' speech (*Phaedra*, 482 ff., *Thyestes*, 446 ff., *Octavia*, 377 ff.); the 'haunted grove' speech (*Thyestes*, 204 ff., *Oedipus*, 530 ff.); the 'king must be obeyed' dialogue (*Thyestes*, 204 ff., *Oedipus*, 509 and 699 ff., *Octavia*, 440 ff.).[2] The speeches of the messengers, usually to report the culminating atrocity or disaster, fall into a stereotyped pattern – the description of the place, the horror of the act, the stoical courage of the sufferer; and the isolation of the speech as a narrative almost detached from the action becomes the more conspicuous when the messenger, as in *Thyestes*, begins with a detailed description of the place, which must have been perfectly well known to those whom he is ostensibly addressing.

1. Introduction to Newton's *Ten Tragedies of Seneca* (see p. 27).
2. The authorship of *Octavia* is, of course, extremely doubtful; see p. 38.

Seneca's use of the Chorus is for the most part flaccid and unconvincing. A traditional farrago of mythology – the labours of Hercules, the loves of Jupiter, escapades of Bacchus, and torments of the damned in Hades – is served up in slightly varied forms, at more or less appropriate occasions. Yet at its best the Senecan chorus supplies examples of his best writing, in the concise lapidary style for which the Latin language is so perfect an instrument – and translation so unsatisfactory a substitute. These peaks occur when the author, restraining his exuberant verbosity and the habit of using all the possible synonyms of one word (wrath, anger, rage, ire; fear, terror, dread – to do the best we can in English) in close proximity, or quoting a string of mythological examples for one idea, brings himself to say one thing only and say it simply – as in the ode on death in *Troades*, 371 ff., the reflections on fate in *Oedipus*, 980 ff., or the thirteen lines on humble life in *Thyestes*, 391 ff.[1] It may be noticed, however, that such passages of philosophical reflection are often inconsistent with the attitudes adopted, even by the Chorus itself, in the main current of

1. Readers to whom the original is not easily accessible may like to have this example of the Latin:

> Stet quicunque volet potens
> aulae culmine lubrico;
> me dulcis saturet quies;
> obscuro positus loco
> leni perfruar otio;
> nullis nota quiritibus
> aetas per tacitum fluat.
> sic cum transierint mei
> nullo cum strepitu dies,
> plebeius moriar senex.
> illi mors gravis incubat
> qui, notus nimis omnibus,
> ignotus moritur sibi.

Thyestes, 391–403

the play. If death is the end of all, and the legends of Hades no more than idle fictions, to what purpose is all the harping on the tortures of Tantalus and Tityos, and whence come the ghosts to disturb the lives of men on earth? If fate is immutable and inevitable, why should the violence of tyrants and murderers be shown as the effective cause of tragic disasters?

If we look among the idiosyncrasies of Seneca's tragic style for 'faults', we can find plenty: excess of rhetoric, irrelevance, iteration, banality, bathos (how could he have passed that line where Oedipus, blindly groping for his final exit, with Jocasta lying dead beside him, pauses to say 'Mind you don't fall over your mother'!). Such lapses are the by-product of the labour of striving to extract the utmost effect from the spoken word; and in the effectiveness of the spoken word was all that mattered in Seneca's conception of drama. He was not a constructor of tragic plots; his plays are not concerned with the moral conflict between good and good which is the essence of 'true' tragedy; he only recognizes the power of evil to destroy good. He does not delay or complicate the issue by any moral dilemma exhibiting the conflict of justifiable but mutually incompatible ambitions; his tragedy is simply a disastrous event foretold and anticipated from the start, and pursued ruthlessly to its end. But nothing can be more horrifyingly final than the Senecan tragic climax. The swift and merciless destruction of Hippolytus, as the result of his father's hasty verdict, with no word spoken between them, has a more awful grandeur than the same event in Euripides' play, where the father and son confront each other in a forensic wrangle over the issue.

With their strong individuality of style, but limited range of dramatic invention, the plays of Seneca, on their arrival in renaissance England, made a powerful but superficial impression. As plays, and models for plays, on the boards of the theatre, they soon dropped dead; but their language, flamboyant with every rhetorical ornament, remained as a compost-heap to enrich the soil of English dramatic verse for a couple of generations.

*

The first printed edition of Seneca's tragedies came from the press of Andreas Gallicus at Ferrara in 1474. Others followed during the next hundred years from all the leading continental presses. Translation or imitation has been traced as far back as 1315, when a tragedy in the classical manner, *Eccerinis*, was produced by Albertino Mussato for the University of Padua. The introduction of the texts into English schools and universities must have been accompanied almost simultaneously by their appearance in acted form, but the earliest identifiable landmark is the performance of *Troades* at Trinity College, Cambridge, in 1551, and of *Oedipus* and others in the next few years. For the decisive impact of Senecan tragedy on the vernacular theatre we must note two events in the years 1559–61: Jasper Heywood's translation of three plays, and the performance of *Gorboduc*, the first original blank-verse tragedy on an English theme; to which we may add, for its importance in the history of English blank verse, the Earl of Surrey's translation of the *Aeneid*.

One might have expected that the form and style adopted by the first translator, and almost unanimously followed by his successors,[1] would have set a pattern for the revival of classical tragedy in English dress on the English stage. But, in fact, the fourteen-syllable rhymed couplet of these translations, though it survived in such plays as Preston's historical thriller *Cambyses* (1570), did not, in general, set an

1. See Appendix I.

example for the theatre – fortunately. The form was more suitable for ballad and narrative verse (and so has some success in the narrative speeches of the plays). The length of line is the outcome of the difficulty of translating Latin sentences into as few English words, but its use, together with the rhyme and the preference for a monosyllabic Anglo-Saxon vocabulary, tended towards expansion of the already verbose original – verbose, that is, in content, though structurally concise.

The translators were: Jasper Heywood (*Troas*, *Thyestes*, *Hercules Furens*), Alexander Neville (*Oedipus*), John Studley (*Agamemnon*, *Medea*, *Hercules Oetaeus*, *Hippolytus*), Thomas Nuce (*Octavia* – in ten-syllable rhymed couplets). Their versions appeared between 1559 and 1567, and in 1581 they were published (with some revisions) in a collected edition by Thomas Newton, who added his version of *Thebais*.[1] None of these translators was a professional dramatist; they were scholars, college fellows, divines. It would probably not occur to them to study the theatrical technique of their originals or of their translations – although they would have been familiar with scholastic performances of classical plays. Carried away by the exuberance of their own 'fourteener' verses, they were tempted to enlarge and embroider descriptive passages, to introduce additional speeches or omit what seemed superfluous. Here is Heywood's apology:

Now as concerninge sondrye places augmented and some altered in this my translation. First forasmuch as this worke seemed unto

1. *Seneca, His Tenne Tragedies translated into English*, edited by Thomas Newton, 1581. Reprinted with an Introduction by T. S. Eliot, The Tudor Translations, Constable, 1927.

E. M. Spearing, *The Tudor Translations of Seneca's Tragedies*, Cambridge, 1912.

Heywood's *Thyestes* is reprinted in *Five Elizabethan Tragedies*, ed. A. K. McIlwraith, Oxford, 1938.

mee in some places unperfite, whether left so of the Author, or
parte of it loste, as tyme devoureth all thinges, I wot not, I have
(where I thought good) with addition of myne owne penne
supplied the wante of some thynges, as the firste Chorus, after the
first acte begynninge thus, O ye to whom etc. Also in the seconde
Acte I have added the speache of Achilles Spright, rysing from
Hell to require the Sacrifice of Polyxena, begynning in this wyse,
Forsaking now etc. Agayne the three laste staves of the Chorus
after the same Acte: and as for the thyrde Chorus which in Seneca
beginneth thus, *Quae vocat sedes?* for as much as nothing is herein
but a heaped number of farre and straunge Countries, considerynge
with my selfe, that the names of so manye unknowen Countreyes,
Mountaynes, Desertes, and Woodes, shoulde have no grace in the
Englishe tounge, but bee a straunge and unpleasant thinge to the
Readers (except I should expounde the Historyes of each one,
which would be farre to tedious), I have in the place thereof made
another, beginninge in this manner, O Jove that leadst etc. Which
alteration may be borne withall, seynge that Chorus is not part of
the substance of the matter.

Heywood may easily be forgiven for boggling at the geographical chorus of *Troades* 814, but he omits to mention
that his substitute is partly a translation of a chorus in
Phaedra.[1] His introduction of the ghost of Achilles is typical
of a tendency which was to persist in the professional
theatre; Seneca, it is sometimes said, was responsible for
the Elizabethan dramatists' addiction to ghosts; in fact,
there are only two ghosts in his *dramatis personae* – Tantalus
in *Thyestes*, and Thyestes in *Agamemnon*; or three, if we
count Agrippina in *Octavia*. Other apparitions, as those of
Achilles and Hector in *Troades*, and Laius in *Oedipus*, play
an important part in the story, but remain off-stage. The
Elizabethans used their ghosts more freely, but often more
subtly, as (apart from the obvious examples in Shakespeare)
in Kyd's *The Spanish Tragedy*. This begins with the arrival

1. See Appendix I, 4.

of a ghost from Hades, but his role is not merely to create
an atmosphere of awe and menace; he is on the contrary an
amiable and rather puzzled ghost, brought by Revenge to
witness the punishment of his murderers, having as yet no
clear idea of the depth of the conspiracy against him, which
is to be revealed in the action of the play, as much to his
enlightenment (as he sits watching) as to that of the
audience.

To return to our Elizabethan translations, there is no
certainty that any of them were acted, though it is likely
that some of them were, in view of the translators' connexion with the universities and, in the case of Neville and
Studley, with the Inns of Court. That the professional
dramatists (and their audiences too) were as well acquainted
with Seneca in Latin as in translation is shown by their
fondness for quotation from the original.[1] At any rate, the
'fourteener' made little impression on the stage; it appears
on occasions, as in the masque in *Cymbeline*, v. 4:

No more, thou thunder-master, show thy spite on mortal flies . . .

But Shakespeare also found it fair game for parody in *A
Midsummer Night's Dream*:

But stay, O spite! But mark, poor knight, what dreadful dole is
    here!
Eyes, do you see? How can it be? O dainty duck, O dear!
Thy mantle good, what, stained with blood! Approach, ye
    Furies fell!
O Fates, come, come, cut thread and thrum; quail, crush,
    conclude, and quell!

It may be conceded, however, that some measure of variety

1. The instances noted, in the appropriate places, in footnotes to
my translations, are derived from J. W. Cunliffe (*The Influence of
Seneca on Elizabethan Tragedy*: Macmillan, 1893) who cites about
twenty quotations.

and individual voice was achieved by the translators. There is vigour in Heywood's version of the Agamemnon–Pyrrhus dialogue (Appendix I. 1, 2, 3), and descriptive power in Neville's *Oedipus* (8, 9) – the more remarkable when it is known that it was written in the translator's sixteenth year, he being then already a B.A. of Cambridge. Studley revels in the Stygian invocations of Medea (11), but he can vary his line from the monosyllabic

If ghost may here be given for ghost, and breath may serve for breath (14)

to the surprisingly concise

    Lo, I enjoy my father's gift; O solitariness! (16)

From their own knowledge of Seneca, and by imitation of one another, the dramatists filled their plays with a Senecan flavouring. An example of the perpetuation of a 'tag' may be seen in the following sequence of variations on a theme. Seneca wrote (*Agamemnon*, 116): *per scelera semper sceleribus tutum est iter* ('the safe way through crime is by [further] crimes' – a somewhat woolly epigram in the first place, meaning 'the safe way to get away with, or cover up, crime . . .'). Studley's translation:

    The safest path to mischiefe is by mischiefe open still.

T. Hughes, *The Misfortunes of Arthur*[1] (1587):

    The safest passage is from bad to worse.

Marston, *The Malcontent* (1604):

    Black deed only through black deed safely flies.

(to which the next speaker replies: 'Pooh! *per scelera semper sceleribus tutum est iter!*')

---

1. From this play Cunliffe quotes passages amounting to about 300 lines of translation or paraphrase from Seneca.

Shakespeare, *Macbeth* (1605):

> Things bad begun make strong themselves by ill.

B. Jonson, *Catiline* (1611):

> The ills that I have done cannot be safe
> But by attempting greater.

Webster, *The White Devil* (1612):

> Small mischiefs are by greater made secure.

Massinger, *The Duke of Milan* (1620):

> One deadly sin, then, help to cure another!

And beside the picking of Seneca's brains[1] by quotation
and imitation, the general tone of Senecan rhetoric was
infused into English drama, even in contexts where it was
least appropriate. Thomas Heywood's *A Woman Killed with
Kindness* (1603) is an example of a 'thriller' of bourgeois
life, with the least possible resemblance in form or setting
to classical tragedy. Servants indulge in such homely talk
as:

> Fie, we have such a household of serving creatures! Unless it
> be Nick and I, there's not one amongst them all can say boo to a
> goose –

and the gentlemen's blank verse can be relaxed and natural-
istic:

> Choose of my men which shall attend on you,
> And he is yours. I will allow you, sir,
> Your man, your gelding, and your table, all
> At mine own charge; be my companion.

1. 'Seneca, let blood line by line and page by page, at length
must needs die to our stage' – Thomas Nashe, Preface to Greene's
Menaphon (1589).

31

Yet the injured Master Frankford, being told of his wife's infidelity, has classical rhetoric at his command:

> Thou hast kill'd me with a weapon whose sharpen'd point
> Hath prick'd quite through and through my shiv'ring heart:
> Drops of cold sweat sit dangling on my hairs,
> Like morning's dew upon the golden flowers,
> And I am plung'd into a strange agony . . .

and, discovering the culprits *in flagrante delicto:*

> O God! O God! that it were possible
> To undo things done; to call back yesterday!
> That Time could turn up his swift sandy glass,
> To untell the days, and to redeem these hours!
> Or that the sun
> Could, rising from the west, draw his coach backward,
> Take from the account of time so many minutes,
> Till he had all these seasons call'd again,
> Those minutes, and those actions done in them,
> Even from her first offence; that I might take her
> As spotless as an angel in my arms!

It was all to the good; the language of Elizabethan drama would not have reached its height of poetic eloquence without the infusion of the classical voice – the Ovidian mythology and the Senecan rhetoric. It is not necessary to see direct borrowing from the Latin in every reminiscent line or phrase; the voice and the manner became naturalized in the English theatre; the invocations, hyperboles, geographical similes and mythological parallels, proliferated out of the compost-heap. When Shakespeare wrote

> Will all great Neptune's ocean wash this blood
> Clean from my hand? . . .

he may not have known that he was producing another version, perhaps the best yet, of a figure employed twice by Seneca and before him by Sophocles.[1] A passage in *Thyestes* (267 ff.) may have run through many variations before it became Lear's

> I will do such things—
> What they are yet I know not – but they shall be
> The terrors of the earth.

The parallels are so frequent that the translator of Seneca must have the curious feeling that he is trying out English constructions which Shakespeare and Marlowe will later improve upon.

To turn from the language to the form and subject-matter of English tragedy is to find a different and more complex process at work. The campaign for the revival of classical form in drama brought the forces of academic classicism into conflict, and a losing battle, with the vigorous though formless and rudely equipped tradition of the popular theatre, with its rambling episodic histories, its serio-comic moralities, and later its Italianate romances and English domestic crime-plays. The scholar-playwrights, looking beyond the merely linguistic possibilities of the classical style, became fascinated with the formal conventions of the Senecan drama and (supported by the Aristotelian precepts) took its austere 'unities' of time and place to be the ideal conditions of tragedy. In which they misunderstood the nature of those conventions. Reduced to literal terms, the action of *Thyestes*, for example, would seem to take place on one spot and within a continuous space of time limited to a few hours. But, in fact, the action

1. See *Phaedra*, 715. J. A. K. Thompson (*Shakespeare and the Classics*, 1952) finds in *Macbeth* the strongest evidences of direct classical influence and concludes that 'Shakespeare, before writing *Macbeth*, must have been reading Seneca, being especially struck by the *Hercules Furens*.'

is placeless and timeless; it presents a series of pictures: the
menace of an ancestral curse – the diabolical spite of Atreus
– the stoical resignation of Thyestes in exile – the deceptive
hospitality of Atreus – the horror-climax of the murders
(described) and the banquet (enacted). It does not matter
where, or at what intervals of time, these scenes are set –
nor what happens between them to link one with another
(and no one asks how Thyestes remained unaware of the
atrocious rite performed with full ceremony at Atreus's
court). Nevertheless, the craze for 'unity' took hold of
the academic mind, despite its impracticability when
literally applied. When the classical manner was adopted
for an English historical tragedy, in Gorboduc,[1] the first
notable attempt of the kind, the result was a drama recalling
the Senecan features of static declamation, symmetrical
conflict, choral commentary, and narrated action (but
shirking the horrific climax), yet diffusely spread over a
passage of years and diversified with dumb-shows to supple-
ment the action and point the moral. For this reason it
drew only qualified approval from Sir Philip Sidney,[2] to
whom the play seemed

full of stately speeches and well-sounding Phrases, climbing to the
height of Seneca his style, and as full of notable morality ... yet
very defectious in the circumstances: which grieveth me, because
it might not remain an exact model of all Tragedies. For it is
faulty both in Place and Time, the two necessary companions of
all corporal actions. ... But if it be so in Gorboduc, how much
more in all the rest? where you shall have Asia of the one side,
and Afric of the other, and so many other under-kingdoms, that
the Player, when he cometh in, must ever begin with telling where
he is.

1. By Thomas Norton and Thomas Sackville; acted 1561 by the
gentlemen of the Inner Temple at Whitehall before the Queen.

2. Apology for Poetry, c. 1580. The whole passage is printed in
Halliday's A Shakespeare Companion, Penguin, 1964.

INTRODUCTION

Experiments continued, the scholastic coteries producing their translations and imitations, and translations of
imitations,[1] and the dramatists drawing upon Seneca for
the enrichment of their verse and elaboration of their
incidents, but showing no inclination to confine their
plot-structure within the classic frame or to re-tell the oft-
told classical myths. The defence of the unities continued to
be maintained in the studies of the academicians, and was
upheld by some of the more classically erudite playwrights
such as Ben Jonson. Echoes of the controversy were to be
heard until the next century, when Pope, for the opposition, gave his opinion that 'to judge of Shakespeare by
Aristotle's rules is like trying a man by the laws of one
country, who acted under those of another'; and Samuel
Johnson took the commonsense view that if you can
imagine the stage to be 'Rome' for the duration of the
play, you can just as easily imagine it to be 'Rome' at one
time and 'Egypt' at another in the course of the same play.

In the meantime the popular theatre, remaining on the
whole faithful to its preference for straggling narrative
plays, was learning to use what it could of the classical
example: first, as we have seen, the flamboyance and
rotundity of the classical language; next, the machinery of
tragic spectacle, the ghosts and horrific incidents – with the
difference that in Seneca the atrocity is the end and climax
to which the whole play points, in the Elizabethan tragedy-
chronicle it is an added relish, to be expected anywhere, at
the beginning, middle, or end of the story. As for the view
that Seneca's 'atrocities' themselves prove the plays to be
unactable and never intended for acting, it must surely

1. Gascoigne's translation of Dolce's (Italian) version of Euripides'
Phoenissae; the Countess of Pembroke's translation of Garnier's
Antonius; Kyd's translation of Garnier's *Cornelia*; the *Meleager*,
Dido, and *Ulysses* of Dr Gager of Christchurch.

35

be noticed that the Elizabethans were no less brutal and rather more resourceful in their exploitation of horror, and even in our own day the 'unactable' *Titus Andronicus* has been staged with artistic power and dignity. Would the spectacle of the dismembered corpse of Hippolytus have been too great a shock for Romans accustomed to the atrocities of the amphitheatre? The Elizabethans had equally strong stomachs; but only in the full flowering of the masterpieces of Marlowe, Jonson, and Shakespeare, does the infusion of Senecan blood into English drama mean not merely a new tone of voice and a new repertoire of blood-shed but a new life and soul. 'Unity', as a technique of play-construction, was Seneca's gift to the classical French drama, but not to ours; yet the kind of unity, or concentration of theme, that turned the humdrum 'tragicall histories' into immortal tragedies, can be traced to the Roman discipline. Out of the welter of battle-scenes and cut-throat feuds emerged the introspective studies of Revenge, Jealousy, Ambition – the passions of Hamlet, Othello, or Macbeth, and the use of 'histories' to exhibit the problems of political power, the corruption or the loneliness of king-ship. These are the kind of topics which lie at the centre of the austerely formal, and at first sight almost inhuman, tragedies of Seneca. Atreus is an autocrat maddened by lust for revenge, Thyestes a disillusioned king with a nostalgia for peace; Theseus a self-confident husband and father blundering into an awful outrage against his son; Agamemnon (in *Troades*) a conqueror chastened by his own success, vainly protesting against vindictive reprisals. Seneca decorates his plays with mythological garnishing, his characters apostrophize the Gods and his choruses muse upon Fate, but what really interests him, and what brings life to his otherwise frigid reproductions of Greek master-pieces, is the exploration of the human conscience, of man's need to know and justify his own motives. This attitude of introspection was the link which Seneca provided between the fatalistic superhumanity of the ancient, and the humanism of the modern drama, and which made possible the fusion of classical uniformity with romantic multiformity in the Elizabethan theatre.

It would not be difficult to trace the progress of these influences in the art of Shakespeare alone. In the early poems the profusion of rhetorical ornament outruns restraint;[1] the first historical plays include experiments in Senecan declamatory or reflective monologue, and use violent action as a recurring and cumulative assault on the spectator's sensibilities (not, as in Seneca, the culmination of the drama; *Titus Andronicus* is the classic example of the distortion of the classical tragedy of revenge, drawing heavily by quotation, imitation, and reproduction, on ancient precedents, but creating only an extravaganza of atrocious deeds with no unifying shape or theme; it would have horrified Seneca.) The early comedies brought refinement of the verbal instrument and a firmer control of

---

1. For instance, *The Rape of Lucrece*, 764–77:

> O comfort-killing Night, image of hell!
> Dim register and notary of shame!
> Black stage for tragedies and murders fell!
> Vast sin-concealing chaos! nurse of blame!
> Blind muffled bawd! dark harbour for defame!
>   Grim cave of death! whispering conspirator,
>   With close-tongu'd treason and the ravisher!
>
> O hateful, vaporous and foggy Night!
> Since thou art guilty of my cureless crime,
> Muster thy mists to meet the eastern light,
> Make war against proportion'd course of time;
> Or if thou wilt permit the sun to climb
>   His wonted height, yet ere he go to bed,
>   Knit poisonous clouds about his golden head.

dramatic form. With the 'Roman' plays came perhaps a deeper understanding of the stoic attitude of self-questioning and the search for a solution of the conflict between reason and passion. And in the greatest tragedies the form, the instrument, and the theme – each owing something, however unconsciously, to the example of Seneca – cohered at last into a perfect whole; but yet not so perfect as to tidy up all the loose ends or exclude the superfluities and irrelevances which make the Elizabethan drama of life a different thing from the Roman sculptured monument of death.

*

The titles and sequence of the Senecan plays differ in the two principal groups of manuscripts. The group 'E' (Codex Etruscus) has: *Hercules, Troades, Phoenissae, Medea, Phaedra, Oedipus, Agamemnon, Thyestes, Hercules.* The group 'A' (various sources) has; *Hercules Furens, Thyestes, Thebais* (for *Phoenissae*), *Hippolytus* (for *Phaedra*), *Oedipus, Troas, Medea, Agamemnon, Octavia, Hercules Oetaeus.*

From the absence of *Octavia* from 'E', and for other reasons, it is believed that this group has prior authority; although it has been suggested that 'A' represents an edition of the plays issued shortly after the death of Seneca, while 'E' represents the collection as it existed in his lifetime, excluding, for obvious reasons, *Octavia.*

In any case, it is clear that the authenticity of *Octavia* is a matter of considerable doubt. There is no reason why Seneca, in the interval between A.D. 62 and his death, should not have amused himself by composing this grim commentary on contemporary events in the form of ancient tragedy. But equally another writer, with some acquaintance with Seneca's style and thought, could have borrowed his pen to produce a passable imitation of a Senecan tragedy, with perhaps a mischievous pleasure in showing Seneca himself involved in the kind of scene which he had so often composed for his actors. The play could evidently not have appeared in its final form (so far as it is final, being as it stands rather imperfectly articulated into acts and choral interludes) before the death of Nero, three years after that of Seneca. One is strongly tempted to assume that Seneca knew more than nothing about it.

. E.F.W.

October 1965

ACKNOWLEDGEMENT

Extracts from the Elizabethan translations of Seneca's tragedies are quoted, by kind permission of Messrs Constable and Co. Ltd, in the form in which they appear in Charles Whibley's edition of Newton's collection of translations (Tudor Translations, Constable, 1927).

THYESTES

THE crime which doomed the House of Pelops to a series of feuds and violent acts from generation to generation was that of Tantalus, a son of Zeus, who served his son Pelops as food at a banquet of the gods. Restored to life by Zeus, Pelops obtained a wife and a kingdom by treachery, and on his death after many other ruthless acts of conquest his throne became a bone of contention between his sons Atreus and Thyestes. Agreements to share the kingdom, or to rule it alternately, were broken more than once; each brother enjoyed periods of prosperity and suffered periods of banishment.

At the time of the play's action, Atreus is in possession and is plotting to entrap his brother by a false show of reconciliation. Thyestes, with his three sons, returns from exile, to be the victim of an atrocity recalling, but surpassing, the crime of their first ancestor. The curse on the house was to live on, the feuds to be repeated in the persons of Agamemnon, son of Atreus, and Aegisthus, son of Thyestes (by his own daughter Pelopia) and in the murder of Clytaemnestra by her son Orestes.

No Greek tragedy on the subject of Thyestes is extant, though a fragment of a *Thyestes* by Sophocles survives. Seneca may have been indebted to a predecessor, L. Varius Rufus, whose tragedy *Thyestes* was performed in 29 B.C. at the games celebrating the victory of Actium.

DRAMATIS PERSONAE

GHOST OF TANTALUS
FURY
ATREUS, *King of Argos*
A MINISTER
THYESTES, *brother of Atreus*
YOUNG TANTALUS, *son of Thyestes*
PLISTHENES (*mute*), *his second son*
THIRD SON (*mute*)
A MESSENGER
CHORUS *of Argive elders*

*

Scene: at the palace of Mycenae

ACT ONE

Ghost of Tantalus, Fury

GHOST: Who hales me from my miserable rest
  Among the dead below, where my starved mouth
  Gapes for the food that runs out of its reach?
  What god bids Tantalus return again
  To this abode he never should have seen?
  Is there some punishment in store for me
  Worse than to stand dry-mouthed in running water,
  Worse than the everlasting yawn of hunger?
  Is there another stone of Sisyphus
  Whose slippery weight my shoulders must support;
  A turning wheel upon whose spokes my limbs
  Must be extended; or a punishment
  Like that of Tityos, whose hollowed bowels
  Are open caverns where foul birds of prey
  Feed on his flesh – each night replenishing
  The losses of the day, to bring tomorrow
  A rich repast for each returning fiend?
  To what new torture have I been assigned?
  O, thou unknown implacable dispenser
  Of torments to the dead, if there can be
  Yet more intolerable penalties –
  Such as the keeper of hell's gaol himself
  Would loathe to look on, such as would affright
  Grim Acheron – to fill my soul with terror,
  Find one for me! For from my loins is sprung
  A generation whose iniquities,
  Whose crimes, of horror never known till now,
  Make all their predecessors' sins look small
  And me an innocent. Does any place in hell
  Still lack a tenant? I can furnish one
  From my posterity. While stands the house

45

Of Pelops, Minos never will be idle.
FURY: On with your task, abominable ghost:
    Let loose the Furies on your impious house.
    Let evil vie with evil, sword with sword;
    Let anger be unchecked, repentance dumb.
    Spurred by insensate rage, let fathers' hate
    Live on, and the long heritage of sin
    Descend to their posterity. Leave none
    The respite for remorse; let crimes be born
    Ever anew and, in their punishment,
    Each single sin give birth to more than one.
    Let those proud brothers each forfeit his throne,[1]
    And be recalled to it again from exile –
    In this strife-riven house Fortune herself
    Will never know which way to turn between them.
    The high shall be brought low, the weak made strong,
    The kingdom tossed by ceaseless waves of chance.
    Let there be culprits banished for their crimes,
    And when restored, by mercy of the gods,
    Returning to their crimes, to make their names
    Hateful to all mankind and to themselves.
    Vengeance shall think no way forbidden her;
    Brother shall flee from brother, sire from son,
    And son from sire; children shall die in shames
    More shameful than their birth; revengeful wives
    Shall menace husbands, armies sail to war
    In lands across the sea, and every soil
    Be soaked with blood; the might of men of battle
    In all the mortal world shall be brought down
    By Lust triumphant. In this house of sin
    Brothers' adultery with brothers' wives
    Shall be the least of sins; all law, all faith,

1. As if outside the supposed time of the play's action, Fury 'foresees' the course of the feud which is now coming to a climax.

All honour shall be dead. Nor shall the heavens
Be unaffected by your evil deeds:
What right have stars to twinkle in the sky?
Why need their lights still ornament the world?
Let night be black, let there be no more day.
Let havoc rule this house; call blood and strife
And death; let every corner of this place
Be filled with the revenge of Tantalus!

   Behold, the pillars shall be wreathed with flowers,
The porches garlanded with festive bay,
The fires heaped high to give you worthy welcome.
Then shall a Thracian tragedy[1] be played
With larger numbers. . . . Is the uncle's hand
Ready? . . . Why does he pause? . . . When will he strike?
Thyestes does not know his children's fate. . . .
Now light the fire and make the cauldron boil! . . .
Divide the bodies into little pieces! . . .
Splash blood on the paternal hearth! Draw up,
And serve the banquet! Here will be one guest
Not unaccustomed to such villainies.

   See, I am giving you a holiday
And a rich feast to satisfy your hunger.
Fill your lean belly, Tantalus; and see,
There will be wine mingled with blood to drink.
I fear I have devised a meal so strange
That *you* will run away from *it*. No, stay!
Where are you off to?

GHOST: To the lake, the river,
The elusive water and the laden tree
Whose fruits avoid my lips. O let me go
Back to my lightless bed, my prison cell!

---

1. The 'Thyestean banquet' has a precedent in the case of Procne
(wife of the Thracian king Tereus) who killed and cooked his son
Itys in revenge for the king's outrage upon her sister Philomela.

Or if my punishment has been too light,
There is another river, Phlegethon –
Let me go there, let me be left to stand
Midstream in waves of everlasting fire.
Hear me, all souls condemned by Fate's decree
To serve your penance: you that cowering sit
Under a vaulted cave, whose imminent fall
Is your eternal terror; you that face
The jaws of hungry lions, or beleaguered
By bands of raving Furies quake with fear;
You that half-burnt ward off a hail of torches –
Hear me! This is the voice of Tantalus,
Who comes in haste to join you. Learn from me,
And be content with your afflictions. When,
Ah, when may I escape this upper world?

FURY: Not till you have put chaos in your house
And with your coming set its kings at war.
Fill them with evil lust for battle, shake
Their raving souls with storms of insane strife.

GHOST: It is my place to suffer punishment,
Not be myself a punishment to others.
Am I commanded now to issue forth
Like noxious vapour boiling from the ground
Or some foul pestilence to spread destruction
Over the face of earth? Am I employed
To do a deed of monstrous wickedness
Against my grandsons? Father of all gods! –
My father, though in shame – let my loud tongue
Itself be sentenced to extremest pain
For this audacity, yet it will speak:
My sons, I warn you! Do not soil your hands
With sinful slaughter, keep your altars clean
Of blood aspersed in impious sacrifice.
I shall stand by you and avert that sin. . . .

Ah, wouldst thou, fiend, brandish thy fearful whip
Before my face, and fright me with the serpents
Writhing about thy horrid head? My belly
Aches with the agony of my old hunger
Awakened at thy bidding. In my blood
A fire of thirst is raging, leaping flames
Consume my vital parts. . . . Lead on, I follow.

FURY: So . . . so . . . cast wide thy spell of madness . . . here,
And here, on every part of this doomed house. . . .
With this . . . this . . . fury be they all possessed,
And envy, thirsting for each others' blood.
So . . . now the house has felt your coming in –
It quaked from top to bottom with the touch
Of your corrupting hand. Enough, well done.
Now take your way back to the lower depths,
Back to your river. The offended earth
Protests under your tread: see how the springs
Recede and shrink, the river beds are dry,
The scarce clouds ravaged by a scorching wind.
All trees are drained of colour, branches bare,
Fruit fallen; and the seas, that washed the shores
So close on either side the narrow Isthmus,
Have fled so far apart, the land between,
Now broader, barely hears their distant roar.
The lake of Lerna is dried up, Alpheus
Has closed his sacred river, and Phoroncus[1]
Is scarcely to be seen; Cithaeron's height
Stands naked of its cloak of snow; in Argos
The elders fear the drought of days gone by.
Behold, the very Lord of Heaven, the Sun
Is loth to drive his chariot forth, nor cares
To hasten on the day that soon must die.

1. Phoroneus, son of Inachus, the first king of Argos; and so used
for the name of the river which was also called Inachus.

CHORUS
If any god loves our Achaean Argos,
Pisa, for chariots known, the twofold harbours
On the twin seas of the Corinthian Isthmus –
If any god looks down upon the far-seen
Heights of Taygetus, where snows of winter
Massed in deep drifts by Scythia's wild north-easter
Melt to the summer winds that sailors wait for –
If any loves the cooling stream, Alpheus,
Running beside the famed Olympian circus –
   May such a god, we pray,
   Regard us with an eye of peace,
   And turn all harm away –
Forbid the ever-repeated alternation
Of crime with crime, spare us a new succession
Of young blood baser than older generations,
Of children apter in sin than were their fathers.
Grant that at last the impious brood descended
From thirsting Tantalus may tire of outrage.
Evil has gone too far – law's rule is powerless,
Even the common bounds of sin exceeded.

Treachery conquered Myrtilus[1] the traitor;
The sea betrayed him as he betrayed his master,
Drowned him, and kept his name, to make a story
Known, to their cost, by all Ionian seamen.
Tantalus' infant son[2] was infamously

1. When Pelops raced his chariot against Oenomaus, King of Elis, for the prize of the king's daughter Hippodamia, he bribed Myrtilus, the king's charioteer, to tamper with the axle and cause an accident. Instead of rewarding Myrtilus, Pelops threw him into the sea (cf. l. 660).

2. This was Pelops, and this was Tantalus's archetypal crime; but Pelops was restored to life by Jupiter, to continue the series of atrocities.

Put to the sword, while running to kiss his father,
Slaughtered, a baby victim upon the altar,
By his own father's hand, and cut to pieces,
Served as a dish to grace the godly tables.
The consequence of this repast was hunger,
Hunger and thirst for all eternity;
  What fitter penalty
  Could any fate decree
For the provider of that bestial banquet!
  Tantalus stands fainting, gasping,
  Empty-mouthed, with food abundant
  Over the sinner's head suspended
  Out of his reach, a prey elusive
  As the wild birds that Phineus[1] hunted.
Trees all around him bend their laden branches
Stooping and swaying with the fruits they offer
In playful mockery of his empty mouthings.
Time and again deluded, now the sufferer,
Famished and desperate with his long torture,
Will not attempt to touch them, turns his head down,
Clenches his teeth and swallows down his hunger –
Only to see the riches of the orchard
Lowered to meet him, juicy apples dancing
On bending branches, goading again his hunger
Till he must shoot out hands to clutch . . . but useless –
Soon as he moves, expecting disappointment,
Up to the sky go all the swinging branches,
Out of his reach flies that autumnal richness.
Thirst follows, an agony equal to the hunger;
  His blood burns hotly, fiery torches
  Dry his veins; he stands demented
  Straining to reach the running river
  Close at his side; at once the water

1. Blinded, and tormented by harpies.

Turns and deserts its empty channel,
Runs from him as he tries to follow,
Leaving, where once a torrent sped,
Dust for his drink from its deep bed.

ACT TWO

Atreus, Minister

ATREUS: Am I a coward, sluggard, impotent,
And – what I count the worst of weaknesses
In a successful king – still unavenged?
After so many crimes, so many sleights
Committed on me by that miscreant brother
In violation of all sacred law,
Is there no more to do but make vain protests?
Is this your anger, Atreus? All the world
By now should be resounding to your arms,
The sea to east and west bearing your fleets;
Fire should be blazing over field and city,
The glint of naked sword on every side.
The thunder of our horsemen must be heard
On every quarter of the Argive land.
The woods must give the enemy no cover,
The mountain tops no site for fortresses.
The people of Mycenae, man by man,
Must take the field and sound the trump of war.
And be it known that whosoever here
Protects or shelters our detested foe,
His penalty is ignominious death.
Ay, may this mighty house of noble Pelops
Fall even on my head, if in its fall
It crush my brother too. Awake, my heart,
And do such deeds as in the time to come
No tongue shall praise, but none refuse to tell.
Some black and bloody deed must be attempted,
Such as my brother might have wished were his.
You cannot say you have avenged a crime

53

Unless you better it.[1] But how to find
An act of vengeance terrible enough
To bring him down? Is he resigned or cowed?
Is he a man to celebrate success
With modesty, or calmly brook eclipse?
Not he; I know that man's rebellious temper;
Nothing will move him; but he can be broken.
Therefore, before he can collect his forces
Or steel his courage, I shall go for him,
Not let him come for me, and find me resting.
Let him destroy me now or be destroyed;
The gage of action lies upon the field
For him to seize who can be quick to take it.

MINISTER: You do not fear your people's disapproval?

ATREUS: Of the advantages of monarchy
The greatest is that subjects are compelled
Not only to endure but to approve
Their master's actions.

MINISTER: Men compelled by fear
To praise, may be by fear compelled to hate.
He who desires to win sincere approval
Will seek it in the heart, not on the tongue.

ATREUS: A moderate man may win sincere approval;
It takes a strong man to enforce feigned praise.
Men must be made to want what they dislike.

MINISTER: Let the king want what's right, who will oppose
    him?

ATREUS: The king who binds himself to want what's right
Sits on a shaky throne.

MINISTER: No throne can stand
Where there is neither shame nor law nor trust
Nor care for sanctity or piety.

---

1. *Scelera non ulcisceris, nisi vincis.* The Latin is quoted in Marston's
Antonio and Mellida (1599).

ATREUS: Sanctity, piety, trust − are luxuries
  For private life. Leave kings to go their own way.
MINISTER: To harm a brother, even a guilty brother,
  Must be a sin.
ATREUS: Whatever might be sin
  Against a brother, can be only justice
  In this man's case. What has he left untouched
  By his unlawful acts, what crime not dared?
  He took my wife by rape, my throne by theft;
  By treachery he won our ancient crown;
  He brought our house to ruin by treachery.
  You know that in the royal byres of Pelops
  We have a famous animal, a ram
  Of mystic origin, king of a flock
  Of valuable beasts; its back is covered
  With an abundant fleece of purest gold,
  And from this fleece is made the golden sceptre
  Borne by each reigning heir of Tantalus.
  The owner of the ram is king; the ram
  Controls the destinies of all our house.
  His pasture, as befits a sacred beast,
  Is in a special precinct safely guarded
  By strong stone walls which circle and protect
  This grazing-ground on which our fates depend.
  My brother planned a bold and treacherous plot −
  My wife, the partner of my nuptial bed,
  Being privy to that most nefarious deed −
  To steal this golden ram. And from that fount
  Springs all this spate of mutual enmity.
  Banished, I wandered lonely and afraid
  Throughout my realm. No portion of my birthright
  Was safe from his rapacity and cunning;
  My wife seduced, my sovereignty disowned,
  My blood disgraced, my progeny suspected.

One thing alone was certain in my life –
My brother's enmity. Then why stand idle?
Where is my resolution? Think of Pelops
And Tantalus; these are the precedents
My hand is called to follow. . . . Tell me, man,
How can I best destroy that hated head?

MINISTER: A sword's point will draw out an enemy's
    breath.

ATREUS: You tell me of the *end* of punishment;
  I ask, *what* punishment? The kindest king
  Can put a man to death; under my rule
  A culprit should be made to beg for death.

MINISTER: Is nothing sacred?

ATREUS: Sanctity, begone! –
  If thou wast ever known within these walls.
  Come all the dread battalions of the Furies!
  Come, seed of strife, Erinys! Come, Megaera,
  With torches armed! My spirit yet lacks fire;
  It would be filled with still more monstrous rage.

MINISTER: What new device will your wild rage invent?

ATREUS: No act that common anger knows. Nothing
  Will I not do! Yet nothing will content me.

MINISTER: By sword?

ATREUS: Too light.

MINISTER: By fire?

ATREUS: Not yet enough.

MINISTER: What other tool can your dire vengeance use?

ATREUS: Himself – Thyestes!

MINISTER: This is worse than vengeance.

ATREUS: It is. My heart is shaken with a storm
  Of passion that confounds it to its centre.
  I am compelled, although I know not whither,
  I am compelled by forces. . . . Hear! the earth
  Groans from its depths; the sky is clear, but thunder

Rumbles, and from the house there came a crash
As if the roof were falling; and our gods,
Shaken, have turned their backs on us. So be it!
Let a black deed be done, which gods above
Will fear to see.

MINISTER: What deed is in your mind?

ATREUS: I know not what. Some deed more wonderful
Than mind can contemplate, more terrible
Than any ordinary act of man,
Beyond the bounds of human nature, fills
My soul and prompts my idle hand to action.
What it will be, I know not. It will be,
I know, something tremendous. . . . Yes, I have it!
Hold hard to this, my soul! This is a deed
Thyestes could be proud of, as can Atreus;
Let them be partners in the doing of it!
Was there not an abominable banquet
Seen in the house of Tereus¹ of Odrysia?
There was; and truth to tell, it was a crime
Most horrible. But I have been forestalled;
My vengeance must contrive a better crime.
Mother and sister of Daulis,² give me guidance!
My case is yours; help and direct my hand! . . .
What if the father could be made to tear
His children into pieces, happily,
With eager appetite – eat his own flesh? . . .
Good, very good. I could be well content
With such a punishment. . . . But now, where is he?
Is Atreus to be innocent much longer?
A picture of the murder, done, complete,
Rises before my eyes . . . the father's mouth

1. See on l. 56.
2. Procne and Philomela. The atrocity occurred in Daulis, or
Phocis, being under the rule of the Odrysian (Thracian) king Tereus.

Devouring his lamented little ones. . . .
What! Is this fear again, my heart? Dost faint
Upon the point of action? Call thy courage up!
In this vile act the most atrocious part
Will be the victim's own.

MINISTER: By what device
Will he be lured to walk into our net?
He looks for danger everywhere.

ATREUS: We could not
Catch him, were he not hoping to catch us.
Already he aspires to win my throne;
To gain this end he would stand up to Jove
Armed with his thunderbolts; to gain this end
He is about to brave the angry sea,
To cross the dangerous shoals of Libyan Syrtis;
For this, he will endure what he most hates –
His brother's sight.

MINISTER: How will he be persuaded
That peace is made?[1] Whom will he trust for that?

ATREUS: Dishonest hope is always credulous.
But I shall give a message to my sons
To carry to their uncle. They will ask him
To quit his vagrant life in foreign lands,
Exchange his penury for royal state,
And be my partner in the rule of Argos.
Should he prove obstinate and spurn these prayers,
His sons, less hardened, tired of deprivation,
And easy to deceive, will listen to them.
But his inveterate determination
To gain the kingdom, added to the weight
Of his misfortunes and dire poverty,

---

1. Atreus has not yet explained that he proposes to trap his brother by an offer of reconciliation; but the Minister obligingly makes that inference.

    Albeit these have toughened his resistance,
    Will surely bring him round.
MINISTER: May not long habit
    Seem to have lightened his afflictions?
ATREUS: No;
    The sense of suffering grows continually.
    A hardship may be easy to accept,
    But very irksome to endure for ever.
MINISTER: My lord, I would advise you to employ
    Some other instruments for your fell purpose.
    Young men are all too apt to learn bad lessons;
    The stratagems that you would have them use
    Against their uncle, they may come in time
    To use against their father. Very often
    A counsellor of crime has found his precepts
    Employed against himself.
ATREUS: They'll learn the ways
    Of crime and villainy, without a master;
    Their kingly life will teach them. Have no fear
    Of their becoming villains; they were born so.
    Besides, what is to your mind harsh and cruel,
    What you call heartless and inhuman conduct,
    May well be happening on the other side.
MINISTER: Your sons will know the trap you are pre-
       paring?
ATREUS: They are not old enough to keep a secret;
    They would betray the plot. It takes a man
    Experienced in defeat to learn discretion.
MINISTER: Would you deceive the very messengers
    By whom you purpose to deceive your enemy?
ATREUS: Yes, so that they at least be innocent
    Of guilt, or blame for their complicity.
    Why should I need to implicate my sons
    In my dark deeds? Let me alone exact

My own revenge. . . . No, no, my heart; no bungling,
No weakening now! If you would spare your sons,
You will be sparing his. No – Agamemnon
Shall be a conscious agent of my plan,
And Menelaus help him with full knowledge.
Their handling of the deed will give me means
To test the truth of their suspected birth.
If they refuse the encounter, if they will not
Help me to my revenge, if they protest
'He is our uncle' – then he is their father.
About it, then. . . . And yet, a timid face
Can give away too much; in great affairs
The unwilling hand is easily detected.
No – my assistants shall be ignorant
Of the importance of their mission. . . . You, sir –
Say nothing of my plan.

MINISTER: I need no telling.
Your words are locked within my breast by fear
And duty – but by duty above all.

CHORUS

At last this royal seat, this ancient race of Inachus,
Sees its old fratricidal feud composed, strife laid to rest.[1]
What senseless folly drove our kings to shed each others'
     blood
And use such sinful means to win possession of a throne?
Were they so covetous of royal citadels of power?

1. That the Chorus, here and again at 546, appear to be ignorant
of Atreus's treacherous intentions, is a considerable strain on the
dramatic convention. Some suppose that the Chorus is absent from
the stage between the acts. But no realistic solution need be looked
for; the Chorus may participate as much, or as little, in the action as
is convenient; here they are assumed to be aware only of the 'overt'
situation – the apparent reconciliation of the brothers.

Did they not know where only perfect kingship can be
   found?

It is not worldly wealth that makes a king,
Nor the rich diadem encompassing
His royal head, nor the proud gaudiness
Of gilded halls and Tyrian purple dress.
A king is he who has no ill to fear,
Whose hand is innocent, whose conscience clear;
Who scorns licentious greed, who has not bowed
To the false favour of the fickle crowd.
The minerals unearthed in western lands,
The ore washed down in Tagus' glittering sands,
Are not for him; nor all the golden grain
Threshed from the harvests of the Libyan plain.
He is the man who faces unafraid
The lightning's glancing stroke; is not dismayed
By storm-tossed seas; whose ship securely braves
The windy rage of Adriatic waves;
Who has escaped alive the soldier's arm,
The brandished steel; who, far removed from harm,
Looks down upon the world, faces his end
With confidence, and greets death as a friend.

Above the king whose broad domain
Covers the far-flung Scythian plain,
The king who holds his court beside
The ruby sea whose blood-red tide
Sparkles with gems, the king who wards
The Caspian pass from Slavic hordes;
Above the king whose feet dare tread
Upon the Danube's icebound bed,
Or him who rules (where'er be these)
The famed silk-farms of the Chinese:

Above all, innocence alone
Commands a kingdom of its own.

This kingdom needs no armed defence,
No horseman, nor that vain pretence
Of Parthian archers who, in flight,
Shoot arrows to prolong the fight.
It has no need of cannon balls
And guns to batter city walls.
To have no fear of anything,
To want not, is to be a king.
This is the kingdom every man
Gives to himself, as each man can.

Let others scale dominion's slippery peak;
Peace and obscurity are all I seek.
Enough for me to live alone, and please
Myself with idleness and leisured ease.
A man whose name his neighbours would not know,
I'd watch my stream of life serenely flow
Through years of quietness, until the day
When an old man, a commoner, passed away.
Death's terrors are for him who, too well known,
Will die a stranger to himself alone.[1]

1. *Qui notus nimis omnibus | ignotus moritur sibi*. The Latin is quoted
in Marston's *The Fawn* (1605).

ACT THREE

Thyestes, Young Tantalus, Plisthenes, and another son

THYESTES: The place that I have most desired to see –
  House of my fathers, majesty of Argos;
  My native soil – the exile's greatest joy,
  The outcast's hope; gods of my fatherland,
  If there be any gods. These now I see
  With my own eyes; and there the sacred walls,
  The Cyclops' work, of more than human grandeur;
  And there the course where the young men resort,
  Where I myself gained honours more than once
  Driving to victory in my father's chariot.
  All Argos, all her people, will be here
  To meet me. I shall meet my brother, Atreus . . .
  No! Back! Go back, man, to the forest's shelter,
  The leafy glades, your life among the beasts,
  Shared with the beasts. This blaze of royalty
  Cannot deceive your eyes with its false show.
  When you are tempted to admire the gift,
  Observe the giver. I was confident
  And happy in a life which most would think
  Intolerable; now my fears return.
  My spirit falters and arrests my body;
  I am unwilling to go on my way.
TANTALUS: Why does my father move with such slow
        steps
  As in a trance, and cast his eyes around
  Seeming to be uncertain of himself?
THYESTES: What, can you doubt, my brain? The course is
        clear
  And needs no anxious thought. A throne? A brother?
  What could be more unworthy of your trust
  Than those uncertain things? Are you afraid

63

Of hardships which you have already tamed
And learnt to overcome? Do you now seek
Escape from comfortable indigence?
No, better far to be a beggar still.
Turn back, while yet you can; get safe away.
TANTALUS: Why, father, what can make you turn away
From home, now you have seen it? Why refuse
To embrace such happiness? Here is your brother
Returned to you in reconciliation;
He gives you back your share of sovereignty,
Makes you yourself again, and reunites
The broken members of our family.
THYESTES: You ask me why, I cannot tell you why
I am afraid; I see no cause for fear,
And yet I am afraid. I would go on;
But I am paralysed, my knees are weak,
My legs refuse to carry me; some force
Repels me from the way I try to go,
As when a ship labours with oar and sail
But oar and sail are powerless to resist
The driving of the current.
TANTALUS: Set aside
Those obstacles that hinder your intention,
And think what prizes wait on your return.
Father, you can be king.
THYESTES: As I can die.
TANTALUS: Power supreme –
THYESTES: Is nothing, when a man
Wants nothing.
TANTALUS: You have sons to follow you.
THYESTES: One kingdom cannot have two kings at once.
TANTALUS: Choose misery when happiness is offered?
THYESTES: Take it from me, my son, great prizes tempt us
By their false aspects, and our fear of hardship

64

Is likewise a delusion. While I stood
Among the great, I stood in daily terror;
The very sword I wore at my own side
I feared. It is the height of happiness
To stand in no man's way,[1] to eat at ease
Reclining on the ground. At humble tables
Food can be eaten without fear; assassins
Will not be found in poor men's cottages;
The poisoned drink is served in cups of gold.
I speak as one who knows, and make my choice
The life of hardship, not prosperity.
Mine is no lofty dwelling-place built high
Upon a mountain top to overawe
The common folk below; I have no ceilings
Lined with white ivory, I need no watch
Outside my door to guard me while I sleep.
I own no fishing fleet, no piers of mine
Intrude their massive blocks upon the sea.
My stomach is no glutton, to be filled
With every nation's tribute; not for me
Are harvests reaped from fields in farthest east.
No man burns incense at a shrine for me;
I am no god with altars to my name
More richly served than those of Jupiter.
Roof-gardens of luxurious foliage
Are not for me; for me no steamy baths
Stoked by the labour of a hundred hands.
My day is not a time for sleep, my night
An endless vigil in the cause of Bacchus.[2]
But neither am I feared by any man;

1. Cf. Appendix II, 7.
2. A passage in Seneca's *Letters*, CXXII, inveighing against luxury,
mentions consecutively 'rooftop gardens' and 'turning night into
day'. The speech of Thyestes is, of course, singularly anachronistic!

My house is undefended, but secure.
Great is my peace, as my estate is small:
Kingdom unlimited, without a kingdom!

TANTALUS: You have no need to ask, nor to refuse,
A kingdom offered to you by a god.
Your brother asks you to be king with him.

THYESTES: Does he? There's danger there; some hidden
trap.

TANTALUS: Brotherly love can often live again
In hearts that once have lost it; true affection
Broken can be repaired.

THYESTES: My brother love me?
Sooner will Ocean wash the Seven Stars,
The fury of the wild Sicilian currents
Rest, the Ionian sea become a field
Of ripening corn, night's darkness be our daylight;
Sooner will water come to terms with fire,
Wind make a peace with sea, or life with death.

TANTALUS: But what harm do you fear?

THYESTES: All kinds of harm.
Why should my fear have limits, when his power
Is boundless as his hate?

TANTALUS: How can he hurt you?

THYESTES: I know – not for myself, for you, my sons,
I know that I must fear the power of Atreus.

TANTALUS: You fear some trap, in spite of all your
caution?

THYESTES: Caution is late, when you are in the trap.
Let us go on, then. But – your father speaks –
Remember this: 'tis you that lead, I follow.

TANTALUS: God will look kindly on your good intentions.
Go boldly on.
    [Enter Atreus, aside]

ATREUS: The net is spread, the game is in the trap.
  I see my brother, with his hateful sons
  Close by his side. Vengeance is now assured.
  I have Thyestes in my hands at last,
  Himself and all he has.[1] I am impatient,
  And find it difficult to curb my wrath.
  Thus does a keen-nosed Umbrian hunting-dog
  In quest of game, while held in leash, silent
  Follow the trail, nose to the ground, obedient
  While still the scent is weak, the quarry distant;
  But at close quarters with his prey, he'll fight
  With every muscle of his neck, protesting
  Against restraint, and strive to slip the leash;
  And when he sniffs the scent of blood, his rage
  Is almost uncontrollable, but still
  Must be controlled. . . . Look at him, how his hair
  Hangs all unkempt over his ruined face;
  His chin unshaved. But we must offer him
  A reassuring welcome. . . .
                              Welcome, brother!
  How glad I am to see you! Let me feel
  That long-desired embrace. . . . Let us forget
  The anger that has parted us; henceforth
  Let love and kinship ever be our law,
  All enmity condemned and put away.
THYESTES: I could plead innocent; but as you come
  In this kind mood, I cannot but confess,
  Freely confess, my brother, I am guilty
  Of all you have believed of me. This love
  Has robbed me of my plea. Only to seem
  Guilty in a devoted brother's eyes

  1. *Venit in nostras manus / tandem Thyestes; venit et totus quidem.*
The Latin is quoted, with variations, in Marston's *Antonio and
Mellida* (1599).

Is guilt enough. I can but plead with tears –
Though no man ever saw me plead before –
And with these hands, that have touched no man's feet.
Be all your anger set aside, your heart
Eased of the tumult of your indignation.
For the assurance of my trust, brother,
My innocent sons shall be your hostages.

ATREUS: Touch not my knees, but come into my arms.
And you three lads, an old man's sentinels,
Embrace me too. Take off that ragged garment,
Brother, its sight offends me, and be dressed
In robes like mine; accept with a good will
Your part and share of our fraternal kingdom.
It cannot but be counted to my credit
That I admit my brother, safe returned,
To the enjoyment of his royal birthright.
To own a kingdom is a man's good fortune;
To give one is an act of charity.

THYESTES: And may the gods, my brother, so reward you
As your good deed deserves. As for the crown,
That mark of royalty would scarce become
This ruined head; this sorely troubled hand
Can never hold a sceptre. Let me live
Unseen, among the humblest of your subjects.

ATREUS: This realm is wide enough to hold two kings.

THYESTES: I know that what is yours is mine, my brother.

ATREUS: What man would spurn abundant fortune's gifts?

THYESTES: The man who knows how fast abundance ebbs.

ATREUS: May I not have this honour that I seek?

THYESTES: Your honour is assured; but what of mine?
I am determined to refuse the crown.

ATREUS: If you refuse your share, I give up mine.

THYESTES: Well . . . I accept the title thrust upon me,
But on condition all my arms, my powers,

And I, shall be devoted to your service.
ATREUS: Come then, and let your venerable head
Suffer the yoke that I shall put upon it.
Then I shall offer to the gods above
The sacrifice I have prepared for them.

CHORUS

Would any man believe it possible?
Atreus, that hard, that bitter man, that man of un-
    repentant cruelty,
Stands checked, awed into impotence, before his brother.
Truly there is no greater power on earth
Than natural affection.
Strife between strangers may go on for ever,
But where it has bound once
The chain of love will always bind again.

Peace had been broken by a storm of strife
For causes not to be despised.
The call to arms was heard,
The tramp of horsemen and the clink of harness,
Bright steel flashed to and fro at the command
Of Mars the God of Battle, armed and angry
And thirsting for fresh blood.
Yet now
Love has conquered the sword,
Bound the contesting hands,
And brought the combatants, despite themselves,
To reconciliation.
Which of the gods has given us this peace
So soon, after such bitter strife?

Loud was the noise of civil war, but yesterday,
Throughout Mycenae. Mothers stood pale with terror

Clutching their infants; wives watched fearfully
While husbands armed, grasping reluctantly
The long-forgotten sword, now dulled
With the rust of peaceful days.
Then there were crumbling walls to be repaired,
Towers, weakening with age, to be restored,
Gates to be hurriedly locked with iron bolts;
While on the battlements the anxious guard
Watched for the night's alarms.
Worse than war is the fearful waiting for war.

Now, stilled is the threat of the killer's sword;
Now, silent the trumpet's thrilling call,
Silent the bugle's piercing note. Deep peace
Comes back to the city, and all is joy again.

So, when the north gales fall upon the Bruttian sea
And breakers roll in from the deep, the caves of Scylla
Echo their pounding beat, and sailors yet ashore
Tremble to see the swirling waters which Charybdis
Greedily swallows down and vomits up again.
Fear grips the brutish Cyclops sitting in the depths
Of Etna's burning crater: will his father soon
Put out with his cascade the everlasting fires
That feed the furnaces of their unresting forge?
Ithaca shakes, and the ill-used Laertes
Expects to see his little kingdom drowned.

But when the winds lay by their force,
The sea lies calmer than a lake,
The ships that feared to cross the deep
Spread their bright sails on every side,
Boats dance upon a level floor
So clear, the eye can count the fishes

Swimming beneath the waters, where
Lately the fury of the gale
Had lashed the waves, and Cyclad islands
Trembled beneath their shock.

No state of life endures; pleasure and pain
Take each their turn; and pleasure's turn is shorter.
Time swiftly changes highest into lowest.
That king – who can give crowns away;
Before whose feet nations have bowed
In fearful homage; at whose nod
The Medes, or Indians, neighbours of the sun,
Or Dahians whom the Parthian horsemen fear,
Have sheathed their swords – himself
Fears for his crown,
Anxiously scans the signs of Fate,
Dreads treacherous Time and the swift chance
That can make all things change.

You – to whom the ruler of earth and ocean
Gives the dread power of life and death – be humble;
That overweening face does not become you.
No threat of yours that makes your subjects tremble
Is greater than that your master holds above you.
Kings of the earth must bow to a higher kingdom.
Some, whom the rising sun sees high exalted,
The same sun may see fallen at its departing.[1]
No man should put his trust in the smile of fortune,
No man abandon hope in a time of trouble.
The Spinner of Fate twines good and bad together,
Never lets fortune rest, keeps all things moving.

1. *Quem dies vidit veniens superbum, / hunc dies vidit fugiens iacentem.*
The Latin is quoted in Marlowe's *Edward II*.

Never was man so sure of the good gods' favour
That he could promise himself a safe tomorrow.
Under God's hand, life's circle is ever revolving,
The swift wheel turning.

ACT FOUR

Messenger, Chorus

MESSENGER: O that some whirling wind would carry me
  Away into the sky, or wrap my head
  In darkest clouds, to banish from my sight
  So foul a deed! O Tantalus, O Pelops!
  This house would fill even your souls with shame.
CHORUS: What is your news?
MESSENGER: What country are we in?
  The land of Argos, and of Sparta, where
  Two brothers[1] dwelt in love and harmony,
  Of Corinth, buttress 'twixt two warring seas –
  Or in the wild Danubian lands that shelter
  Fugitive Vandals, or the eternal snows
  Of Caucasus, the nomad Scyths' domain?
  What country is it that can be the scene
  Of such unspeakable abomination?
CHORUS: Whatever evil you have seen, reveal it.
MESSENGER: First let the tumult of my mind be stilled,
  And fear release my body from its grip.
  A picture of the brutal deed still floats
  Before my eyes. Carry me far away,
  Wild winds! Far from this place! Take me away
  To where the journey of the daylight ends!
CHORUS: You only hold us longer in suspense;
  Describe this deed you shudder at, and name
  The author of it; nay, I ask not 'who',
  But 'which of them'. Come, speak without delay.
MESSENGER: Part of the royal house of Pelops stands
  Upon the summit of the citadel,
  Facing the west, and at its outer edge

1. Castor and Pollux.

73

It towers above the city like a mountain
Ready to crush the people, should they rise
In insolent revolt against their kings.
Within this building is a huge apartment
Spacious enough to hold a multitude,
A hall of dazzling brilliance; golden beams
Rest upon handsome many-coloured pillars.
Behind this public space, to which the people
Freely resort, extends the private palace,
Room after room, of great luxuriance.
Deep in the secret heart of this domain,
Down in a hollow, is an ancient grove,
The sanctuary of the royal house.
Here grow no trees of pleasant aspect, none
That any pruner's knife has cultivated;
Yew and dark cypress and black ilex twine
A tangled canopy of shade; above,
A tall oak towers and dominates the grove.
This is the place in which the royal sons
Of Tantalus consult the auspices
And pray for help in danger or defeat.
The trees are hung with offerings, with horns
That called to battle, pieces of the chariot[1]
Won at the sea of Myrto – when the wheels
Of the defeated car were treacherously
Loosed from the axle; trophies of every crime
Committed by this family are here;
And here is hung the Phrygian crown of Pelops,
A painted cloak from a barbarian foe,
And many other spoils of victory.
A spring, under the shadow of the trees,
Forlornly drips and spreads its sluggish water
Into a sombre pool; like that dark river

1. See note on l. 140.

Styx, by whose name the gods are known to swear
Under this ground, at dead of night, 'tis said
The gods of death are heard to utter groans;
Chains rattle in the grove, and spirits cry.
There sights are seen that mortals quake to hear of.
The ghosts of men of ancient time emerge
From their old tombs and wander in the wood;
Spectres more strange than any known elsewhere
Invade the place; flames flicker on the trees,
And neighbouring roofs appear to be on fire,
Though no fire burns within. Sometimes the grove
Is filled with sounds of barking, thrice repeated;
Sometimes gigantic phantoms haunt the palace.
Daylight brings no relief from these alarms;
The grove's own darkness is the dark of night,
And even at high noon the ghostly powers
Retain their sway. Here worshippers
Receive responses from the oracles,
And at such times the Fates' decrees are cried
In thundering voices from the shrine; a god
Speaks, and the cave gives forth a hollow sound.
    Into this place came Atreus, like a man
Possessed with madness, with his brother's children
Dragged at his heels. The altars are prepared. . . .
But oh, what words are fit to tell what happened? . . .
He tied the princes' hands behind their backs,
And bound their hapless heads with purple fillets.
Incense was used, and consecrated wine,
The salt and meal dropped from the butcher's knife
Upon the victims' heads, all solemn rites
Fulfilled, to make this act of infamy
A proper ritual.

CHORUS: Who held the knife?

MESSENGER: *He* was the sacrificial priest, *his* voice

Boldly intoned the liturgy of death
And spoke the funeral prayers; beside the altar
He stood alone; and then laid his own hand
Upon the three appointed to be slain,
Placed them before him, and took up the knife.
He saw that all was done; and all was done
According to the rites of sacrifice.
A shudder shook the grove; the palace rocked
Over the trembling earth, and seemed to hang
As if uncertain whether it should fall
This way or that; and on the left a star
Traced out an angry furrow in the sky.
The sacrificial wine was changed to blood;
The diadem upon the royal head
Fell, twice or three times, to the ground; tears dripped
From ivory in the temples. Every man
Was moved to horror at these prodigies;
Atreus alone, intent upon his purpose,
Remained immovable, even defiant
Against the menacing gods. Without delay
He strode up to the altar and there stood
With scowling eyes, glaring this way and that.
A hungry tiger in an Indian forest,
Coming upon two steers, will stand in doubt,
Greedy for both, which victim to attack,
Baring his teeth at one, then at the other,
Holding his ravenous appetite in check
While making up his mind. Just so was Atreus
Eyeing the victims doomed to satisfy
His impious vengeance: which shall be the first
For slaughter, which the second head to fall?
As if it mattered! But he won't be hurried –
He wants to have his ghastly deed performed
In proper order.

CHORUS: Which was slaughtered first?
MESSENGER: The first – no one can say that Atreus failed
    In duty to his ancestors! – the first
    Was dedicated to his grandfather:
    The first to be dispatched was Tantalus.
CHORUS: What look, what bearing did the young man
        show
    In face of death?
MESSENGER: He held himself erect,
    Unflinching; prayers, that would have died unheard,
    He scorned to utter. With a savage blow
    The king drove in the sword, and pressed it home
    Until his hand was at the throat; the body
    Stood, with the sword plucked out, as if deciding
    Which way to fall, then fell against the king.
    Immediately the brutal murderer
    Seized Plisthenes and dragged him to the altar
    To add his body to his brother's, struck
    And hacked the head off; the truncated corpse
    Fell forward to the ground, and from the head
    That rolled away a faint last sob was heard.
CHORUS: And after those two butcheries, what next?
    A third, or did he spare the youngest child?
MESSENGER: Think of a tawny lion in Armenia
    Crouching amid the vanquished carcases
    Of a whole herd of oxen, jaws agape
    And wet with blood, his hunger satisfied
    But not his fury; he will stalk the bulls
    This way and that, and still with flagging speed
    And slackening mouth make passes at the calves:
    So Atreus, still with fury unassuaged,
    His sword now reeking with two victims' blood,
    Fell on the third, and with no thought of mercy
    For the defenceless child whom he attacked

So violently, pierced the body through;
The sword that entered by the breast was seen
Protruding from the back; the boy fell dead,
His spurting blood damped out the altar fires
And through both wounds his spirit fled away.

CHORUS: Inhuman outrage.

MESSENGER: Do you shudder now?
If this had been the end of his foul deed,
You could have called him innocent.

CHORUS: What more?
What more stupendous, more atrocious crime
Can man conceive?

MESSENGER: No, this was not the end,
Only a step upon the villain's way.

CHORUS: Could he do more? He threw the bodies out
For beasts to maul – denied them funeral fire?

MESSENGER: Denied them fire! Ah, would that that were
      so!
Would that he had denied them burial,
Denied them the consuming flames, left them
To be a meal for birds, a hideous banquet
For savage beasts! Well might their father pray
For what most fathers would abhor to see –
The unburied bodies of his sons. O sin
Incredible to any age of man,
And for the men of ages yet to come
A thing to be declared impossible! . . .
The entrails torn from the warm bodies lay
Quivering, veins still throbbing, shocked hearts beating.
Atreus picked at the pieces, scrutinized
The message of the Fates, noted the signs
In the internal organs hot with blood.
Finding no blemish in the sacrifice,
He was content, and ready to prepare

The banquet for his brother; hacked the bodies
Limb from limb – detached the outstretched arms
Close to the shoulders – severed the ligaments
That tie the elbow joints – stripped every part
And roughly wrenched each separate bone away –
All this he did himself; only the faces,
And trusting suppliant hands, he left intact.
And soon the meat is on the spits, the fat
Drips over a slow fire, while other parts
Are tossed to boil in singing copper pans.
The fire seems loth to touch the roasting flesh;
Two or three times it has to be repaired
To feed the crackling hearth, and still, reluctant
To do as it is told, burns sulkily.
The liver on the spits was heard to squeal;
Which cried the more, the bodies or the fires,
It would be hard to say. Above the flames
A pitch-black smoke ascended, and this too
Refused to rise up to the roof, but hung
A thick and noisome cloud, filling the house
With hideous vapours. Then . . . O patient Phoebus!
Thy light was sunk in darkness at mid-day
And thou hadst fled – thou shouldst have left us sooner!
The father bites into his children's bodies,
Chews his own flesh in his accursed mouth.
Drowsy with wine, his glistening hair anointed
With scented oil, he crams his mouth with food
Till it can hold no more. O doomed Thyestes!
This is the one good part of your misfortune:
You know not what you suffer. Not for long
Will this be true. The Lord of Heaven, the Sun
May turn his chariot back and drive away;
Black night may rise untimely from the east,
And total darkness in the midst of day

Veil this atrocious deed; but you must see
And know your own misfortune to the full.

CHORUS

O Father of all earth and all that lives,
Whose rising banishes the lesser lights
That make the dark night beautiful:
Why hast thou turned aside
From thy appointed path?
Why hast thou blotted out the day
And fled from heaven's centre? Why,
O Phoebus, hast thou turned thy face from us?
Vesper, the herald of the close of day,
Is not yet here to usher in the stars;
Thy wheel has not yet passed the western gate
Where, with their day's work done,
Thy steeds should be unyoked. We have not heard
The third note of the trumpet telling us
That day is over.
Ploughmen will stand amazed –
Suddenly supper-time, and oxen not yet ready to rest!

What can have forced you, Sun, from your heavenly road?
What can have made your horses bolt from their fixed
    course?
Are the Giants escaped from their prison and threatening
    war?
Has tortured Tityos found strength in his breast again
    to renew his old aggression?
Or has Typhoeus stretched his muscles to throw off his
    mountain burden?
Is Ossa to be piled on Pelion again
To build a bridge for the Phlegrean Giants' assault?[1]

1. The region of Phlegra in Macedonia was associated with the
revolt of the Giants against Olympus.

Is all the order of the universe plunged into chaos?
Will there be no more East and no more West?
The mother of the daylight, dewy Dawn,
Who never fails to give the chariot-reins
Into the hands of Phoebus, now with horror sees
Her kingdom's frontiers in confusion;
It is strange work for her
To lead the tired horses to the water,
To see them sink their steaming necks into the sea.
The Sun himself is like a stranger lost in a strange land,
Meeting the morning as he goes to rest,
Calling for darkness when no night has come.
The stars have not appeared, there is no light in all the
       sky,
No moon to break the darkness.

What darkness it may be, we cannot tell,
But pray that it be nothing else than night.

This is the fear, the fear that knocks at the heart,
That the whole world is now to fall in the ruin
Which Fate foretells; that Chaos will come again
To bury the world of gods and men; that Nature
A second time will wipe out all the lands
That cover the earth and the seas that lie around them,
And all the stars that scatter their bright lights
Across the universe.
Never again will the Lord of Stars lift his undying fire
To guide the march of time and give his signals to the
       world
For summer and for autumn. Never again
Will there be Moon to catch the Sun's fire in her face
And take night's terrors from us, as she runs, outstripping
Her brother's pace upon her shorter orbit.

All mingled into one vast void will fall
The multitude of gods.

That belt of constellations that marks out the passage of
    the years,
The highway of the holy stars that lies oblique across the
    zones,
Will fall away, and see the stars fall with it.
The *Ram*, at whose approach, even before the spring's
    full warmth,
Ships may spread sails to balmy zephyrs – he who once
Carried the frightened Helle[1] over the sea,
Into the sea himself will fall.
The *Bull*, who holds the Hyades between his shining
    horns,
Falling will drag the *Gemini* down, and down will fall
The bent-armed *Crab*.
Leo, resplendent with the fires of summer,
Victim of Hercules, will fall again.
Virgo will fall, back to the earth that once she knew;
Libra's true-balanced scales will fall, and after them
Sharp *Scorpio*. So too the aged *Chiron*,[2]
With feathered arrows and Thessalian bow,
Will lose both bow and arrows. *Capricornus*,
Slow winter's icy harbinger, will fall and break the urn
Of the unknown one whom we call *Aquarius*;[3]
And last of the twelve signs, the *Fish*, will disappear.
Into the universal deluge will the *Wain* descend,
Which never touched the sea before;

1. See note on *The Trojan Women*, 1034.
2. Chiron the Centaur, in several myths a guardian and tutor of young demigods (cf. *The Trojan Women*, 830), is identified with *Sagittarius*.
3. In the Latin 'will break your urn, whoever you are'. There appears to be no myth explaining the origin of *Aquarius*.

The *Snake*, like a meandering river sliding
Between the *Bears*; and the great *Dragon's* smaller neigh-
    bour,
The freezing *Cynosura*;[1] and the slow-footed watcher
Beside the wagon, *Arctophylax*,[2] will be shaken
And fall into the deep.

And are we chosen out of all earth's children
To perish in the last catastrophe
Of a disjointed universe? Are we
To see the world's end come?
A cruel fate brought us to birth, if we
Have lived to lose the Sun, or if our sins
Have driven him away.
But we must not complain, nor fear;
Too fond of life is he who would not die
When all the world dies with him.

        1. Or *Ursa Minor*.
        2. 'Keeper of the Bear', alias *Boötes*.

ACT FIVE

Atreus, Thyestes

ATREUS: I walk among the stars! Above the world
My proud head reaches up to heaven's height!
Mine is the kingdom and the glory now,
Mine the ancestral throne. I need no gods;
I have attained the summit of my wishes.[1]
Well done – and more than well. I ask no more. . . .
No more? Enough? Nay, but I will do more.
I will yet see this father eat his fill
Of his dead offspring. Shame need not deter me;
Daylight is gone. Yes . . . I need have no fear
While heaven itself is empty; gods have fled;
Would I could stop them, drag them back by force
And make them see this banquet of revenge!
Yet *he* shall see it; that will be enough.
Day hides its face, but I will bring a light
Into your darkness, brother, and unseal
Your sorrows from the night that covers them.
You have sat long enough at your repast,
Now it is time to rouse you from your rest
And change that happy smile. I need Thyestes
Sober, to face so terrible a sight. . . .
   Slaves, open wide the doors! Let all men see
Our hall, our temple of festivity!
   Now . . . to watch his face! . . . to see its colour
Change, when he sees the faces of his sons!
To listen to his first tormented cries,
To see his body stiffen with the shock
As if struck dead. This will be my reward

1. *Dimitto superos; summa votorum attigi.* The Latin is quoted in Marston's *Antonio and Mellida* (1599).

For all my pains – I must not only see him
Broken, but watch the breaking when it comes. . . .
    There – now the doors are open and the hall
Is bright with torches. There, upon a couch
Of gold and purple he reclines full length,
His left hand propping up his drunken head. . . .
His stomach heaves. . . . Now I am god of gods
And king of kings! My prayers are more than
    answered. . . .
He has fed full, and now he drinks again
From a great silver goblet. Drink it up!
There's blood to spare from all those slaughtered cattle,
Of colour to match well with that old wine. . . .
Ay, try that cup to finish off the banquet! . . .
I want to see him drinking up that potion
Made with his children's blood; he would have drunk
Mine if he could! . . . Now he begins to sing
A song of jollity . . . his wits are wandering.

THYESTES: Heart, dulled with long despair,
          Rise up, and banish care.
          Let fear and sorrow flee;
          Begone, chill poverty
          That banishment must know.
          Begone, the shame
          That clings to those brought low.

          Man, think not of your plight
          When down, but of the height
          From which you fell.[1] 'Twas good
          When, fallen from where you stood

1. *Magis unde cadas quam quo refert.* The Latin is quoted in Marston's
Antonio and Mellida.

Upon a dizzy peak, you found
Your footing firm on level ground.
'Twas good, that in your state
Of humbled misery
You stood under the weight
Of ruined royalty
With back unbowed and head held high,
An undefeated soul
Courageous in calamity.

Away, then, every mark
Of ill, away the dark
Shadows of destiny!
Greet happy days with happy face;
Forget the old,
And put a new Thyestes in his place.

And yet, with those that have known evil days
One fault remains: the good time, when it comes,
Seems unbelievable; they will not trust it.
Fortune may smile again,
Those that have felt her heavy hand
Have little heart for laughter.

Grief, dost thou pluck my sleeve again?
Dost thou deny me this day's happiness?
Grief, dost thou rise unbidden, unprovoked,
And wouldst thou have me weep?
Dost thou forbid me crown my head with flowers?
She does, she does. . . .
So, there they go . . . roses of summer. . . .
Now they are off. And what is this?
My scented and anointed hair
Stands stiff with horror . . . tears on my cheeks

Not of my bidding . . . sobs in my voice
When I would speak. . . .
'Tis sorrow's way; she will not be denied
The tears that she has grown to love. Weep then!
Yes! I will weep, though in this time of joy.
Yes! I will weep and howl
And tear these Tyrian purple clothes. My brain
Forewarns me of a thing
That I shall have to weep for by and bye;
It knows the coming evil; just as sailors
Know that a storm is brewing, when the sea
Begins to rise and swell, though no wind blows.

Why, fool, what griefs, what dangers
Does your imagination see?
Believe your brother with an open heart.
Your fears, whatever they may be,
Are either groundless, or too late. . . .
It is no use; against my will some fear pervades my being;
I have no cause to weep, yet tears start from my eyes.
Is it for grief, or fear? Can a man weep
For too much happiness?

ATREUS: Brother, we two must celebrate together
    This memorable day, which will confirm
    My kingdom and assure my confidence
    In everlasting peace.
THYESTES: I have dined well;
    And you have wined me well. Only one thing
    Can add a culmination to my pleasure –
    That I should share my pleasure with my sons.
ATREUS: Consider them already with you here
    In your embrace. They are, and will be, with you
    For evermore. No member of your family

87

Can now be taken from you. You shall see,
As you desire, their faces very soon,
And I shall see a father well content
Rejoicing in the presence of his loved ones.
Your cup shall be filled full; have no more fear.
Your sons are taking part in the enjoyment
Of festive fare – all the young folk together;
They shall be sent for. Let me offer you
A cup of wine from our ancestral vintage.

THYESTES: I shall accept your hospitable toast,
  Brother, with pleasure. A libation first
  To our paternal gods; then drain the cup. . . .
  But what is this? My hand will not obey me,
  The cup grows heavy, I can hardly lift it.
  The wine I try to drink avoids my lips –
  Some trick? – the liquor dribbles down my chin. . . .
  And see, the table rocked, the floor is shaking.
  The torches' light sinks low; the sky itself
  Hangs dull and heavy, seeming to be lost
  Between the daylight and the dark. And why –
  The ceiling of the heavens seems to shake
  With violent convulsions – more and more!
  The murk grows darker than the deepest darkness,
  Night is engulfed in night; all stars have fled.
  Whatever be this peril, may it spare
  My brother and my sons; on my vile head
  Let the storm break. But let me see my children!

ATREUS: I shall; no day shall ever take them from you.

THYESTES: What agitation in my stomach swells?
  What moves within me? Some protesting burden
  Lies on my heart, and in my breast a voice
  That is not mine is groaning. O my children!
  Where are you? Come! Your ailing father calls you.
  If I can see your faces, all my pain

Will soon be ended. Do I hear them? Where?

ATREUS [*exhibiting the children's heads*]: Embrace your
    children, father! They are here
Beside you. Do you recognize your sons?

THYESTES: I recognize my brother! Canst thou bear,
    O Earth, the weight of so much wickedness?
    Wilt thou not break, and drown thyself and us
    In the infernal Styx? Wilt thou not open
    Into a vast abyss and sink in chaos
    Kingdom and king? Not overturn Mycenae
    And tear it stone by stone from its foundations?
    We two should now be joined with Tantalus.
    Unlock thy gates, O Earth, open them wide,
    And to whatever dungeon lower lies
    Than Tartarus, where our forefathers are,
    Dispatch us quickly, down the steep descent
    Into thy awful bosom, there to lie
    Entombed under the weight of Acheron.
    Above our heads let guilty spirits float,
    Above our prison let the fierce hot flood
    Of Phlegethon stir up the scorching sands! . . .
    Dost thou lie idle, Earth, unmoved, inert?
    The gods are fled.

ATREUS: But here are your dear sons,
    Whom you have asked to see. Receive them gladly.
    Kiss them, make much of them, embrace them all.
    Your brother will not stop you.

THYESTES: Treachery!
    Was this our pact? Is this your brotherly love
    And reconciliation? Is this peace?
    What can I ask for now? Not as a father
    To have my children given back to me
    Alive; but as a brother I will beg
    This from my brother, which can be no loss

89

To his most infamous revenge: to give
A funeral to my sons. Can you not give me
Something which you will see immediately
Thrown on the fire? A gift, not to be kept,
But to be lost, is all this father asks.

ATREUS: You have them – all that now remains of them;
And all that is not here – is with you too.

THYESTES: What, are they lying out for birds of prey
To make a meal of? Are they set aside
For savage beasts or creatures of the field?

ATREUS: *You*, you yourself have dined on your sons' flesh!
You have consumed this monstrous banquet!

THYESTES: Gods!
This was the sight you could not bear to see!
This was the sin that drove the daylight back
To where it came from. O what words can tell,
What grieving can assuage my agony?
There are not words enough to speak of it.
Here are their severed heads, I see, their hands
Chopped off, the feet left from their broken legs,
The leavings of their father's gluttony.
My stomach moves; the sin within me strives
To find escape – cannot escape its prison.
Lend me your sword, brother, lend me that sword
Already glutted with my blood; its blade
Shall set my children free. You will not? Hands,
Beat on this breast until it break in pieces! . . .
No! Strike not, wretch! We must respect the dead.
When was such horror seen – when, in the days
Of Heniochus upon the awful crags
Of barren Caucasus, or in Procrustes' den,
The terror of the land of Attica?
I press my sons to death – they press their father.
Is sin illimitable?

ATREUS: There are bounds
To limit wilful sin; but sin's requital
Acknowledges no limits. I have done
Too little yet. I should have drained their blood
Warm from their wounds into your open mouth;
You should have drunk it from their living bodies.
I was too hasty, I rebuffed my rage;
I did it all myself – drove in the sword
To slay them at the altar, washed my hearth
With sacrificial blood, cut off the limbs
From the dead bodies, chopped them into pieces,
And threw the pieces into boiling cauldrons
Or had them slowly roasted on the fire;
Sinews and limbs I severed, warm with life;
I saw the meat impaled on slender spits
And heard it squealing; I heaped up the fires.
I should have made the father do all this!
His torture came too late; he never knew
What he was doing when his cursed teeth
Gnawed at those bones! His children never knew it!

THYESTES: Hear him, all seas that wash the winding shores!
Gods, wheresoe'er ye be, now fled from us,
Hear all this wickedness! Hear, powers below,
Hear, Earth! And thou, deep night of Tartarus,
Give ear to these my prayers; to thee alone
I come; thy starless dark, like this black day,
Alone can look upon my misery.
I will not pray for any evil thing;
I will ask nothing for myself – what good
Could ever now be mine? For you I pray:
Almighty ruler of the sky, great king
Of heaven's realm – wrap all the universe
In awful darkness, let the winds make war,
From every quarter of the sky let thunder

91

Loudly resound; not with thy gentler hand
That tempers its assault upon the homes
Of innocent men, but with that hand of wrath
Which overthrew the triple-mountained pile,
Ay, and the mountain-topping Giants too,
Prepare thy weapons and discharge thy fires.
Avenge the darkness of this stolen day,
Send thunderbolts and lightnings to supply
The place of this lost sun. Thou hast no need
To weigh the issue; count us guilty, both;
Or else on me alone pronounce thy sentence.
Strike at this head, let triple forks of fire
Impale this breast – how else should I expect
To give my sons a burial, or commit
Their bodies to the final flames, if not
To be burnt up myself? . . . Ah, will the gods not hear?
Have they no weapon to destroy the sinner?
Then may eternal night endure, may darkness
Cover these vast immeasurable sins
For evermore. Sun, never move again,
And I shall be content.

ATREUS: Well done, my hands!
This is my true reward. My wicked work
Would have been wasted, if I had not heard
Those cries of agony. Now I am sure
My sons are mine again, reborn to me;
The slur upon my fatherhood is lifted.

THYESTES: What cause could you have had to hate the
    children?[1]

ATREUS: That they[2] were yours.

THYESTES: Their father's sons. . .?

1. Meaning his own sons.
2. Meaning *his*, Agamemnon and Menelaus, suspected of being
begotten by Thyestes (cf. l. 327).

ATREUS: I know
  They *were* their father's,[1] and I am content.
THYESTES: Now, by the gods that make us love our own –
ATREUS: Why not the gods of marriage?
THYESTES: Is a fault
  To be requited with more wickedness?
ATREUS: I know why you are angry; 'tis your grief
  That you were cheated of the crime you purposed.
  You weep, not that you ate this loathsome meal,
  But that you had not cooked it! Your intent,
  I know, was to prepare a like repast
  And serve it to your unsuspecting brother;
  To seize *my* children, with their mother's aid,
  And make an end of them, as I of yours –
  And would have done it, but for one thing only:
  You thought you were their father.
THYESTES: My revenge
  The gods will give. I have no other wish
  But to entrust to them your punishment.
ATREUS: As I do yours, into your children's hands.

Exeunt

  1. i.e. 'mine'; but it is difficult to be sure whether this ambiguity
was the author's intention or only the result of the compression of
the Latin, particularly in Thyestes' exclamation *gnatos parenti* – sons
to their father! An alternative interpretation is: THY. How were
(my) children at fault? AT. In being yours. THY. (You could give)
sons to their father (to eat)! AT. Yes, and I am happy to know that
they were really yours. – Still the difficulty remains, why does
Atreus now feel assured of his own sons' legitimacy?

PHAEDRA

(or Hippolytus)

By his marriage with Antiope (Hippolyta), the queen of the Amazons, Theseus had one son Hippolytus. Preferring the goddess Diana to Venus, this young man devoted himself to athletic and rural exercises, and despised the love of women. Having murdered his wife Antiope and married Phaedra, daughter of the Cretan king Minos, Theseus absented himself on an expedition to the underworld to help his friend Peirithous abduct Persephone. Phaedra became enamoured of her handsome stepson and resolved to tempt him, though much tormented by her consciousness of sin and by the taint of evil tradition in her family. Her mother, Pasiphae, was also the mother, by a bestial union, of the bull-man Minotaur; this monster had been confined in the labyrinth of Knossos until sought out and killed by Theseus – whom Phaedra's sister Ariadne aided with her clue of thread.

The mass of legend associated with Theseus has many variations; its main course is charted by Plutarch in his *Life of Theseus*. Ovid's *Heroides* IV (*Phaedra to Hippolytus*), is a source from which Seneca's picture of Phaedra's passion may have derived some of its typically Roman colour. The *Hippolytus* of Euripides is the prototype (and only surviving version) in Greek tragedy.

DRAMATIS PERSONAE

THESEUS, *King of Athens*
PHAEDRA, *second wife of Theseus*
HIPPOLYTUS, *son of Theseus and Antiope*
NURSE
MESSENGER
CHORUS *of Athenian citizens*
Companions of Hippolytus

*

Scene: Athens, at the palace of Theseus

PRELUDE

Hippolytus and Companions

HIPPOLYTUS: Men of the land of Cecrops, come
  Range round the leafy woods! Away
  To the mountain tops! Swiftly afoot
  Spread wide your ways, to the glades that lie
  In the shadow of Parnes' height, to the river
  That thrashes its rapid course along
  The vale of Thria; climb to the hills
  White-topped with never-melting snow
    From northern skies.

For some, another way, where groves
Of alder weave a shade, where meadows
Kissed by the dewy breath of Zephyr
Lie, where the spring grass hears his call;
Or where Ilissos' stripling stream
Idles beside starved fields, bare sands
Scored into niggard channels.
Others, away by the western road
To the open pass of Marathon,
Where the suckling dams at evening graze
With their young behind them. Some, go down
Where the warm south breezes thaw the frost
  Of the hard Acharnian plain.

Who will climb to sweet Hymettus,
Who to Aphidnae's little hill?
The arc of Sunium that swings
Into the sea; there is a place
Long undespoiled, that asks for hunting.
Lovers of woods in all their glory,

Phlya awaits you, where the wild boar
Lurks, to the farmers' terror, a fighter
With many a victim to his credit.

Come, loose the hounds, the quiet ones;
But keep those wild Molossians leashed,
And the Cretan fighters, their tough necks
Can tug the collar. Those Spartans too
Are a lively breed, thirsting for blood;
Be sure to keep them well reined in.
Their time will come; we shall hear their voices
Raising the echoes in the mountains.
First you must let them get their heads down
Sniffing the air with their shrewd noses,
To pick up the scent around the coverts
Before the sun comes up, while footprints
    Pattern the dewy grass.

Up with the heavy nets, the coarse ones
Will need a hefty shoulder; and here
Are the finer snares. And take a line
Of coloured feathers, to intercept
    And trap the silly creatures.
You can be our javelin-thrower –
You, take the heavy broad-head spear,
It needs both hands at once – you, beater,
Stalk the game and cry him out
Full speed from his lair – and when we've caught him,
You shall knife the innards from him.

And come Thou to thy servant's side,
Huntress Divine, whose sovereign will
The secret heart of earth obeys;
Whose arrows fly swift to their mark

In any beast that stoops to drink
At cold Araxes' side, or paws
The ice of Ister. Thine the arm
That slays Gaetulian lions, thine
That hunts the Cretan stag; thine too
The lighter hand that pricks the deer.
Thou meet'st the tiger's mottled breast,
The shaggy bison's back, the span
Of the wild auroch's spreading horns.
No creature feeds in fields so far –
Under the rich Arabian trees,
On arid Garamantian plains,
Where the Sarmatian nomad roams,
Upon the high rough Pyrenees,
Or in Hyrcanian ravines –
    But it must fear Diana's bow.

Fortune attends the worshipper
Who has found favour at thy shrine;
Thy power goes with him to the fields,
His nets hold fast their captured prey,
No creature's feet break down his snares,
A laden wain brings back his spoils,
His hounds return with blooded mouths,
And all the country fellows join
Rejoicing in the long march home.

Hark, the dogs are baying; that is the sign
That thou art with me, Goddess. Now to the woods;
This way will take me quickly to the long road
That lies ahead.

ACT ONE

Phaedra, Nurse

PHAEDRA: O Crete, great land, great mistress of wide seas,
　Whose ships in countless numbers reach all shores,
　Faring across the ocean – to Assyria,
　To every coast, wherever the Sea God
　Permits a prow to cleave its way to land:
　Why have you banished me, a hostage bound
　To a hostile house, wife to an alien lord,
　To spend my days in tears and wretchedness?
　Where is my lord? Away – that is how Theseus
　Observes his marriage vows – on a bold venture
　Through the deep darkness of the underworld
　From which no man returns, comrade in arms
　To an audacious suitor who will steal
　And carry off a bride straight from the throne
　Of the King of Death. So Theseus follows him,
　Partner in his mad escapade; no fear,
　No shame, deters him. Lust and lawless marriage
　In hell Hippolytus's father seeks.
　　But I have other, greater pain to bear;
　No rest at night, no balm of sleep relieves
　My troubled soul. It thrives and grows – my pain
　Burns in me like the burning heart of Etna.
　My loom stands still, the wool drops from my hands;
　I have no heart to make my offerings
　At the gods' temples, or to take my place
　Among the dances of the Attic women
　Torch-bearing in dark rites around their altars.
　I cannot make pure prayers or honest vows
　To their presiding goddess, to whose care
　This land was given. I take pleasure now

In following the hunt, starting wild game,
A strong spear in this tender hand. Why, why,
My soul? What does it mean? What is this passion
For woods and fields? Is this the evil spell
That bound my mother, my unhappy mother? ...
Our love has gone astray in the woods. ... O mother,
I feel for you. I know how you were forced
By monstrous doom into audacious love
For that brute beast, bull of a roaming herd;
An angry beast, untamed and lecherous,
His wild mates all obeyed him – yet he loved.
What god will pity me? Where is a Daedalus
To find a cure for my complaint? That craftsman,
Master of Attic arts, who built a prison
To hold our Cretan monster in seclusion,
Could not, if he were here, do anything
To lighten my distress. This comes from Venus;
She hates all children of her enemy
The Sun,[1] and now through us she takes revenge
For what was done to her – the chains that bound her
In the arms of Mars; on all the tribe of Phoebus
She lays a load of shame. Love lies not lightly
On any daughter of the house of Minos;
We know no love that is not bound to sin.

NURSE: Nay, noble wife of Theseus, child of Jove,
Cleanse your pure heart at once of such vile thoughts;
Smother the flame and give no countenance
To evil hopes. Stand up to Love and rout him
At the first assault, that is the surest way
To win without a fall; once humour him,
Cherish the pleasant bane – 'twill be too late
Then to refuse the yoke you have accepted.
I am not blind, I know how royal pride,

1. Phaedra's mother Pasiphae was a daughter of the Sun.

Stubborn, and deaf to truth, abhors correction.
I am ready for my end, whate'er it be;
The old have courage, freedom is near for them.
To choose the good is the first rule of life,
And not to falter on the way; next best
Is to have shame and know where sin must stop.
Why, my poor mistress, why are you resolved
To heap fresh infamy upon your house,
With sin worse than your mother's? Wilful sin
Is a worse evil than unnatural passion;
That comes by fate, but sin comes from our nature.
You think, because your husband's eyes are closed
To all this upper world, that you are free
To sin without fear? No, you are mistaken;
Though Theseus may be safely out of sight
In Lethe's depths, walking the shores of Styx,
Perhaps for ever – what of him who rules
The hundred cities and the wide sea roads,
Your father? Will he let such sin be hidden?
Parents are watchful, and their care is wise.
And even if we do conceal your crime,
By our devices, from all human eyes,
There is your mother's father, He above
Who sheds his light upon the earth; and He,
Father of all the gods, who shakes the world
With hail of fiery bolts from his bright hand.
Will you believe that you can do this thing
Out of the sight of your all-seeing grandsires?
Again, let us suppose the good gods choose
To hide forbidden love; let us suppose
They lend to lawless intercourse protection
Denied to greater crimes – think of the price,
The penalty within, the conscious heart's
Deep dread, the mind burdened with guilt, the soul

That dare not face itself. Some may have sinned
With safety, none with conscience unperturbed.[1]
No – you must kill these fires of impious love,
This crime which every barbarous land abhors,
From which the Getan nomads, and the Scythian
Wild tribes and Taurian savages abstain.
Purge your thoughts clean of this abomination;
Learn from your mother; dare no strange affection.
Do you intend to be the common spouse
Of son and father, to conceive in sin
Two husbands' progeny at once? . . . Go, then!
Confound all nature with your wicked passions!
Let there be monsters still! Your brother's house[2]
Requires a tenant. Has it come to this?
Will nature waive her laws, will the world hear
Of monstrous prodigies each time love comes
To a Cretan woman?

PHAEDRA: All you say is true,
Good nurse. Unreason drives me into evil.
I walk upon the brink with open eyes;
Wise counsel calls, but I cannot turn back
To hear it; when a sailor tries to drive
His laden vessel counter to the tides,
His toil is all in vain, his helpless ship
Swims at the mercy of the current. Reason? . . .
What good can reason do? Unreason reigns
Supreme, a potent god commands my heart,
The invincible winged god, who rules all earth,
Who strikes and scorches Jove with his fierce fire.
The God of War has felt that flame; the forger
Of triple thunderbolts himself has felt it;
The feeder of the never-sleeping furnace

1. Cf. Appendix II, 5.
2. The prison, now empty, which contained the Minotaur.

In Etna's depths can feel this tiny flame;
Phoebus is lord of the bow, but one small boy
With more unerring aim can shoot an arrow
Straight to his heart, for he is everywhere,
Menacing heaven and earth.

NURSE: That love is god
Is the vile fiction of unbridled lust
Which, for its licence, gives to lawless passion
The name of an imagined deity.
Venus from Eryx, we are to believe,
Sends her son wandering over all the earth,
And he, skyborne, shoots out his wicked darts
From one small hand – the littlest of the gods
Endowed with such almighty power! Vain fancies
Conceived by crazy minds, they are all false!
Venus' divinity and Cupid's arrows!
Too much contentment and prosperity,
And self-indulgence, lead to new desires;
Then lust comes in, good fortune's fatal friend;
Everyday fare no longer satisfies,
Plain houses and cheap ware are not enough.
Why, tell me, does this sickness seldom taint
A humble home but strikes where life is soft?
Why is pure love found under lowly roofs,
And why do common people generally
Have wholesome appetites where modest means
Teach self-control – while wealth, propped up by power,
Always asks more than its fair share of things?
A man who can do much would like to do
More than he can. But there – you know what conduct
Is fitting for the great ones of the land;
Await your lord's return with fear and reverence.

PHAEDRA: I fear no man's return. Love is my sovereign.
And when has any man set eyes again

Upon this bowl of sky, having descended
Once to the silence of perpetual night?

NURSE: Never trust Pluto; though he keeps the key
Of his infernal realm, and has his hound
To guard the gates of death beside the Styx,
If any man can find the way, despite him,
That man is Theseus; he will find the way.

PHAEDRA: Perhaps he will forgive me for my love.

NURSE: He had no mercy for a virtuous wife;
That foreign one, Antiope, had cause
To know his wrath. But, be it possible
To charm an angry husband, who of us
Will move the obstinate young man? Women . . .
He hates the whole sex, he avoids them all,
He has no heart, he dedicates his youth
To single life; marriage is not for him –
Which proves him a true Amazonian.

PHAEDRA: Ah, let him never leave the white hillsides,
The rugged rocks down which he lightly leaps,
Across the mountains and through thickest woods
I mean to follow him.

NURSE: And will he stop
To pay attention to your blandishments?
Will he exchange his virgin exercises
For the illicit rites of Venus? Will
His hatred cease for you, when, very like,
It is for hate of you he hates all women?
No prayers can ever turn that man.

PHAEDRA: He is
A creature of the wild; have we not known
Wild creatures to be overcome by love?

NURSE: He'll run from you –

PHAEDRA: – run, even through the sea,
I'll follow still.

NURSE: Do you forget your father?

PHAEDRA: No, nor my mother.

NURSE: But he hates all women.

PHAEDRA: The less I'll fear a rival.

NURSE: And your husband
Will soon be here.

PHAEDRA: What, with Peirithous?

NURSE: Your father will be here.

PHAEDRA: He will have pity,
The father of Ariadne.

NURSE: Oh, by this heart
Worn out with age and care, these silvered hairs,
This breast you loved, I do implore you, child,
To stop this folly. Be your own best friend;
The wish for health is half the remedy.

PHAEDRA: Well, have your way. Shame and nobility
Live in me still. If love will not obey,
It must be vanquished; honour shall be kept
Unstained. One way, then, only one way out
Of danger still remains. I'll join my husband.
By death I shall avert transgression.

NURSE: No!
That is too rash; restrain that impulse, child!
Hold these hot thoughts in check. Yourself to say
That you deserve to die, is proof enough
That you deserve to live.

PHAEDRA: But I must die,
Of that I am resolved. The manner, how,
Is yet to find. A noose? A sword? A leap
Precipitate from the high rock of Pallas?

NURSE: Leap to your death? Shall these old bones allow it?
Curb that wild will. No one returns from death.

PHAEDRA: No one that means to die, and ought to die,
Can be forbidden to die. This hand must fight

108

To save my honour.

NURSE: Mistress, only joy
Of my spent age, hear me: is your heart heavy
With this immoderate passion? Then ignore
The tongue of reputation. Reputation
Takes no account of truth; it often harms
The innocent, and treats the guilty well.
This is what you must do, try out the strength
Of that perverse austerity. I'll do it;
I'll speak to the young savage presently
And bend the stiffness of his stubborn will.

CHORUS

O daughter of the never gentle sea,
Goddess divine, mother of Cupids twain –
   For twofold is his power; with fire
      And arrows sharp he plays
      His wanton game,
   A smile upon his wicked face
      As he prepares his bow
      With never erring aim.

He can send madness to consume the heart,
A flame of hidden fire to dry the blood.
      His wound makes little show,
   But eats into the secret soul.
He is a boy who gives his enemy
      No peace; the wide world over,
Ever alert, he makes his arrows fly.

The land that sees the sun newborn, the land
      Beside the western gates,
   The lands that burn under the Crab,
And those that the wild plainsman cultivates

Under the cold Great Bear –
Love's fire is everywhere.
Love stirs the leaping flame of youth,
And warms the dying ash of age,
Kindles the first fire in a maiden's heart,
   Brings gods from heaven to walk the earth
      In strange disguises.

Phoebus came down to Thessaly,[1]
To be a neatherd; left his lyre and quill,
   And learnt to use a scaled reed-pipe
      To call the cattle home.
Time and again, the very god who made
Heaven and the clouds, assumed a humbler shape:[2]
      A bird, with white wings waving –
A voice, sweeter than any swan's last song –
A lusty grim-faced bull, stooping to carry
A playful maiden on his back and away
To a world his brother owned, not his;
   In he plunged and mastered it,
Paddling with his hoofs for oars, anxious
   As any boatman for the safety
      Of his stolen cargo.

The shining goddess of the darkened sky[3]
   Knew love, gave up her rule of night
   And left her chariot of light
To other hands, her brother's; he found out
A way to handle the nocturnal equipage

1. When he served as herdsman to King Admetus (cf. Euripides,
Alcestis).
2. The disguises of Jupiter: the swan which loved Leda – the bull
which carried Europa into the sea (Neptune's province).
3. The Moon, descending to earth for love of Endymion.

Around its narrower course, but with his weight
 The wheels drove hard and night ran late
 Delaying the return of day.
   So too Alcmena's son[1]
 Dropped quiver and lion-skin – that huge
 And formidable garment – and allowed
His shaggy hair to be reduced to order
 And emerald rings to grace his fingers,
 Bound his legs with yellow ribbons,
 Cased his feet in golden slippers,
And with a hand that used to wield a club
 Spun yarn upon a twirling spindle.
 Thus in an oriental land,
 In a rich court of wealthy Lydia,
Was seen, instead of the wild lion's mane,
A silky robe of Tyrian workmanship
 Upon that back which once held up
   The kingdom of the sky.

   Great is the power,
   And baneful, of that flame,
 As they whom it has touched can tell.
Where the earth's edge is skirted by the sea,
Where bright stars ride across the upper world,
   The pitiless child holds sway.
Under the waters the blue Nereid hosts
Do not escape his darts; nor can the sea
   Wash that flame's scars away.

   Love drives the desperate bull
   To battle for his herd.
When danger threatens any of his wives,

1. Hercules, sentenced to serve at women's tasks for Omphale,
queen of Lydia (cf. Ovid, *Heroides*, IX).

The meekest stag will fight.
At such a time, as the black Indian knows,
The motley tiger is a menace; boars
Whet their sharp tusks and fleck their cheeks with foam.

The Punic lion shakes his mane,
And speaks his passion with a roar.
Love moves, and the whole forest roars again.
Love moves the monsters of the senseless sea,
And the bull elephant in Luca's fields.[1]
All nature is his prey;
Nothing escapes; at the command of Love
Old angers die, and enmity gives way.
And, let us not forget, this malady can take
A hard stepmother's cruelty away.

1. If this is the meaning of *Lucae boves*, animals used by Pyrrhus
in Lucania in his war against the Romans.

ACT TWO

Nurse, Phaedra, Hippolytus

CHORUS: Nurse, have you news? How is it with the queen?
   Does she yet find relief from her great torment?
NURSE: There is no hope; there can be no relief
   From suffering such as hers; the rabid fire
   Will never end. The fever silently
   Burns in her heart; only her face betrays
   The inner anguish which she tries to hide.
   Her eyes are bright as flame, while her wan face
   She hides from daylight; nothing long contents
   Her wandering mind; this way and that she turns,
   Her body racked with shifting pain. Sometimes
   Stumbling she falls as if she'd live no longer,
   Cannot hold up her head, then, calm again,
   Lies down to rest, but with no thought of sleep
   Weeps all night long. Now 'Lift me up' she cries,
   Then 'Lay me down'. 'Unbind my hair' – and soon
   She'll have it braided up again; no dress
   Pleases her long, but she will have it changed.
   She takes no interest in her food or health;
   She wanders aimlessly, her strength all spent –
   How different from the old activity,
   The bright blush painting those clear cheeks! Ravaged
   With care her body now, feeble her tread,
   Lost all the grace of that sweet loveliness!
   Those eyes, the very torches of the sun,
   Reflect no trace of what was once their birthright.
   Tears flood her face; upon her cheek drops down
   The incessant dew, as on the slopes of Taurus
   The warm rain falls to melt away the snow. . . .
      Now they are opening the palace doors,

And there she lies upon a golden couch . . .
Throwing her customary garments off. . . .
She will have none of them . . . she is deranged.
PHAEDRA [*seen within*]: Out of my sight, slaves, take these
        broidered robes,
    Of gold and purple! Take that Tyrian scarlet,
    And silkstuff culled from far-off Seric[1] trees.
    Give me a light robe and a simple sash,
    No necklace at my throat, no pendant pearl
    From Indian seas hung in my ear; my hair –
    Let it be loose and free of Syrian perfume. . . .
    So . . . falling anyhow about my neck . . .
    Down to my shoulders . . . let it toss in the wind
    As I run . . . the left hand reaching for the quiver,
    The right hand wielding a Thessalian spear.
    I shall be like the mother of Hippolytus –
    That cruel one – a woman of Maeotis
    Or Tanäis, leading her warriors
    From frozen Pontus on to Attic soil. . . .
    Hair knotted up . . . or falling free . . . her side
    Protected by a crescent shield; so I
    Will away to the woods. . . .
CHORUS: Do not weep over her.
    Grief cannot help the afflicted. Let your prayers
    Invoke the virgin goddess of the wild.
        [*The doors are closed*]
NURSE: Queen of the forests, Thou who walk'st
    apart
    On the high hills, goddess alone among
    The lonely mountains: turn thou into good
    These ill-portending omens. Hecate,[2]
    Of triple aspect, great divinity
    Of groves and woods, bright lantern of the sky,

1. Chinese.   2. Moon.

Light of the world, making night beautiful
With thy recurrent beams ... ay, with us now
To bless our work! Bend the hard heart
Of that stern youth. Let him relent and hear us.
Soften his iron soul; teach him to love;
Let him too feel that flame; capture his heart;
Let love's law win again that silent, cold,
Reluctant man. For this let all thy powers
Work with us – as we pray thy face may shine
And no cloud dim the glory of thy crescent,
No dark Thessalian witchcraft draw thee down
From where thou ridest through the night, no shepherd
Make thee his thrall.[1] O Goddess, hear our cry!
Come, and be gracious to our supplication! ...

    Yonder I see the man himself. He comes
To make an act of worship, and alone. ...
What better time? Here is the chance, the place,
The opportunity. I must be artful.
Am I afraid? It is no easy thing
To be the agent of an evil business
Dictated by another; royalty
Commands, and he who fears to disobey
Must banish honour from his thoughts. Conscience
Is always royalty's worst minister. ...

HIPPOLYTUS: Good nurse, what brings your old feet toil-
    ing hither –
Your face so sad – and trouble in your brow?
My father – surely all is well with him?
And Phaedra? And their two sons?

NURSE: Have no fear.
The kingdom prospers, and good fortune smiles
Upon the royal house. More cause that you
Should smile upon good fortune. I am grieved

        1. As Endymion; cf. above, 309.

And anxious for you, that you lay this hard
Relentless discipline upon yourself.
When fate compels, a man may well be wretched;
But go out of your way to look for trouble,
Torment yourself – then you deserve to lose
The gifts you had no use for. You are young;
Then be young! Free that heart! Salute the night
With fire and revelry! Let Bacchus lift
That heavy load of sadness from your soul.
Life is to be enjoyed; it quickly passes.
Now is the time for ease, the time for youth
To know the joy of love. Let your heart live!
Why do you sleep alone? Unlock those chains
That bind your joyless youth; seize pleasure now,
Give it the reign; the best days of your life
Must not be left to drain away. God gives
Each age its proper occupation, guides
Man's life from step to step; joy is for youth,
The frown for old men's faces. Why should you
Bridle yourself and stifle your true nature?
A farmer reaps the richest crop from fields
In which the blade, when young, was free to thrive
In healthy soil; that tree will top its fellows,
Which has not been cut back or pruned away
By niggling hands. A noble nature needs
The food of healthy freedom, if true worth
Is to bring forth the fruit of good achievement.
Are you some churlish woodsman, ignorant
Of life's true meaning, giving up your youth
To melancholy, hating the name of Venus?
Is this what man was born for – toil and hardship,
Horse-taming, war and bloody battlefields?
Why, are there not already deaths enough
Of different kinds, by sea, by sword, by malice,

Preying upon mankind? Nor need we these –
We find our own way to the eternal dark
Without their aid. Who could praise single life
But youth that asks no future? Have your way
And all that lives will be one passing swarm,
A single generation, doomed to perish.
Did not the Father of the universe
Take thought, having observed Fate's grasping hand,
To find a way how loss might be repaired
By new creation? Why – if from our life
We banish Venus, who replenishes
And recreates our dwindling stock, the earth
Will soon become a desert, drear and ugly,
The sea a dead sea, where there are no fish,
The sky will have no birds, the woods no beasts,
The air will be a place where nothing moves
Except the passing winds. Therefore I say,
Let nature's instinct guide your life; be seen
Here in the city; meet your fellow-men.

HIPPOLYTUS: There is no other life so free, so pure,
So true to man's primeval laws – as this,
Life far from city walls, a rustic life.[1]
No rage of avarice eats out the hearts
Of simple countrymen who love the mountains.
The winds of popularity, mob rule
Which no good man can trust, the bite of envy,
The treachery of favour, cannot touch them.
The countryman is no king's slave, nor asks
For empty honours, angling after kingship.
He seeks no perishable wealth, he lives
Free of ambition, free of fear. Base jealousy's
Despicable sharp tooth bites not at him.

1. Compare this speech with similar thoughts in *Thyestes*, 446 ff.
It may remind us also of Shakespeare's *3 Henry VI*, ii. 5.

He is a stranger to the sins that breed
In populous cities, has no need to wake
In guilty fear at every passing sound,
Or guard his speech with lies. The rich man's house,
Pillared and porticoed, the ostentation
Of gold-encrusted ceilings, tempt not him.
He takes no part in pious sacrifices,
Lavish expense of blood, sprinkling of meal
Over a hundred head of snow-white oxen
Stooping for slaughter. Free and innocent
In the open air the countryman commands
His unencumbered land. He can be crafty,
But only in the setting of shrewd snares
For animals; and after the day's toil
His bath is the Ilissos, cooled with snow.
He will be roaming on the riverside
Where swift Alpheus flows, or in the depths
Of some dark wood, some hushed retreat beside
Lerna's pellucid water, clean and cold;
The only sound the shrill bird's cry, the stir
Of ancient beech and ash touched by the breeze.
He loves to rest beside some straying brook,
To sleep on naked ground; a waterfall,
Perhaps, pours copiously down, a stream
Winds prattling pleasantly through fresh-sprung flowers.
His food is easily supplied; wild fruits
Shaken from trees, and berries picked from shrubs
Keep hunger off. Banquets in regal style
He heartily detests; what danger lurks
In the gold cups of high society!
What pleasure in a drink scooped by bare hands
From running water! Sleep comes easily
To care-free bodies on uncushioned beds.
Unlike the sinner seeking furtive joys

In darkened bedchambers, behind closed doors,
In the recesses of the tortuous palace
In which he hides his shame – the countryman
Seeks light and open air, and lives his life
Under the eye of heaven.

                    So, I think,
Men lived in the olden days, the men who shared
Their life on earth with gods.[1] They had no gold
To excite their blind desires. No legal landmarks –
Stones to give laws to families of men –
Divided field from field. There were no ships
Striking out confidently through the sea;
What sea they knew was near at hand. No cities
Stood within massive many-towered ramparts;
There were no soldiers armed with cruel steel,
No catapults bombarding bolted gates
With heavy stones. The land was not enslaved
To any master's will, the soil not subject
To teams of oxen. Man made no demands,
But self-productive fields supplied his needs.
What wealth the woods contained, they freely gave;
Homes were as nature built them – cool dark caves.
This state of peace was wickedly destroyed
By the accursed lust for gain, blind hate,
And all the reckless passions which ignite
And dominate man's soul: the thirst for power,
Whetted by blood; strong preying upon weak;
Might standing in the place of right. Bare hands
Were the first weapons; then came stones and clubs.
That was before the slender cornel shaft
With tapered iron point was made, or longsword
Slung from the belt; before the crested helmet

1. The legend of the ages of man, a commonplace of Latin poetry,
appears again in *Octavia*, 397 ff.

Proclaimed the oncoming foe; the rage for battle
Was weapon enough in those days. But the War God
Devised new kinds of strategy, and death
In myriad shapes, until the whole earth's soil
Was stained with blood and all the sea grew red.
There was no stopping it, crime walked unchecked
Through every home of man, no shape of sin
Lacked its example. Brother fell to brother,
Sons slew their fathers, wives shed husbands' blood,
Mothers, defying nature's law, destroyed
Their infants ere they lived. Stepmothers –
What can one say of them? – wild beasts
Have more compassion. Woman, say what you will,
Is the prime mover of all wickedness;
Expert in every evil art, woman
Lays siege to man; for her adulteries
Cities have burned, nation made war on nation,
Multitudes perished in the fall of kingdoms.
Let one example speak for all: Medea,
Aegeus' wife, proclaims all women damned.
NURSE: If some have been at fault, must all be damned?
HIPPOLYTUS: I hate them all; I dread, I shun, I loathe them.
I choose – whether by reason, rage, or instinct –
I choose to hate them. Can you marry fire
To water? Can ships safely sail the quicksands?
Can Tethys make the sun rise in the west?
Can wild wolves smile on does? No more can I
Consent to have a tender thought for woman.
NURSE: It has been known for Love to put a bridle
On fractious tempers, and to cast out hate.
Think of the women whom your mother ruled;
Fighters they were, yet knew the bonds of Venus –
Witness yourself, their one surviving son.[1]

1. The Amazons were said to destroy all their male children.

HIPPOLYTUS: One thing consoles me for my mother's
      death:
  There is no woman now whom I must love.
NURSE: He will not listen; he throws back my words
  As some unshakable hard rock, immune
  On every side to the assaulting sea,
  Flings back the waters. . . .
                          But here Phaedra comes,
  In such impatient haste, no hand can stop her.
  How will Fate shape the outcome of this passion? . . .
  She has fallen as if dead; the pallor of death
  Is in her face. . . . Lift up your head, my child.
  Is there not something you can say? Hippolytus
  Is here with you, and has you in his arms.
PHAEDRA: I had been glad to lose myself. . . . Who drags
      me
  Back to my misery? Who gives me back
  My load of anguish?
HIPPOLYTUS: How can you refuse
  The blessed gift of life brought back to you?
PHAEDRA [aside]: O soul, be bold . . . have courage . . . do
      not shirk
  Your self-taught precept. Speak up fearlessly;
  One who asks faintly asks to be refused.
  My course of wickedness was long ago
  More than half run; it is too late for shame;
  I have already loved unlawfully.
  If I go on the way I have begun,
  I may perhaps conceal my sin in marriage.
  Success can justify some evil actions.
  Then courage, heart! . . . [To Hippolytus] May I have
      words with you
  In private? If there is any friend with you,
  Dismiss him.

HIPPOLYTUS: There is no one who can hear us.

PHAEDRA: But yet ... my lips refuse to frame the words
  I meant to speak; one strong power gives me voice,
  Another, stronger, takes that voice away.
  Be witness, all ye gods, that my desire –

HIPPOLYTUS: Something your heart desires but cannot
    speak of?

PHAEDRA: Light troubles speak, the heaviest have no
    voice.[1]

HIPPOLYTUS: Yet tell me what your trouble is, mother.

PHAEDRA: Mother – that is too fine and great a title
  For my condition; better a lower one –
  Sister, Hippolytus – or call me servant;
  Yes, servant; I will do you *any* service –
  Bid me to go through driven snow, gladly
  I'd walk across the frozen heights of Pindus;
  Send me through fire or battle, I'd not fear
  To breast drawn swords. Be regent in my place,
  And let me be your slave; it is your right
  To rule, my duty only to obey.
  It is no part of women's work to hold
  The reins of government. You, in the prime
  And flower of your youth, should rule your people;
  Your birthright gives you power. Only protect
  Your slave, and take your suppliant to your arms!
  Have pity for a widow –

HIPPOLYTUS: God avert
  The omen of that word! My father lives
  And he will very soon return unharmed.

PHAEDRA: The master of the silent prison-house

1. *Curae leves loquuntur, ingentes stupent.* The Latin is quoted in
The Return from Parnassus (anon. c. 1600), in *Sir Thomas More* (anon.
1590–1600), and (with a variation) in Tourneur's *The Revenger's
Tragedy* (1607).

Of death allows a traveller no way
Back to the world he came from; will he allow
A ravisher[1] to return? Unless we think
Pluto himself sits by, smiling on love!

HIPPOLYTUS: Yet I believe the kindly powers of heaven
Will bring him back. Until our prayers are answered,
I will be guardian, as in duty bound,
Of my dear brothers; and my care of you
Will make you never think of widowhood.
I shall be with you in my father's place.

PHAEDRA [aside]: Could he say more? O tempting voice of
       love!
Fond lovers' hope! I must entreat again. . . .
[To Hippolytus]
Yet pity me; hear my heart's silent prayer;
I long to speak, yet am ashamed –

HIPPOLYTUS: What ails you?

PHAEDRA: Such trouble as you would not think a step-
       mother
Would have to bear.

HIPPOLYTUS: You set me riddles to guess.
Can you speak plainly?

PHAEDRA: Madness is in my heart;
It is consumed by love, a wild fire raging
Secretly in my body, in my blood,
Like flames that lick across a roof of timber.

HIPPOLYTUS: Love – why, your innocent love for Theseus,
       how
Can that be madness?

PHAEDRA: This is the truth, Hippolytus:
The face of Theseus is the face I love –
The youthful face of former years – the cheek

  1. Referring to Theseus as the abettor of Peirithous in the rape of
Proserpine.

That had been smooth, pencilled with its first beard –
The moment when he saw the Cnossian monster's
Labyrinth prison – when he wound the thread
Along the twisting alleys. Ah, the splendour!
His gentle face, below the banded hair,
Shone with the golden glow of modesty.
His arms were tender, but with muscle strong;
And in his face there was the face of Phoebe,
Your ancestor – or Phoebus, mine; but yet
More like your own. Yes, yes, I see him now –
So was he when he won his enemy's[1] favour –
Just so – his head held high; though in your looks
The natural grace, unkempt, is still more splendid.
Your father is all here in you; here too
Is something of your mother's sternness, lending
As great an added dignity – your face
Is Greek but with a trace of Scythian roughness.
If *you* could have been there beside your father
The day he crossed the sea to Crete, my sister[2]
Would rather have spun out her ball of thread
For you. And O my sister, help me now!
Now, from wherever in the starry sky
Your bright face shines, come to my aid in this
The same perplexity as was your own:
Two sisters fallen victims to one house,
You to the father, I to the son! . . .
[*To Hippolytus*]   Behold,
The daughter of a king kneels at your feet!
Spotless, unstained, and innocent of sin,
Till now; but now, for love of you alone,
No longer what I was. Not without purpose

1. Minos of Crete, who allowed him to court his daughter
Ariadne.
2. Ariadne.

Have I abased myself in prayer; this day
Must end my misery, or end my life.
Have pity on my love –

HIPPOLYTUS: Almighty God!
God of all gods! Canst thou hear things so foul
And not be moved? Canst see – and not be moved?[1]
For what cause shall the sky be rent with thunder
If no cloud dims it now? Let ruin wreck
The firmament, and black night hide the day!
Let stars run back and all their courses turn
Into confusion! Thou too, king of stars,
Lord Sun resplendent, art thou looking down
Upon thy daughter's wickedness? Wilt thou
Not veil thy light and flee into the darkness?
Ruler of gods in heaven and men on earth,
Why is thy hand not armed, will not thy torch
Of triple fire set all the world ablaze?
Hurl against me thy thunderbolt, thy spear,
And let me be consumed in instant fire.
I am the sinner; I deserve to die;
I have found favour with my stepmother.
[To Phaedra]
So, did I seem fit sport for filthy amours?
Was I, of all men, picked by you to be
The easy instrument of your foul crime?
Is my austerity rewarded thus? O woman,
First of all womankind in wickedness,
Worse than your mother! – as your sin is worse
Than hers who was the mother of a monster.
Once did she sin, and – though long afterwards –
The nature of that sin was brought to light

1. *Magne regnator deum, / tam lentus audis scelera, tam lentus vides?*
The Latin is quoted, with a variation, in *Titus Andronicus*, IV. I. See
also Appendix I, 28 and 30.

By the crossed offspring of her womb, her crime
Revealed in her freak infant's brutish visage.
And from that mother's womb you too were born!
O three times bless'd, and four times, by the hand
Of generous fate, are those whom enmity
And malice have consumed, cut down, destroyed.
Father, I envy you; you had a stepmother,
The Colchian woman,[1] but my enemy
Is one far worse, far deadlier than she.

PHAEDRA: I know the fate that has pursued our house;
What we should shun we must desire. Yet knowing,
I cannot help myself. Even through fire,
Through raging seas, through rivers in full flood,
Over the mountain heights, I shall pursue you.
No matter where you go, I shall go with you,
Mad for your love. Once more, contemptuous man,
I stoop to kiss the ground before your feet.

HIPPOLYTUS: Keep off those wanton hands from my chaste
body!
What! Does she fling herself into my arms?
Here is my sword to see full justice done. . . .
I have her by the hair, this shameless head
In my left hand . . . O Goddess of the Bow,
Never did blood more justly stain thy altar.

PHAEDRA: Hippolytus! My prayer is answered now,
My mind made whole. More than my prayer is granted,
Now I can die by your hand, saved from sin.

HIPPOLYTUS: Rather than that, go, live, obtain no boon
From me! . . . Let this contaminated sword
Never again come near my spotless side! . . .
Will Tanäis wash me clean, will the wild waves
Of far Maeotis, feeding the Pontic sea?
No; nor great Neptune in his whole wide ocean

1. Medea.

126

Drown this great weight of sin.[1] Woods and wild
    creatures! ...
NURSE: Now all the evil is exposed. What then?
Shall resolution faint or fail? Not so.
We must prefer a counter charge against him,
Take up the case ourselves and prove him guilty
Of violation. Crime must cover crime.
The safest shield in danger is attack.
When the offence is private, who shall say
Which of us sinned and which was sinned against? ...
    Help us, all Athens! Help, you faithful slaves!
Rape is afoot, a ravisher, Hippolytus,
Attacking, assaulting us, threatening death!
Menacing a chaste woman with drawn sword. ...
Ay, here it is, the sword, left when he fled
In frightened haste, being surprised in the act;
We have it to prove his guilt. But the poor queen –
We must revive her first. No, let her hair,
Torn and disordered, stay as it is, for proof
Of the terrible thing she has suffered. Carry her
Indoors. ... Come back to life, dear mistress. ... Nay,
You need not beat your breast, and turn away
As if to avoid our eyes; an accident
Cannot stain innocence, without intention.

CHORUS

Swift was his flight as the wildest gale,
Swifter than Corus cloud-compelling,
Swifter than flames of fire that stream
From a star that flies before the wind.

1. This concept (repeated in *Hercules Furens*, 1323) has fathered a
long line of imitations, of which Macbeth's 'Will all great Neptune's
ocean ...' is a sufficiently familiar example. Nor can it be credited
to Seneca's invention; cf. Sophocles, *O.T.*, 1227.

What though thy beauty, youth, be set beside all
Beauty of ancient time in fame's account, where
Olden days are remembered; all the brighter
Then shall thy beauty seem; never so brightly
Shines the full-circled moon, her crescent closing
Into an orb of fire, her chariot speeding
Through the long night, when Phoebe's face resplendent
Dims every smaller star. The star of evening,
Hesperus, has such grace, bringing the darkness
At the approach of night, up from his sea-bath
Rising refreshed; so beautiful is the Day Star
   Ending the darkness.

   Bacchus, from India thyrsus-dancing,
   Ageless for ever, hair unshorn,
   A vine-leaf wand thy tiger-tamer,
   Thy horned head delicately turbaned –
   Nothing hast thou more beautiful
Than the crisp curls of young Hippolytus.
What is thy beauty worth? All the world knows
Whom Phaedra's sister loved, who loved not thee.[1]

   O beauty, but a dubious boon
Art thou to man, brief gift of little stay,
   Lent for a while and all too soon
      Passing away . . .
   Passing . . . as the fields' spring glory
   Fades in the summer's heat, when fiercely
   Burns the high sun at noon, when night's
   Wheels roll too rapidly. As lilies
   Languish and their leaves grow pale,
The head must lose the glory of its hair,
      The glowing cheek of youth

   1. Ariadne, only when deserted by Theseus, unwillingly accepted
Dionysus (Bacchus).

Be ravaged by the hand of time.
Each day that passes takes its toll
Of body's beauty. Beauty cannot stay;
Would any wise man trust so frail a thing?
　　　Then use it while you may.
Time is the enemy, silently
Working beneath; worse after worse,
　　　Hour follows hour away.

And would you fly to empty places?
Beauty will be no safer there,
Where few feet walk. Hide in the forest,
And at high noon a wanton rout
Of sporting Naiads will surround you;
Such as trap comely youths in rivers;[1]
Dryads, who chase the woodland Pans,
Will lie in wait to wake your slumbers.

Or else the Moon, whose birth
The old Arcadians saw, older than she,
　　　Will spy you from her starry height
　　　And leave her chariot of light
To run untended.[2] Did we not see her blush
A while ago? Yet there was no dull cloud
Veiling her face. We were alarmed to see
　　　Our lady thus disturbed; we thought
　　　Thessalian spells had been at work
　　　To draw her down; we beat our gongs;
And it was you she pined for, you
　　　That stopped the Moon; to look on you
The goddess of the night had paused in her career.

Ah, would you spare that face from winter's frost,

1. As Hylas.
2. As she did for love of Endymion (cf. above, 309 and 422); but
a different explanation is suggested here!

Let it less often greet the summer's sun,
  Purer than Parian marble then
  Would be its loveliness. That firm,
That manly bearing – what a grace is there,
What grave old wisdom in that solemn brow!
That neck is not less lovely than Apollo's,
  Whose flowing tresses, unconfined,
  Flow down, as robe and ornament,
Over his shoulders; yet your rougher crown
Of short and tousled hair becomes you well.

There is no god so brutal, so ferocious,
But you would be a match for him, so great
Your strength, your body's bulk. Young still,
You have a broader chest than warring Mars
      And arms like Hercules.
      If you should choose to ride,
You'd show a defter hand upon the rein
Than Castor's, mastering his Spartan Cyllarus.[1]
Finger a bowstring, draw with all your might,
      Your shaft will surely fly
Farther than the most expert Cretan archer
      Can shoot his slender reed;
Or, like the Parthian, shoot your arrows high
  Into the air; not one will fail
  To bring a bird down; every one
  Will find its mark in living flesh
  And snatch its prize out of the sky.

Rare is the man – look in the roll of time –
To whom great beauty has not been great cost.
May kind gods spare you, that your beauty live
  To pass into the house of age
Where at the end all beauty must be lost.

          1. The horse, or centaur, ridden by Castor.

ACT THREE
Nurse, Theseus, Phaedra

CHORUS: Is there no end to the audacity
   Of an impetuous woman, crazed with passion?
   The youth is guiltless and the queen intends
   To charge him with a heinous crime. What infamy!
   For evidence she'll show her tangled hair,
   Her tear-stained face, her whole head's beauty marred.
   She has her plot prepared by every art
   Known to her sex. . . .
                        But who is this that comes,
   With kingly mien and head borne high? His face
   Is like the face of young Peirithous,
   But for the bloodless pallor of his cheeks,
   And the unsightly hair, matted and stiff.
   Theseus it is! He has returned to earth! . . .

THESEUS: From my long sojourn in eternal night's
   Dark universe, the spacious prison-house
   Of souls departed, now at last escaped
   I scarce know how to suffer with my eyes
   This long-desired light. Four years of harvest
   Triptolemus[1] has granted to Eleusis –
   Four equinoxes under Libra passed,
   While I have been held captive by a task
   Of strange necessity and doubtful issue,
   Bearing the pains of death and life at once;
   For, being as dead, I still retained of life
   The sense of suffering. I owe my freedom
   To Hercules, who brought me back to earth
   When he returned with the dog Cerberus
   Captured and carried off from hell. But now

  1. The ward and pupil of Demeter, taught men the art of agriculture and was worshipped at Eleusis.

My strength is spent, my former powers exhausted,
My steps unsteady. A laborious journey
It was indeed, from Phlegethon below
To this world far above – running from death
And following Hercules.
                                    But what is this?
Do I hear cries of lamentation? What?
Who can tell me? Can there be grief and sorrow
And tears to meet me at my door? Fit welcome,
In truth it may be, for a guest from hell.
NURSE: Phaedra your wife is fixed in her resolve
   To die; she will not listen to our tears;
   She is at the door of death.
THESEUS: Why, for what cause?
   Why should she die? Her husband has come home.
NURSE: The very reason hastening her death.
THESEUS: That riddle must contain some serious matter.
   Speak out, and tell me what it is that ails her.
NURSE: She will tell no one. Secretly she grieves;
   Whatever pain is driving her to death,
   She means to take it with her. Come, sir, come;
   There is no time to lose.
THESEUS: Unbar the doors
   Of the royal house.
   [*Doors are opened and Phaedra is seen*]
                        Dear consort of my bed,
   Is this your welcome for your lord's return,
   Your greeting to your long-awaited husband?
   Put down that sword! Allay my fears. Tell me
   What trouble drives you to escape from life.
PHAEDRA: Ah, noble Theseus – by your royal sceptre,
   Your living children, and your life restored,
   And by my body that shall soon be ashes –
   Do not forbid my death.

THESEUS: Why must you die?

PHAEDRA: To tell the cause is to destroy the purpose.

THESEUS: No one shall hear your reason, but myself.

PHAEDRA: Chaste wives least trust their secrets to their
  husbands.

THESEUS: Your secret will be safe with me; speak out.

PHAEDRA: A secret is best kept when shared with no one.

THESEUS: We shall protect you from all means of death.

PHAEDRA: Death cannot hide from one who means to die.

THESEUS: Is it to expiate some sin? What sin?

PHAEDRA: My being alive.

THESEUS: Are my tears nothing to you?

PHAEDRA: To die lamented is to die content.

THESEUS: Nothing will move her silence. The old nurse
  Shall tell – we'll have her bound and scourged
  Till she reveal all that my wife withholds.
  Put chains upon her! See if the whip will draw
  The secret out of her.

PHAEDRA: No! I will tell you.

THESEUS: Well? . . . Can you only turn your face away
  So woebegone . . . hiding under your sleeve
  The tears that now begin to flood your cheeks?

PHAEDRA: O be my witness, God, Creator, Father
  Of all the gods in heaven! And Thou, bright flame
  Of heavenly light, progenitor of my house!
  Besieged with pleadings, I resisted them;
  Threatened with swords, my will was never weakened;
  Yet violence was used upon my body.
  For this, my blood must wash my honour clean.

THESEUS: Tell me, what man has stolen my good name?

PHAEDRA: The last whom you would think of.

THESEUS: I must know.

PHAEDRA: Learn from this sword, which the adulterer
  Left, in alarm, fearing a hue and cry.

THESEUS: O God, what crime, what monstrous villainy
This shows me! In this polished ivory hilt
The intricate engraved designs proclaim
The rank of the Athenian royal house. . . .
Which way did he escape?

PHAEDRA: These servants saw him
Running away as quickly as he could
In great alarm.

THESEUS: By all the sanctity
Of human faith, by Him who rules the heavens,
And Him who moves the seas, the second realm –
Whence came this foul infection, this corruption
Into our blood? Could this man have been bred
On Grecian soil, or in the Scythian Taurus,
The Colchian Phasis? Every stock returns
To its ancestral type, degenerate blood
Retains the nature of its primal source.
This is that warrior people's native[1] vice –
To abrogate legitimate love, and sell
Chaste women's bodies in the public market.
Vile race, that never bowed to the control
Of more enlightened laws! Even the beasts
Abhor forbidden union, instinct teaches
Proper respect for laws of generation.
   So much for that cold look, that mask of gravity!
That uncouth style of dress, that affectation
Of old time-honoured ways, modest behaviour
And stern rigidity of character!
O base deceit, keeping true feelings close –
Fair face without, and foul intent within!
Lechery masked by modesty, assurance
Cloaked by reserve, sin screened by sanctity!

   1. The Amazons – but the indictment here is hardly justified or
logical.

Liars praise truth, and weaklings feign endurance!
   Was it for me, you wild man of the woods,
With your untouched, untamed virginity –
Was it for me your first assault was destined?
Was it my bed you chose, so impiously,
For this inauguration of your manhood?
How gladly now I thank the heavenly gods
That I had put Antiope to death
With my own hand, and did not leave her here,
Your mother, at your mercy, while I travelled
Down to the Stygian pit. Escape me, will you,
And flee to distant lands unknown to man?
Take refuge, if you will, beyond the Ocean
At earth's extremest edge; go and inhabit
Worlds that lie upside-down beneath our feet;
Traverse the perilous tracts of arctic north
And hide in its remotest wastes; outrun
The reach of winter, pass the bounds of snow,
Leave the loud wrath of Boreas behind,
Fly faster than his ice-cold breath can follow –
Yet you shall pay for your iniquities.
Run where you may, I shall be on your heels;
Hide anywhere, and I shall hunt you down.
No place can be so far, so closed, so private,
So unexplored, so inaccessible –
We shall explore it. Nothing shall bar our way;
You know where I have lately been. If weapons
Cannot be aimed at you, my curses can
And will be. Neptune granted me, his son,
Three prayers which he would honour, and by oath
Upon the name of Styx confirmed his promise.
   Fulfil it now, great Ruler of the Sea!
Unwelcome though it be, grant me this boon:
Grant that the day shall never dawn again

Upon Hippolytus; let my young son
Go down to meet his father's enemies
The spirits of the dead. To me, thy son,
O father, render this abhorrent service,
This last of thy three promised gifts; which I
Would not have claimed, but for the hateful need
Which now compels me. I forebore to claim it
Even when I was in the pit of hell,
Braving the wrath of Dis and the dread hand
Of the infernal king. Can you refuse,
O father, now to make your promise good? ...
Not yet? Is there no sound upon the waters?
Summon the winds, and cover up the night
With black clouds; pluck the stars, the sky, away;
Empty the sea, fetching from farthest Ocean
The billowy multitudes at thy command!

CHORUS

O Nature, whence all gods proceed;
   And Thou, King of Olympian light,
Whose hand makes stars and planets speed
   Round the high axis of the night:
If thou canst guide with ceaseless care
   The heavenly bodies in their train,
To make the woods in winter bare
   And in the springtime green again,
Until the summer's Lion burns
   To bring the ripening seed to birth
And every force of nature turns
   To gentleness upon the earth –
Why, if such power is in thy hand
   To balance by an ordered plan
The mass of things, why dost thou stand
   So far from the affairs of man?

Thou dost not care to help the good
   Nor punish men of evil mind.
Man lives by chance, to Fate subdued,
   And evil thrives, for Fate is blind.
Vile lust has banished purity,
   Vice sits enthroned in royal state;
Mobs give to knaves authority
   And serve them even while they hate.
Poor is the prize sour virtue gains,
   Want lies in wait for honesty,
Sin reigns supreme. What good remains
   In shame, what worth in dignity?

ACT FOUR

Messenger, Theseus

CHORUS: Why does a messenger come hurrying hither
  With tears of sorrow watering his cheeks?
MESSENGER: A hard and cruel fate is mine, heavy
  The burden of my service. Why was I
  Chosen to bring the news I dare not tell?
THESEUS: Speak out, and have no fear; tell all the worst
  That has befallen us. I am prepared.
MESSENGER: My tongue wants words to tell this grievous
    woe.
THESEUS: Say what last stroke has crushed our fallen
    house.
MESSENGER: Weep for Hippolytus, for he is dead!
THESEUS: My son is dead, I knew already; now
  A miscreant has died. Say how he died.
MESSENGER: With desperate steps he hurried from the
    town
  As fast as any way could take him. Quickly
  He yoked his restive steeds and bridled them
  With buckled curbs. Then, muttering all the while,
  Cursing his native land, and crying aloud
  His father's name, wildly he drove away,
  With flying reins and whirling lash. At once
  A peal of thunder broke across the sea,
  Which rose to meet the stars. No wind disturbed
  The salty surface, the untroubled sky
  Uttered no sound; the storm that shook the sea,
  So calm till then, was native to itself,
  But fiercer than the rage of southern Auster
  Lashing the straits of Sicily; and wilder
  Than the Ionian waters tossing high

When northern Corus reigns, when rocks are shaken
By mighty billows, and the head of Leucas
Whitened by the spray. The whole great main
Was piled into a towering mass; the ocean,
Big-bellied with a monster, rolled to land.
This was no ship-destroying cataclysm,
Its fury was directed at the shores,
Whereon the waves came tumbling thick and fast.
And what was this strange burden that the tide
Bore in its swelling womb? Was some new island
Raising its head to light? Was this the birth
Of one more Cyclad? Now the rising waters
Covered the sacred reef of Epidaurus,
And the notorious Scironian rocks,
And all the Isthmus in between the seas.
      Amazed we watched, and wondered, while the whole
Sea roared, and the surrounding cliffs roared back.
Each pinnacle was wet with driven spray
Blown out and sucked back by the swirling waters;
As when the huge spouting leviathan's
Wide mouth blows out the water as he rides
Across the ocean. Then, a tremor shook
The mass of water and it burst apart
And threw on to the shore a thing – a thing
Of evil, far more foul than any fear
Of ours could have conceived; and after it
The sea rushed on towards us, in the wake
Of that abominable apparition. . . .
My fear still trembles on my lips. . . . How vast,
How horrible of shape the creature was!
A bull – dark blue about the rising neck,
Sea-green the shaggy forelock on its brow,
Hairy the ears, eyes shot with varied hues,
That of the leader of a mountain herd,

And that of some sea-creature – fiery red,
And lustrous with the purple of the sea.
Thick muscles rippled on its massive neck,
And through the gaping nostrils draughts of air
Hissed horribly. Its breast and dewlaps dripped
Green slimy moss, and all along its flanks
Red seaweed clung. The hinder parts were drawn
Into some nameless shape, a scaly length
Of tail enormous trailed behind the monster.
Of such a shape might be the deep-sea shark
Which crushes or devours the swiftest ships.
Earth shook, and every animal took flight
In terror from the fields, and every herdsman
Was too amazed to follow up his cattle.
Wild beasts broke from their coverts everywhere,
And everywhere the huntsman, frozen stiff
With fear, stood trembling. Only Hippolytus
Was unafraid; his horses took alarm,
But with the rein he held them hard and mastered
Their panic with the voice they knew so well.

   The road that skirts the margin of the sea
Turns through a deep ravine between the hills
Towards the country. Here the monster paused
To whet its anger and prepare for battle.
Then, having practised to its satisfaction
And limbered up its powers, with wrath renewed
It charged ahead, so fast the flying feet
Scarce touched the ground beneath; and then it stopped,
Confronting with a scowl the quivering horses.
Your son stood boldly up and faced the beast
With fearless challenge and unaltered mien,
And in a voice as loud as thunder cried:
'This bogey cannot frighten me! I know
How to fight bulls; it was my father's trade.'

But suddenly his horses jumped the reins,
Swerved off the road, taking the chariot with them,
And raced across the rocks, this way and that,
Wherever their wild terror took them. Still,
Like a ship's helmsman on a heaving sea
Holding his course head-on into the breakers,
Pitting his skill against their force – the youth
Guided his chariot. Tugging at the bit
With tightened reins, or flaying with the whip,
He kept control; while his competitor
Hung on to him – now drawing level, now
Wheeling around to face him, scaring him
From all directions; till at last, full tilt,
The horrible horned monster of the sea
Charged from the front, and there was no escaping.
    At this, the maddened horses broke all bounds
And in their struggle to throw off the yoke
Reared up, hurling their driver to the ground.
Headlong he plunged and, in his fall caught up
In the entangling straps, the more he wrestled
The more he knotted up the gripping harness.
The horses knew what they had done; the chariot
Was lighter, and they had no master now;
Fear took control, and where it led they followed.
So was it when the horses in the sky,
Feeling an unknown rider at their back,
Hating to have the car of daylight lent
To a pretender Sun, flung Phaethon down
From his wild orbit in the upper air.
The ground was reddened with a trail of blood;
His head was dashed from rock to rock, his hair
Torn off by thorns, his handsome face despoiled
By flinty stones; wound after wound destroyed
For ever that ill-fated comeliness.

The speeding wheels trundled the dying body
Until it caught upon a half-burnt tree-stump,
Sharp as a stake, which pierced the groin and held him
Transfixed; and while the man hung there impaled,
The car stood still, the horses at a loss
Checked by the accident. Then they break loose,
Even though they break their master. Now half dead
His flesh is ripped by brambles, gored by spines
Of thorny thickets, broken into pieces
Hanging on every tree. And sadly now
His servants and companions search the ground
Wherever the long trail of blood marks out
The passage of the torn and dragged Hippolytus.
The dogs join in the melancholy chase
Tracking the fragments of their master's body.
But still the efforts of the searching mourners
Have not recovered all the corpse. That beauty,
That form, to come to this! That youth, resplendent
Beside his royal father, star ascendant,
Heir to the throne – now they are gathering him
In scattered remnants to his resting-place
Upon a funeral pyre.

THESEUS: O potent nature,
How strong a bond of blood is thine to tie
A parent's heart! Even against our will
We know and love thee. As my son was guilty,
I wished him dead; as he is lost, I mourn him.

MESSENGER: What he has willed, no man may rightly
      mourn.

THESEUS: This is the very summit of calamity,
When fate makes us demand what we must loathe.

MESSENGER: If you still harbour hate, why are you weep-
      ing?

THESEUS: I weep, not that I lost, but that I killed him.

PHAEDRA

CHORUS

What awful revolutions accident
  Brings in the lives of men!
  Truly the hand of Fate
Is kinder to the humble; punishment
  From heaven falls less heavily
  On those of less estate.
Peace and obscurity make most content,
In lowly homes old age sleeps easily.

  The highest mountain-tops
Catch every wind that blows, from east, from south,
  The wild assaults of Boreas,
      And rains of Corus.
Green valleys seldom feel the stroke of thunder,[1]
  But the high Caucasus
And Phrygian forests of the Mother Goddess
  Quake at the voice of Jupiter
  And fear his armoury.
  For Jupiter is on his guard
And strikes whatever comes too near the sky.
  The thunder rumbles round his throne,
But no great harm can come to common folk
      Who dwell in modest homes.

The wings of time fly unpredictably,
Fate hurries on, and keeps no promises.
Here was a man, returning thankfully
To look upon bright day and starry sky
After his sojourn in the dark; what sorrow
Greets his homecoming! In his father's house
He has received a welcome far more woeful
      Than in the pit of hell.

1. *Raros patitur fulminis ictus umida vallis*. The Latin is quoted in
Sir Thomas More (anon. 1590–1600).

143

Pallas, whom all the Attic race adore:
Theseus thy son has come back from the dead
And lives to see the heaven above; but thou,
Pure goddess, owest no recompense for this
To thy stern uncle's grasping hand; death's king
Has still his victim, and the debt is paid.

ACT FIVE

Theseus, Phaedra

CHORUS: A voice crying from the high palace! What!
  Phaedra comes, sword in hand, distraught. Ah, why?...
  [*Enter Phaedra*]
THESEUS: What is this madness, woman, crazed with grief,
  Why come you with a sword and loud lament
  Over a body which you hate?
PHAEDRA: On me,
  On me let the deep ocean's angry lord
  Let fall his wrath! Let all the blue sea's monsters,
  All that were ever brought to birth afar
  In the deep lap of Tethys, all that Ocean
  Bears in the farthest tides of his wild waters,
  Come against me. O Theseus, ever cruel!
  Never a bringer of joy on your return
  To those that waited for you; first a father,[1]
  And now a son, have died for your homecoming.
  For love of one wife, hatred of another,
  Guilty in both, you have destroyed your house.

  [*The remains of Hippolytus have been brought back*]
  Hippolytus! Is this how I must find you?
  Is this what I have made of you? What creature –
  Some Sinis, some Procrustes? – Cretan bull
  Bellowing in a Daedalian labyrinth,
  Horned hybrid – can have torn you into pieces?
  Alas, where now is all your beauty gone,
  And where those eyes that were my stars? Can I
  Believe you dead? Come back a little while,
  And hear me speak to you – I'll speak no shame.

  1. Aegeus, who died, deceived by the false signal of the black
sails, on Theseus' return from Crete.

Then with this hand I'll pay my debt to you;
Into this wicked heart I'll thrust the sword
That shall set Phaedra free from life and sin.
So through the waters, through the Stygian stream
And the Tartarean lake, and burning rivers,[1]
I shall still follow you, mad for your love.
Here is my offering for the dead . . . this veil . . .
And from my wounded brow this lock of hair. . . .
Take them. Although we could not live as one,
We can still die together. . . .
                              Die then, Phaedra;
If thou art undefiled, die for thy husband;
If thou hast sinned, die for thy love. For how
Could I again approach my husband's bed
Now that such evil has dishonoured it?
This would have been the crowning sin, to ask,
As if repentant, to be loved again.
O Death, sole remedy for errant love,
O Death, lost honour's only ornament,
To thee I fly; receive me in thy mercy.
But hear this first, O Athens; hear this, father –
But more malevolent than any stepmother –
I told you lies, alleged untruthfully
The offence on which my own mad heart was set.
You, father, punished where there was no need.
The innocent boy, charged with inchastity,
Lies dead, untouched by sin, untouched by shame.
Hippolytus, be vindicated now!
My guilty breast awaits the avenging sword;
My blood is shed to pay the dues of death
For one who never sinned. Father, your son

---

1. *Per Styga, per amnes igneos amens sequor.* (Was the anagram intended?) *Titus Andronicus*, II. 1 quotes '*per Styga per manes vehor*', but there is no MS authority for this variant.

Is taken from you; let his stepmother
Teach you your duty now: begone to Hades!
   [*She kills herself*]
THESEUS: Hide me, O prison of pale Death! Hide me, ye
    caves
Of Taenarus, and Lethe's river, for whose arms
The miserable yearn! Let your dank waters drown
My sins, sink my iniquity in endless pain!
Come, sea, come, savage monsters of the main, come all
The brood of Proteus from the ocean's farthest deep.
For having triumphed in my evil victory
Let me be dragged down to the bottom of the sea!
Father, too ready hast thou been to lend thy ear
To my impetuous prayers; how can I now deserve
Merciful death, when I have sent my son to die
As none have died before, when I have torn his body
And scattered it afield, when I, making myself
The ruthless punisher of a fictitious crime,
Have thrown upon myself the veritable guilt?
Hell, heaven, and ocean I have sated with my sins;
Known in three worlds, there is no fourth estate for me.
   Did I return for this? Was I allowed
A way back to this light, only to see
Death twice, two violent deaths, lose wife and son
And with one torch kindle the funeral pyres
Of one I loved and one whom I begot?
This light that is my darkness, Hercules,
You won for me. Let Dis take back his gift!
Let me rejoin the dead! . . . Blasphemous prayer –
And vain – to ask a second chance of death.
Devise your own fit sentence, man of blood!
You have a skill in murder, have invented
Wondrous devices of terrible destruction.
How should I do it? . . . a pine-branch bent to the ground,

Pegged down, then loosed, to fly into the air,
Ripping a body in half, like a sawn plank?
Or the steep drop from the Scironian cliffs?[1]
Or worse things, such as I myself have seen
Men suffer under Phlegethon, damned souls
Imprisoned in a sea of fire. I know
What punishment, what resting-place, awaits me.
Sinners in hell, resign your tasks to me!
The stone of aged Sisyphus shall rest
Upon these shoulders, these two hands shall toil
Under the weight of it. Elusive water,
Just out of reach, shall tantalize these lips.
The deadly vulture shall leave Tityos alone
And fly at me, mine shall those entrails be
That grow for ever to supply fresh food
For suffering. The father[2] of my friend
Peirithous shall rest, and in his place
My body shall be carried round and round
Upon the ever-turning wheel. Be opened,
Earth! And receive me, awful emptiness!
This time my journey to the shadow world
Will have just cause: I go to seek my son.
King of the dead, have no more fear of me;
I come with pure intent. Make me a guest
In your eternal home, where I shall stay
For ever. . . . Ah, the gods are deaf to prayers –
Yet they would answer readily enough
If I were praying for some evil purpose.
CHORUS: Theseus, time without end is time enough

1. Sinis, the deviser of the pine-tree death, and Sciron, who
hurled victims over the cliffs, were two marauders of the Megarid
coast, both overthrown by Theseus in his younger days. They are
alluded to above, 1169 and 1023.
2. Ixion.

For your lament. Now let due rites be done
In your son's honour; let us put away
This vilely ravaged and dismembered body.

THESEUS: Yes, bring your burden, bring me those remains
Of his beloved body, though the parts
Be heaped in no right order. Can this be
Hippolytus? Oh, what a sin was mine!
I murdered you; and more, as if one crime
Were not enough, nor I alone to blame,
I had to ask my father for his aid
In plotting this vile act against my son.
Now I can thank him for his generosity! . . .
What sorrow can be greater than bereavement
At life's dead end? Unhappy man,
Take in your arms these relics, all you have
That was your son! Kneel and embrace these limbs
And take them to your sorrow-laden breast.

CHORUS: You, sir, shall set in order these remains
Of your son's broken body, and restore
The mingled fragments to their place. Put here
His strong right hand . . . and here the left,
Which used to hold the reins so skilfully. . . .
I recognize the shape of this left side.
Alas, how much of him is lost, and lies
Far from our weeping!

THESEUS: Trembling hands, be firm
For this sad service; cheeks, dry up your tears!
Here is a father building, limb by limb,
A body for his son. . . . Here is a piece,
Misshapen, horrible, each side of it
Injured and torn. What part of you it is
I cannot tell, but it is part of you.
So . . . put it there . . . not where it ought to be,
But where there is a place for it. Was this

149

The face that shone as brightly as a star,
The face that turned all enemies' eyes aside?
Has so much beauty come to this? O cruelty
Of Fate! O kindness, ill-bestowed, of gods!
See how a father's prayer brought back his son! . . .

  Receive these last gifts from your father's hand;
These, as each part of you is borne to burial,
Shall go into the fire. . . .

               Open the doors
Of this polluted palace, fouled with blood!
Let there be lamentation loud and full
Through all this Attic land! . . . Let some prepare
The royal pyre; others, search the fields
For any portions of the corpse still lost. . . .

  This one . . . let a deep pit of earth conceal,
And soil lie heavy on her cursed head.

Exeunt

THE
TROJAN WOMEN

TROY has fallen. Outside the ruined and smouldering city, a group of Trojan women are waiting to be carried away on the Greek ships to the homes of their captors. Two acts of vengeance remain to be consummated: the destruction of Hector's son Astyanax, the last heir to Troy's defeated royal house; and the sacrifice of Polyxena, daughter of Priam, as an expiation due to the ghost of Achilles. Prominent among the captive women are Hecuba, the widow of Priam, and Andromache, the widow of Hector, the two mothers on whom the shock of these brutal blows most heavily falls.

The play is derived from the *Hecuba* and *The Trojan Women* of Euripides, but breaks new ground in the scene of dispute between Agamemnon and Pyrrhus and in Andromache's struggle to save her child from Ulysses.

The title appears as 'Troades' in one group of manuscripts and as 'Troas' in another – which would mean 'the Trojan woman' or 'the Trojan story'. The singular title is the one generally known to the Elizabethan translators.

DRAMATIS PERSONAE

HECUBA, *widow of King Priam*
ANDROMACHE, *widow of Hector*
ASTYANAX, *her son, a child*
HELEN
POLYXENA, *daughter of Hecuba*
AGAMEMNON, *commander of the Greeks*
PYRRHUS, *son of Achilles*
ULYSSES
TALTHYBIUS, *a Greek herald*
CALCHAS, *a prophet*
AN ELDER
A MESSENGER
CHORUS *of captive Trojan women*
Greek soldiers

*

Scene: at Troy, outside the ruined city, near the tomb of Hector

ACT ONE

Hecuba, Chorus

HECUBA: The man who puts his trust in kingly power,
The potentate wielding authority
In his high court, having no fear of gods
And their capricious will, the man who takes
His happy state for granted – let that man
Look upon me, and upon thee, O Troy.
Here is the proof, the strongest ever given
By Fate, to show on what uncertain ground
The pomp of power stands. Here lies in ruin
The masterpiece of gods, the tower of Asia.
To her defence allies had come from far,
From the nine mouths of frozen Tanäis,
And from the birthplace of the dawn, where Tigris
Pours his hot stream into the ruby sea;
Hither had come the queen of virgin tribes[1]
Whose frontiers face the nomad Scythians
And threaten foemen on the Pontic shore.
Yet she was vanquished; yet she was destroyed;
Great Pergamum lies low; her massive walls,
With all their towering beauty, are brought down,
Her houses all in ashes. Flames still leap
Around the royal palace, smoke goes up
From every corner of the wide domain
Of prince Assaracus,[2] but even fire
Cannot delay the conquerors' plundering hands.
The town is looted even while it burns.

1. The Amazons.
2. Great-grandfather of Aeneas; one of the founders of Troy,
with his brother Ilos (hence *Ilium*) and father Tros.

Billows of smoke conceal the sky; dense clouds
Blacken the daylight with a pall of soot,
The reek of Ilium. There the victor stands,
His vengeance not yet satisfied; with Troy's
Slow death before his eyes, now the destroyer
Forgives her ten years' toil. Her agony
Appalls him too, and even seeing her vanquished
He hardly can believe such victory
Was possible. Already ravishers
Are carrying away the spoils of Troy,
More booty than a thousand ships can hold.

    Hear this, ye powers of heaven, ye gods above
That ever fight against me; this I swear
By the ashes of my home, by Phrygia's king
Now lying under all the Troy he ruled;
And by the ghost of him[1] who, while he stood,
Kept Troy upright; by all you lesser ghosts,
My many many children: all this woe,
All the disasters that were once foretold
(Although her god forbade us to believe her)
By the impassioned voice of Phoebus' bride,[2]
All these things I, I Hecuba foresaw –
When I was pregnant with a son, I saw
What was to come, and spoke my fears; Cassandra
Was not the first unheeded prophetess.
And who has laid these fires among your streets?
Not the sharp Ithacan,[3] nor his companion[4]
In nightly escapades, nor traitor Sinon;[5]

1. Hector.
2. Cassandra.
3. Ulysses.
4. Diomede, his nocturnal exploit described in *Iliad*, x.
  5. The Greek pretended deserter who persuaded the Trojans to
admit the Wooden Horse (*Aeneid*, 11).

That fire was mine, my hand had lit the faggots[1]
Whose blaze consumes you now.

                              But why should I,
An aged lingering relic, now lament
Over the ruins of a fallen city?
Troy's doom is now old history. Remember,
Unhappy woman, what you have lately seen:
The execrable murder of a king –
Achilles' son (who could believe such sin?)
At the king's altar, sword in hand, his left
Clutching the king's hair – how he savagely
Forced the head back and drove the foul blade deep
Into the old man's throat; and when in triumph
He drew it out again, it came out dry.
What other man would not have stayed his rage,
What man would not have spared an aged life
Already at the door of death, or feared
The witnessing gods and the divine respect
Of royalty overthrown? There Priam lies,
Father of many kings, and has no tomb;
Troy blazes, but there is no fire for him.
And still the gods are not yet satisfied;
The lots are being drawn, assigning wives
And daughters of the royal house of Priam
To their new masters; I shall be one of them,
A prize whom no one wants. They take their pick,
One claiming Hector's wife, one Helenus',
And one Antenor's wife; even Cassandra
Does not lack suitors; my name is the one
They fear to draw, mine is the only name
That still holds terror for a Greek. Come, friends,
Can you no longer weep? Come, let me hear you,

---

1. This fancy probably has reference to the legend that Hecuba in
her pregnancy dreamed that she brought forth fiery torches.

Friends and fellow-prisoners; beat your breasts;
Honour the name of Troy. Let your laments
Be heard on Ida, fatal judgement-seat[1]
And source of all our woe.

CHORUS: Well may you ask us to weep;
It is no new thing, we are well acquainted with tears.
Year after year we have wept,
Since a traveller from Troy[2] set foot ashore
At Amyclae in Greece,
Since a ship of Cybele's holy pine
Sailed over the sea.
Ten snows have whitened Ida's head,
Ten times her woods have built our funeral pyres,
Ten harvests has the reaper, at his peril,
Gathered in the Sigean fields;
And we have known no day without its grief.
Now we have cause to weep afresh.
Weep, women, weep! And you, our queen,
Raise your poor hands.
Let our mistress lead, and her lowly servants will follow;
Mourning is the work we all know well.

HECUBA: You are my faithful friends in my time of sorrow.
Loose your hair, let it fall on your bowed shoulders,
Let it be dirtied in the hot dust of Troy.
Fill your hands with dust, it is all we can take
Away from Troy.
Let every arm be stretched forth; loosen your garments
And tie them around you, be naked to the womb –
Do you still want to cover your breast, shy prisoner –
For what husband's sake?
Tie your cloaks round your dropped tunics, women;
Hands must be free to beat the mad rhythm of lament.

1. The place of the Judgement of Paris.
2. Paris, coming to abduct Helen.

Good ... good ... I like to see you thus,
My women of Troy.

Now let me hear you weep again;
Weep as you never wept before.
This is for Hector.

CHORUS: We have loosed our hair, as for many a death
    before;
Tangled it falls from its knot;
We have smeared warm ash on our faces.
We have bared our shoulders and tied our fallen gar-
    ments round our loins;
Our naked bosoms cry for the beating hand.
Work, Grief, with all your might!
Let our cries be heard on the Rhoetian shore;
Let Echo throw them back from her mountain caves —
Not only our last syllables as at other times,
But every word of our lament for Troy.
Let us be heard on every sea,
And in all the sky.
Hands, spare not your strength;
Heavily beat the breast;
What was enough before is not sufficient now.
This is for Hector.

HECUBA: Yes, Hector, for you I am striking these arms,
For you these bleeding shoulders;
For you a mother's hands tear at her breast;
For you I beat my head.
Here, where I scarred my flesh at your funeral,
Let the wound open again and the blood pour down.
You were our country's tower,
Her stay against the Fates,
Shield of the Trojans when they wearied.
You were our wall,
On your shoulders for ten years our city stood;

With you she fell.
Hector's last day of life
Was the end of his country's life . . .
Enough for Hector. Let a new dirge be sung.
This is for Priam.

CHORUS: Ruler of Phrygia, hear our mourning.
Father, twice captive, receive our tears.
All that has befallen Troy, under your rule,
Has twice befallen her.
Twice she has faced the arrows of Hercules,[1]
Twice seen her walls assaulted by Grecian arms.
Now, after the burial of Hecuba's children,
After the funerals of all the princely family,
Your death, father,
Ends the long procession to the grave.
Headless now you lie on the Sigean sands,
A victim slain in the sight of Jupiter.

HECUBA: No! Change that strain, daughters of Troy!
You must not pity my Priam's death.
'Priam is happy' you must cry.
He has gone free into the deep of death;
He will never wear the yoke of a conquering Greek.
He will never face again the sons of Atreus
Or the treacherous Ulysses; not for him
The prisoner's part in an Argive triumph,
The shoulder bowed under victor's trophies.
No one will bind those hands that held a sceptre;
He will not be seen paraded through Mycenae,
Running behind Agamemnon's chariot
With golden shackles on his wrists.

CHORUS: 'Happy is Priam', we cry.
He has taken his kingdom with him.

1. First, when Hercules attacked Troy, in the reign of Laomedon;
second, when Hercules' arrows were used by Philoctetes.

Now he walks through the safe shadows of Elysian
     groves,
Happy among the pious dead;
He will join Hector there.
Happy is Priam, happy is every man
That has died in battle
And taken with him his life's fulfilment.

ACT TWO

Talthybius, Pyrrhus, Agamemnon, Calchas

TALTHYBIUS: How long the waiting! Ever the long delay
   When Greek ships lie at anchor, waiting to sail
   In search of war, waiting to sail for home!
CHORUS: What are they waiting for? Why are the ships
   Held back? What god forbids their homeward voyage?
TALTHYBIUS: I shudder to tell; I shake with fear. I saw –
   Who will believe portents more terrible
   Than can be true? – and yet I saw them all.
   The first rays of the Sky God had but grazed
   The mountain tops, light chasing dark away,
   When from earth's hidden depths a roar was heard,
   And a convulsion tore her inside out.
   The tree-tops rocked, forest and sacred grove
   Echoed the thunder; Ida was split in two,
   And rocks came tumbling down. Not only earth
   Did shake; the sea stood still, knowing her son
   Achilles to be near. A rift appeared,
   Caves yawned, hell gaped, earth parted and revealed
   A way from worlds below to worlds above.
   His tomb was burst asunder and there stood
   The living ghost of the Thessalian leader,
   Just as he looked when he was conquering Thrace
   In practice for the punishment of Troy;
   Or when he smote the white-plumed son[1] of Neptune;
   Or when, with bloody slaughter in the field,
   He choked the rivers with his dead, and Xanthus,
   Turned out of its accustomed course, became
   A creeping swamp of gore; or when he stood

1. Cycnus, slain by Achilles on the island of Tenedos.

Proud and victorious in his chariot,
Dragging great Hector – dragging Troy – behind him.
And now in every quarter of the coast
His angry voice was heard: 'Go, cowards, go!
Steal off, leaving unpaid the debt you owe
To my departed spirit; go, hoist sail
And launch your thankless fleet upon my sea!
It cost you dearly once, and shall again,
To appease Achilles' wrath. Polyxena
Was promised me; let her be sacrificed
Over my ashes; by the hand of Pyrrhus;
And let my tomb be watered with her blood.'
And with those awful words he took his leave
Of this world's light, and went back to the dead.
As he descended, earth was joined again
And its deep caverns closed. The sea lies calm
And motionless, the wind is gentle now,
Only a ripple whispers on the water,
And we have heard the Tritons from the deep
Singing the hymn of marriage.

PYRRHUS [to Agamemnon]: So, when you spread your sails
        in eager haste
To cross the sea for home, you had forgotten –
You had forgotten Achilles, it appears.
You had no thought for him whose single hand
Had so struck Troy, her fall might be delayed
But only this remained, to see which way
Her towers would fall. Now, willing you may be,
And anxious, as you say, to grant his wish –
It is too late; already all your chiefs
Have claimed their spoils. What lesser prize is left,
Fit to be given for valour such as his?
Is it a little debt we owe to him,
When, though advised to stay away from war

And live his life out in tranquillity,
Passing the years of Nestor, he renounced
His mother's plot to hide him in disguise,[1]
Meaning to prove himself in arms a man?
And did not then his prentice hand receive
Its baptism of blood, of royal blood,
When that unfriendly king, rude Telephus,
Would bar him from the warring land of Mysia –
And lived to learn how strong, yet merciful,
That hand could be? Thebes fell to his assault,
Eëtion was overthrown and saw
His kingdom lost. A like fate overtook
The little hill-town Lyrnesus; and more –
The famous place where Briseis was taken;
Chryse, where kings had fought, laid low; and Tenedos,
Whose story is well known; then Scyros,
Rich pasture land of Thracian flocks; and Lesbos,
Breakwater of the Aegean sea; and Cilla,
Beloved by Phoebus; nor do we forget
The land washed by the spring flood of Caÿcus.

   And all this havoc, all this scourge of nations,
These countless cities scattered to the winds
As by some huge tornado, might have been
For any other man the crown and summit
Of a career of glorious victory.
Achilles took them in his stride. He came;
My father came to you with this behind him.
All these his other glorious wars he fought
As practice for one war. But leave aside
His other exploits; with but one alone
He could have been content – with Hector. Troy?
My father conquered Troy; you have but spoiled it.

   1. When his mother, Thetis, hid him in the disguise of a girl at
the court of Lycomedes, king of Scyros.

It is my joy to tell the famous deeds
Of my illustrious sire – how Hector fell
In *his* own father's sight; how Memnon fell
Before his uncle's eyes; grieving for him,
His stricken mother's face was overcast
And that day's dawn was dull.[1] Even the victor
Was harrowed at the sight of his own act;
That was the first time that Achilles learnt
A goddess's son could die. Then our last foe,
The Amazon queen, fell to his sword. Achilles
Deserves all you can pay, if the account
Be rightly reckoned – even if he should ask
A young girl's life – from Argos – or Mycenae.
Do you deny it? Do you now condemn
What once has been allowed, or think it brutal
To sacrifice a daughter of King Priam
To the son of Peleus? You once sacrificed
A daughter of your own for Helen's sake.
I only claim what precedent approves.

AGAMEMNON: Young men cannot restrain their violence;
It is their common fault. The zeal of youth
Inspires them generally; Pyrrhus here
Is driven by his father's spirit too.
But I have borne the boasts and menaces
Of that proud son of Aeacus ere now,
And have not flinched. Who has most power to act,
Should have most power to endure. What then?
Do you think fit to soil the honoured shade
Of an illustrious leader with foul murder?
Ere you do that, you would do well to learn
What acts are fitting for a conqueror,
What penalties for the conquered. Power unchecked
Has never lasted long; tempered with reason

1. Aurora, the Dawn, was the mother of Memnon.

It can endure. Wherever Fortune's hand
Has lifted and upheld the power of man
Over his fellow-men, there it behoves him
To hold his privilege in check, to fear
Each change of wind and the too generous gods.
Greatness can fall at a touch; my victory
Has taught me that. If Troy's fall makes us proud
And insolent, we Greeks, let us remember,
Are standing in the place from which she fell.
I own I have been guilty, I have been headstrong
In exercise of power, I have been proud;
But now that spirit has been broken in me,
And broken by that thing which, in another,
Might well have caused it – by the gift of Fortune.
Priam has made me proud – and made me fearful.
    Why then should I think kingship anything
But name, o'erlaid with shallow gilt, a brow
Adorned with a mock diadem? A chance,
A moment, may sweep all these things away –
And, like as not, without the aid of ships
Numbered in thousands, or a ten years' war;
Not all find Fortune's hand so long suspended.
If I may speak my mind – forgive me, Argos –
I own I wanted to see Phrygia conquered,
Conquered and punished; but reduced to ruin,
Razed to the ground – I would have spared her that.
Would that I had! No power on earth can curb
The invader's lust, no hand restrain the licence
Of victory let loose upon the night.
If anything of what we did that night
Could have been called inhuman or unseemly,
It was the work of anger, and of darkness –
Itself a spur to cruelty – the work
Of the triumphant sword, whose appetite,

Once it has tasted blood, outruns all reason.
If anything of ruined Troy can live,
Then let it live; vengeance enough, and more,
Has been exacted. A princess to die,
A sacrificial victim, to imbrue
The ashes of the dead – a brutal murder
Called by the name of marriage – never! No!
That I will not allow. For upon me
The guilt of all comes back. Who, having the right
To ban wrongdoing, bans it not, commands it.

PYRRHUS: So shall Achilles' soul not have its due?

AGAMEMNON: It shall. All men on earth shall sing his
          praise
And lands unknown shall hear of his great name.
If blood must flow to give his ashes rest,
Let there be slaughtered finest Phrygian cattle;
Shed blood for which no mother's eyes need weep.
Where is such custom known? Where is man's life
Poured out in payment to the human dead?
Your duty is to shield your father's name
From hatred and dishonour, not ask us
To serve him with an act of brutal vengeance.

PYRRHUS: Oh, you are puffed with pride, now that success
And safety have set up your confidence.
You did not use to be so bold, when danger
Was drumming the alarm – great king of kings!
No doubt your thoughts have turned to love again;
Some new-found mistress fires your passion. Why
Should you so often be the only one
To win a prize? Well, I shall give Achilles,
With my own hands, the victim he demands.
If you refuse to give her up, I'll find
Another, a better gift, a gift more worthy
To be the gift of Pyrrhus. This right hand

Has too long paused from shedding kingly blood.
Priam needs company.

AGAMEMNON: Pyrrhus deserves,
I'll not deny, the credit for that deed,
His noblest exploit in the war, the murder
Of Priam, his father's suppliant.

PYRRHUS: I know
Who were his suppliants, and his enemies.
Priam at least made his appeal in person;
You would not dare to make your own request;
You skulked in safety, you were too afraid
To meet your enemy; the king of Ithaca,
And Ajax, had to do the asking for you.[1]

AGAMEMNON: Your father was no coward, I suppose,
That day when Greeks were dying all around him,
Their ships in flames, and he lay indolent,
Far from all thought of battle, lazily
Strumming sweet music on a tinkling lyre.

PYRRHUS: The songs Achilles sang, you may be sure,
Daunted great Hector more than all your armour
Which scared him not a jot; in that dread hour
Peace reigned in the Thessalian camp.

AGAMEMNON: And there
Was peace, I think, for Hector's father too.[2]

PYRRHUS: It is a lordly act to spare a king.

AGAMEMNON: And yet you raised your hand to kill a king?

PYRRHUS: It may be mercy to grant death, not life.

AGAMEMNON: And now in mercy you would have a
          maiden
Slaughtered upon a tomb?

PYRRHUS: Since when have you

1. As told in *Iliad*, IX.
2. When he came to ransom Hector's body, and was kindly
treated by Achilles (*Iliad*, XXIV).

Thought it a crime to sacrifice a maiden?

AGAMEMNON: A king must put his country above his
children.

PYRRHUS: No law forbids a prisoner's punishment.

AGAMEMNON: Where law does not forbid, shame may
forbid.

PYRRHUS: The victor has the right to please himself.

AGAMEMNON: Who has most right, should least indulge
his pleasure.

PYRRHUS: Dare you say that to those who for ten years
Endured your tyranny – till Pyrrhus freed them?

AGAMEMNON: Is this the breed of Scyros?

PYRRHUS: Scyros breeds
No brother-feuds.

AGAMEMNON: An island in the sea!

PYRRHUS: Our mother sea! For Atreus and Thyestes –
We know their noble lineage.

AGAMEMNON: And yours?
Son of a girl raped by a boy Achilles,
A stripling –

PYRRHUS: An Achilles, by his birthright
Lord of all spheres of heavenly dominion –
The sea through Thetis, the infernal world
Through Aeacus, the heavens through Jupiter.

AGAMEMNON: Whom Paris killed –

PYRRHUS: Whom no immortal god
Dare challenge to his face.

AGAMEMNON: I could find punishment to stop that tongue
And curb that insolence. But my sword too
Knows how to spare a prisoner in my power.
Let us have Calchas here, the interpreter
Of heaven's will; let someone bring him hither.
If the Fates ask, I will not fail to give.

  [Enter Calchas]

Calchas, you loosed the knot that held our fleet
Back from this war; your skill unlocks the sky;
Your art can read the message of the Fates
In flesh of beasts, the thunder of the heavens,
The flaming passage of a shooting star –
And many a time I have paid heavily
For your pronouncements. Calchas, tell me now
What our god wills; instruct us by your wisdom.

CALCHAS: For fate's permission to depart, the price
Is as before. A young girl must be given
In sacrifice on the Thessalian's tomb.
She must be dressed as a Thessalian bride –
Or Mycenean, or Ionian –
Pyrrhus himself must give the bride away
To his father, so that she be duly wedded.
That is not all our ships are waiting for:
A debt is to be paid in nobler blood
Than that of Priam's daughter. One more victim
The Fates demand; and he must fall to death
From the top of Troy . . . Priam's grandson . . . Hector's
      son.
That done, your thousand ships may take the sea.

CHORUS

Is it the truth, or but an idle tale
    To give false comfort to our fears,
That the soul lives on when the body is laid to rest,
    When the wife has sealed the husband's eyes,
        When the last sun has set,
When the ashes are shut into the solemn urn?

Do we in vain give up our life to death?
Has the poor mortal still more time to live?
        Or do we wholly die?

Does nothing remain of us,
After the breath has fled and the spirit of life
Gone, to be mingled with the air above us,
After the fire has been laid to the naked body?

Swift as the feet of Pegasus, Time will gather
    All to itself –
  All that the sun looks down upon,
    From east to west;
  All that the blue sea touches
With its morning and its evening tides.

Onward we speed to our fate –
As fast as the twelve signs speeding through the sky,
As the stars' king turning the cycle of the years,
  As Hecate, running her chequered course –
    Onward we speed.
  To reach the river, by whose name
  The gods themselves take oath, that is
    To be no more.

As smoke from burning fire floats away,
  A quickly vanishing dark smudge;
As clouds, one moment lowering, are dispersed
    By cold north winds;
So will this spirit, this master of our being,
    Pass away.

There is nothing after death; and death is nothing –
Only the finishing post of life's short race.
Ambitious, give up your hopes; anxious, your fears.
Vast Chaos, and the hungry mouth of Time,
  Consume us all.
Death is inseparable; it destroys the body,

And does not spare the soul.
For Taenarus – the realm of the grim king –
The jealous hound that guards the infernal gate –
   These are all idle tales, fables,
   The stories of a troubled dream.
You ask, where will you be when you are dead?
   Where the unborn are.

ACT THREE

Andromache, an Elder, Astyanax, Ulysses

ANDROMACHE: O women of Troy, now do you pull at
    your hair,
  And beat your sorrowful breasts? Now do you flood
  Your cheeks with weeping? Have we endured so little –
  Is weeping enough? It is only now you have seen
  The fall of Troy; I saw it long ago,
  When the murderer dragged the body – my own dear
    body –
  At his chariot-wheels; when the load of Hector's weight
  Made those wheels creak and groan. That was my hour
  Of utter downfall and destruction.
  For what has happened since, I have no feeling;
  My senses are all dead and numbed by pain.
  I should by now have given the Greeks the slip
  And gone the way my husband went – to death –
  But for this child, who puts restraint on me;
  He will not let me die; for his sake now
  I must still ask the mercy of the gods,
  And must prolong my time of suffering.
  For him I must deny myself that comfort,
  Which is the only comfort in great sorrow,
  Freedom from fear. All hope of better things
  Is lost; the way to worse lies open still.
  When hope is gone, fear is ten times more fearful.
ELDER: Is some new fear yet added to your griefs?
ANDROMACHE: Out of our great calamity still greater
  Calamity is grown. Troy falls, but yet
  We have not seen her end.
ELDER: Can the gods wish
  Greater disaster to fall on us, and what

Can they contrive?

ANDROMACHE: The doors of deepest death
  Have been unlocked, the caves of darkness opened;
  As if we vanquished had not feared enough,
  Our buried enemies from the pit of hell
  Are coming back to earth; nor is the way
  From death to life allowed to Greeks alone –
  No, death treats all alike. And while one ghost[1]
  Is spreading terror through all Troy, another
  Night-haunting vision fills my dreams with dread.

ELDER: What vision? Tell us what it is you fear.

ANDROMACHE: The first half of the night had passed in
        peace,
  The Seven Stars turned their shining wain for home,
  When I found rest, such as I had not known
  For long in my despair, and for a while
  My weary cheeks were soothed with sleep – if senses
  Dazed beyond feeling can be said to sleep.
  Suddenly Hector stood before my eyes –
  But not the man who stormed the Grecian camp,
  Attacked their ships with brands from Ida's woods,
  Spread havoc in their ranks, fought a pretender
  Bearing Achilles' arms and won them from him.[2]
  Gone was the light of battle from his eyes;
  His face was weary and dispirited,
  A face too like my own, ravaged with grief,
  Half hidden under unkempt hair. But yet
  It was a joy to see him. 'Wake,' he said,
  Shaking his head at me. 'Wake, faithful wife,
  And save our son from danger. You must hide him.
  No other way can save him. Do not weep.
  You weep for Troy's fall? Would that it were over!

  1. That of Achilles.
  2. Patroclus, fighting in Achilles' armour (*Iliad*, XVI).

Come, lose no time, but get our son and heir
Away at once to any place but this.'
Frozen with fear and horror I awoke.
It was not of my son that I thought first;
I looked for Hector, turning frightened eyes
This way and that, but the deluding ghost
Slipped silently away from my embrace.

   And now, my son – true son of your great father,
Phrygia's one hope, all that our shattered house
Has left, sole offspring of our ancient blood,
Last of our old, our too illustrious line:
Child in your father's image – ah, too like;
This was my Hector's face, his walk, his carriage;
These were his brave strong hands, his rising shoulders,
His stern commanding brow, the hair he shook
About his tossing head. O little son,
You have been born too soon for Troy, too late
To be your mother's comfort. Shall we see
That happy day – will the time ever come,
When you will be Troy's saviour and avenger,
To set our city on her feet once more,
And bring her scattered people home again,
And to restore her name to Phrygia,
Our fatherland? I dare not make that prayer,
Knowing my fate; enough to pray for life,
All that a prisoner can ask.

                                    But now,
Alas, where can I hide you? Where can fear
Find refuge? Troy's great citadel,
The envy and the wonder of the world,
With all her treasure and her mighty walls
Which gods had built, is now a mound of dust;
Fire has consumed it; of the whole vast city
There now remains no fragment large enough

To hide a little child. What place will serve
To baffle the pursuit? . . . My husband's tomb –
A hallowed place, which even the enemy
Must reverence. . . . His father Priam spent all
To make it huge and handsome – the old king
Was prodigal in grief . . . I'll put the child
Into his father's care . . . what better place? . . .
Ah, but my limbs grow cold with sweat; I fear
The ominous presence of this place of death.

ELDER: When out of danger you can pick and choose;
In time of trouble seize what help there is.

ANDROMACHE: Is there not danger, hide him where we
         may,
The place may be betrayed?

ELDER: Let no one see.

ANDROMACHE: What if the enemy come searching for
         him?

ELDER: He perished in the city's fall. Many
Have owed their lives to rumours of their death.

ANDROMACHE: There is small hope for him; his noble
         birth
Lies heavy on his head. He will be caught;
And then what good will hiding him have done?

ELDER: The conqueror is never again so cruel,
Once his first rage is spent.

ANDROMACHE: O son, what place
Is far and inaccessible enough
To keep you safe? Where can we turn for help
In our extremity? Who will protect us?
Hector! Defend your loved ones now, as ever!
This is your loving wife – guard thou
The treasure she has stolen – keep him safe
With your dear ashes – let him live again! . . .
Son, go into the tomb . . . ah, you shrink back;

176

You do not like to hide? It shows your breeding;
You are ashamed to be afraid. But now
You must forget your manly pride, forget
Your courage of former days; now you must wear
The nature that misfortune puts upon you.
You see . . . all that is left of us . . . we three –
A tomb, a child, a captive woman . . . no,
We cannot fight against our fate. Be brave,
And go into this holy place in which
Your father rests. If Fortune can be kind
To those who suffer, you will live; if not,
Here is your grave.[1]

   [*The boy enters the tomb*]

ELDER: He is safe behind the gates.
  Now go; and keep away, lest by your fear
  You cause his hiding-place to be discovered.
ANDROMACHE: One may fear less when one is near the
      danger.
  But if you wish it, I will go away.
ELDER: But wait . . . be silent and refrain from mourning.
  Our enemy, the villainous Cephallenian,[2]
  Is on his way.
ANDROMACHE: Open, O earth! O husband,
  Command the earth to open to its centre
  And hide my treasure in the Stygian deep!
  Ulysses comes, and, by his crafty looks
  And walk, he has some evil plot in mind. . . .

ULYSSES: Sent as the instrument of cruel Fate,
  Let me first say that though I speak the words
  You must not think them mine; this is the voice

---

   1. *Fata si miseros iuvant / habes salutem; fata si vitam negant, / habes
sepulcrum.* The Latin is quoted in *The Spanish Tragedy*, III. 13 (*c.* 1589).
   2. Ulysses, from the island adjacent to Ithaca.

Of all the Greek commanders: Hector's son
Still stands between them and their long-sought homes,
And him the Fates demand. While there remains
A son of Hector and Andromache
To put fresh heart into the conquered Trojans,
Doubtful unrest and a precarious truce
Remain to plague the Greeks; fear at their backs
Will never let them lay their weapons down.

ANDROMACHE: Is this the teaching of your prophet
    Calchas?

ULYSSES: Without the teaching of our prophet Calchas,
We heard as much from Hector; and his power
To terrify lives in his son; true stock
Grows in the likeness of its ancestors.
You'll see a young calf running with the herd,
Before his horns have sprouted, and tomorrow,
With neck upreared and head held high, he's king
And leader in his father's place. A sapling
Sprung from a broken trunk grows up in no time
Tall as its parent, spreading a canopy
Across the sky and throwing shade on earth.
The embers of a dead fire, carelessly
Left unquenched, will spring to life again.
I know that grief is no impartial judge;
But if you weigh the matter honestly,
You cannot find it in your heart to blame
The veteran of ten winters and ten summers
Who dreads more war, new battles, and a Troy
Not laid to rest for good. A future Hector –
That is the one great bugbear of the Greeks.
You must relieve them of that fear. Our ships
Are at the water's edge; only one thing
Delays their sailing; for this cause alone
The whole fleet waits. Pray do not think me heartless,

For coming to demand the son of Hector;
The lot fell upon me; I would as soon
Have gone to fetch Orestes. Will you not bear
The same loss that your conqueror had to bear?[1]

ANDROMACHE: Alas, my son, if only you were now
Within your mother's reach – if I could know
Where you are now, or what has happened to you
Since you were stolen from me! Nothing now
Can turn me from a mother's duty – no,
Not though my breast were pierced with enemy spears,
My hands bound fast with searing chains, my body
Enclosed in hottest fire. My son, where are you?
What fate has come upon you? Are you wandering
Lost in the countryside? Or have you perished
In the vast conflagration of our home?
Has some brute victor gloated in his triumph
Over your blood? Has some wild beast devoured you
And left your mangled corpse as carrion
For birds of Ida?

ULYSSES: Let us have no lies.
You cannot easily deceive Ulysses.
I have outwitted mothers' stratagems –
And goddesses' too – ere now. Give up these tricks.
Where is your son?

ANDROMACHE: Ay, where is Hector? Where
Is Priam? Where are all the Trojan dead?
You ask for one; I ask, where are they all?

ULYSSES: Then, if not willingly, under compulsion
You shall be made to speak.

ANDROMACHE: Nothing can harm
One who can die, must die, and longs to die.

ULYSSES: A nearer sight of death can stop proud mouths.

ANDROMACHE: If you would rule Andromache by fear,

1. Agamemnon's sacrifice of Iphigenia.

Deny her death, not life: death is my prayer.

ULYSSES: Then let us have the scourge, and fire, and torture
Of every kind, till suffering compels you
To tell the truth which you are trying to hide.
Pain will dig out the secrets of your heart.
Necessity can master mother-love.

ANDROMACHE: Show me your fire, your scourge, your
instruments
Of foulest torture – hunger, raging thirst,
All pains there are, swords in this flesh, a prison's
Rank darkness – all that rage, and fear, can dare!

ULYSSES: Vain hope – to hide what you must soon reveal.

ANDROMACHE: A mother on her mettle knows no fear.

ULYSSES: You take your proud stand on a parent's love;
That same love, let me tell you, prompts us Greeks
To guard our children too. After ten years
Of weary war, ten years away from home,
I should be less alarmed by Calchas' warnings
If only for myself I feared the outcome;
But this means war for my Telemachus.

ANDROMACHE: Then here is good news for the Greeks,
Ulysses;
Give it I must, though much against my will.
Grief can no longer keep her burden secret.
The sons of Atreus shall rejoice; and you,
The Greeks' familiar messenger of joy,
Tell the glad tidings: Hector's son is dead.

ULYSSES: Can they believe it true – upon your oath?

ANDROMACHE: Yes. As I pray for every penalty
My conqueror can exact, and that my death
May be an easy one, my body lie
Buried in my own land, and that the soil
Of his own land lie light on Hector's head –
So do I take my oath my son is lost

To the light of day and lies among the dead,
Entombed with all the obsequies of death.
ULYSSES: Then Fate is satisfied, the seed of Hector
Exterminated, peace secured for ever.
I shall be glad to tell the Greeks this news. . . .
　　　　But wait – Ulysses may convince the Greeks;
What is convincing him? A mother's word?
Yet it were strange a mother should invent
So sad a story and not fear to speak
The ominous word of death. Omens are real
To those who have no worse to fear. This woman
Has sworn an oath that all she says is true;
If she is not afraid of perjury,
She must have something worse to fear – but what?
Now is the time for all your art, my man;
Now use your craft and skill, now show yourself
The real Ulysses. Truth cannot be lost.
Observe that mother carefully; she mourns,
She weeps and groans; and see how restlessly
She moves this way and that, paying attention
With anxious ears to any passing word.
That means she's more afraid than sorrowful.
I must be artful with her. . . .
　　　　　　　　　　　Madam,
Most times it would be proper to console
A sorrowing parent's grief. But you, poor mother,
Must be called happy that you have no son.
He was to die a cruel death – thrown headlong
From yonder tower, the only one remaining
Upright amid the ruins of your city.
ANDROMACHE: My limbs grow weak and shiver; my
　　　　heart fails;
My blood is cold as ice. . . .
ULYSSES:　　　　　　　　Yes, she is frightened.

This is the clue that I must follow; fear
Reveals the mother's guile; she must fear more. . . .
Away, men, quickly! Find this enemy
Cunningly hidden from us by his mother,
This final menace to our nation. Find him
And dig him out, wherever his covert is,
And bring him here to us. . . . You've caught him? Good!
Let's have him here at once! . . .

                                You tremble?
You looked that way? Surely the boy is dead?

ANDROMACHE: Would that I still had any cause to
    tremble!
Only long habit now makes me afraid;
Old lessons are not easily forgotten.

ULYSSES: So – since it seems the sacrificial rite
Owed to these walls has been anticipated,
Since the poor child has met a kindlier fate
And cannot now obey our prophet's orders,
This is what Calchas further asks: that we,
To obtain a blessing for our home-going ships,
Shall be allowed to pull down Hector's tomb
From top to bottom, and disperse his ashes
Over the sea. The boy has cheated us
Of his appointed death; we must lay hands
Upon this sacred resting-place.

ANDROMACHE [aside]:   Alas,
What can I do? Two fears divide my heart –
Fear for my son, and for the hallowed dust
Of my lost husband. Which will be the stronger?
Hear me, ye pitiless gods – and hear me, husband's
Dear soul, now verily among the gods –
All that I love in my dear son is Hector.
O let him live, that I may see again
My Hector's face! . . . Yet must I see your ashes

Dug from the grave and drowned? Your broken bones
Flung piecemeal on the ocean? . . . Rather than that,
Let the child die. Am I his mother, then,
And can I see him sent to infamous death?
Am I to see him tossed from that high tower?
Yes, I shall bear it; I shall have the strength
To bear it – but not see my Hector's bones
Ill-treated by his conquerors. . . . And yet
He is now safe in the hands of Fate – the other
Can still feel pain. . . . One must be saved – ah, which? –
You must decide. Can there be any doubt
Where duty lies? Hector, your husband, calls. . . .
Nay, you are wrong; there are two Hectors here;
And one of them still breathes, and still may live
To avenge his father's death. Save both, you cannot.
It must be one of them. Then, O my soul,
Let him be saved, who is the Argive fear.

ULYSSES: I shall obey the order of the prophet
And have this tomb destroyed.

ANDROMACHE: Have we not paid
A ransom for the tomb?

ULYSSES: Still I shall do it;
We'll have the sepulchre thrown down and dragged
From its high mound.

ANDROMACHE: O heaven's powers, protect us!
Achilles, keep your word! Pyrrhus, defend
Your father's gift!

ULYSSES: This monument will soon
Be levelled to the ground.

ANDROMACHE: Worse sacrilege
Than any yet committed by the Greeks.
Temples you have despoiled, even of gods
That served your purpose, but your violence
Has spared the dead. I will not let you do it;

Armed though you are, I'll fight you with bare hands;
Passion will give me strength. If Amazons
Could quell your troops of Argives; if a Maenad
Could march out in her madness, god-possessed,
Armed with a thyrsus, to amaze the woodlands
And strike, with power she never knew was hers,
And never feel a wound herself; so I
Will charge into the battle to defend
This sepulchre and die beside its dust.

ULYSSES: What are you waiting for, men? Do you fear
A woman's angry cries and useless rage?
Do as I tell you instantly.

ANDROMACHE: No, no!
Destroy me rather with your swords, here, here! . . .
O Hector, Hector, break your prison of death!
Throw off the earth and overpower Ulysses!
Your ghost has power enough. Greeks, do you see him?
Do you see Hector now, the sword he grasps,
The firebrands whirling? Does none see him but I?

ULYSSES: Down with it all to the ground.

ANDROMACHE: Have you the heart
To bury son and husband in one ruin?
Could you not ask the Greeks for mercy? Oh!
The tomb's huge weight will crush the one within!
Oh let him die, poor child, as best he can,
In any place but this – let not the son
Be crushed beneath his father's bones, or father
Be bruised beneath the son!
                              Here at your knees,
I fall to pray, Ulysses; at your feet
My hand, that has touched no man's feet before.
Have pity for a mother; hear her prayers
With patience and with kindness; as the gods
Have raised you up, so the more gently lay

Your hand upon the fallen. What charity
You lend to the unfortunate, you lend
To your own fortune. Therefore, as you pray
For safe return to your own chaste wife's bed;
As for your aged father's life you pray,
That he may live to have you home again;
And for your son, that he may take your place,
Exceeding all your hopes in grace and nature,
Older than any of his ancestors,
And greater than his father; so have pity,
Have pity on a mother: nothing else
Remains to comfort me in my affliction.

ULYSSES: Show us your son – then let us hear your prayers.

ANDROMACHE: Come from your hiding-place. . . .
   Poor little thing, that your fond mother
   Tried to steal away. . . .

   He is here, you see, Ulysses –
   The bane of your thousand ships. . . .

   Offer your hand.
   Kneel at your master's feet;
   Touch them and worship him.
   You need not be ashamed to accept what Fate
   Puts upon the unfortunate.
   You may think no longer now
   Of your royal ancestors,
   Forget your grandfather's domain
   Of all the world.
   Put Hector out of mind.
   Play now the prisoner's part
   On bended knee.
   And weep – though your own fate
   Be not yet real to you –

Weep, child,
As you see your mother weep. . . .

An earlier Troy once saw a child,
A king, in tears; when the young Priam
Made Hercules relent from cruelty.
There was that angry man, whose strength
Could overpower any beast,
Who broke into the doors of death
And found a way back from the dark –
Yet one small enemy's tears defeated him.
'Take up the reins, my boy,' he said.
'Sit in your father's place: be king;
And be a better king.' So was it
To be in that man's power.
The lenient ire of Hercules
Should be your lesson;
Or is it only his armed strength
You look for now?
You have a suppliant at your feet
As worthy as his ancestor,
And for his life he pleads.
As for the throne of Troy, with that let Fortune
Do what she will.

ULYSSES: I am not deaf to a grieved mother's plea;
    But all the mothers of Greece concern me more.
    With that child's life great grief must grow for them.
ANDROMACHE: You think that he will bring to life again
    All this – this smoking ruin of a city?
    Will his two hands rebuild the towers of Troy?
    If that is Troy's one hope, she has no hope.
    Troy, fallen as she is, can never be
    A Troy which any man can fear again.

You think his father's courage will inspire
This child? A father tumbled in the dust!
And even had he lived, the end of Troy
Would soon have quenched that courage; no man's
        courage
Outlives defeat. If we must pay the debt,
What greater price can you demand but this –
The yoke of service on his royal neck;
Make him your slave; can that be too much mercy
For royalty to ask?

ULYSSES: Not from Ulysses;
But it is more than Calchas will allow.

ANDROMACHE: O arch-contriver of deceit and crime!
Whose open valour never killed a foe;
Whose cunning wiles have been the cause of death
To your own people. Now you put the blame
Upon the prophet and the innocent gods?
Not so, this outrage is your own invention.
The famous fighter in the dark has found
Courage to dare a deed alone in daylight –
Courage enough to kill a child.

ULYSSES: The Greeks
Know all about the courage of Ulysses,
And Trojans more than enough. But time is short;
We cannot spend the whole day bandying words;
Our anchors are aweigh; we must be gone.

ANDROMACHE: Yet grant me just a little time, to pay
A mother's last attentions to her son –
One last embrace to fill my hungry grief.

ULYSSES: I only wish I could have mercy on you;
But yet, as much as is within my duty
I can allow, a few more moments' grace.
Make what lament you wish; it lightens sorrow.

ANDROMACHE: Alas, beloved treasure of our house

That is no more, last of the Trojan dead,
The dreaded enemy of Greeks, my own
Last hope now lost – ah, how I fondly prayed
Your fame might be the equal of your father's
In deeds of war, your years of life be long
As your grandfather's. God has refused those prayers.
You should have been the holder of the sceptre,
King in Troy's royal hall; you should have been
The people's lawgiver, and conqueror
Of nations; should have scourged the flying Greeks
And dragged the corpse of Pyrrhus in the dust.
That cannot be. Now we shall never see
Your little hand holding a little weapon,
As you join bravely in the hunt for beasts
Across the glades; no solemn feast days now
Will see you riding in the Trojan Games,[1]
Prince of our youth, leading the flying squadrons.
There'll be no dancing in the age-old rites
Around our altars, no more nimble leaping
When the wild music of curved horns salutes
Our Trojan temples. Ah, what a death, more cruel
Than any stroke of Mars! A scene more tragic
Than our great Hector's death these walls must watch.

ULYSSES: Now, mother, it is time to check these tears;
Great grief, unchecked, will never make an end.

ANDROMACHE: No, let me weep, only a little longer,
Ulysses, I beseech you; let me weep
A little yet, and let me lay my hand
Upon his eyes while he still lives. . . . So young
To die . . . and yet already to be feared. . . .
Go now; your Troy awaits you; go, to freedom,
To join those Trojans who are free.

1. An equestrian exercise, attributed to Trojan tradition, was
practised in Rome, and is recalled in *Aeneid*, v. 545 ff.

ASTYANAX: No! Mother!

ANDROMACHE: No, do not cling to me; these hands you
    clutch
  Cannot protect you now. When a young calf
  Hears a wild lion roar and cowers in terror
  Close to its mother's side, the angry beast
  Comes on the more and scares the mother away!
  He grabs the smaller prize in his huge jaws,
  Crushes and carries him away; so he,
  Our enemy, will snatch you from my breast.
  Here are my kisses, and my tears, for you,
  My son . . . and these torn tresses; take of me
  All that you can and go to meet your father.
  And take him these few words of my last cry:
  'If the departed can have any thought
  Of this world's cares, and if love does not die
  In funeral fires, will you allow your wife
  Andromache to be a Greek lord's slave?
  Are you so cruel? Can you lie inert,
  Unheeding, while Achilles comes upon us?' . . .
  Take, as I said, this hair, these tears, last relics
  Of my poor husband's funeral; take my kiss,
  And give it to your father. Let me keep
  This garment; it will be your mother's comfort . . .
  It has been touched by the beloved tomb,
  And the beloved dead . . . some of his dust
  May still be here . . . perhaps my lips can feel it. . . .

ULYSSES: This moaning will go on for ever! Take him!
  Remove this thing that keeps the Greek fleet waiting!

CHORUS

What future home awaits us prisoners?
Hills of Thessaly, vale of Tempe,
Phthia, whence soldiers mostly come,

Stony Trachis where fine herds breed,
Iolchos, queen of the wide sea?
Or Crete, broad island of a hundred cities?
The little town of Gortynis, dry Tricce,
Mothone nestling among trickling streams
In Oeta's woods – whose arrows
Have twice hailed ruin on Troy?

Pleuron, Diana's enemy?
The broad bay of Troezen?
Or Olenus, where homes are few and far?
Or Pelion, great domain of Prothoüs,
Last of three steps to heaven; that was where
Chiron[1] was tutor to a boy already
Eager for battle; sprawled in his mountain den,
The giant strummed his lyre and sang war-songs
To whet that early appetite for strife.

What of Carystos, quarry of coloured marble?
Or Chalcis, treading the edge of that wild sea
Tossed by the ceaseless current of Euripus?
There is Calydnae, easy to reach
In any wind – and Gonoessa,
Where the wind never stops – Enispe,
Swept by the terrible north gales.
Or Peparethos, off the Attic shore?
Eleusis, proud of mysteries
That none may speak of?

And the home of Ajax – the first Salamis;[2]
Calydon, famous for the fierce wild boar;

1. The centaur who taught the boy Achilles.
2. Distinguished from the Salamis in Cyprus, reputed to have
been founded by Teucer.

The swamps of Titaressos, a sluggish river
Meandering till it plunges under the sea.
Bessa, and Scarphe? And old Nestor's home,
Pylos? Pharis? Jupiter's Pisa? Elis –
Prizes of victory are well known there.

Oh, let the winds of fortune
Carry us where they will!
Make us a gift to any place they choose!
But Sparta – save us, O gods,
From Sparta, the bane of Troy,
And bane of the Greeks! Or Argos,
Or cruel Pelops' town,
Mycenae! save us too
From little Zacynthus and its little sister
Neritos – and the dangerous treacherous reefs
Of Ithaca!

What will your fate be, Hecuba?
What master will take you away,
Into what land, for all to see?
In what king's country must you die?

ACT FOUR

Helen, Andromache, Polyxena, Hecuba, Pyrrhus

HELEN: If marriage must be fraught with death and woe,
A time for tears and bloody murder, Helen
May well be chosen for its minister,
Since after their defeat I am still forced
To be obnoxious to the Phrygians.
On me it falls to tell the bride this lie
About her marriage with Achilles' son;
I am to see her dressed and decorated
In Grecian fashion, find the artful words
To tempt her to her doom; by my deceit
The sister of Paris must be lured to death.
But it is well that she should be deceived;
It will be easier for her; to die,
Without the fear of death, is easy death.
So let the task be quickly done; the guilt
Of crime enforced rests only on its author. . . .
    Dear princess of the Dardan house, at last
A good god looks more kindly on the fallen;
A happy marriage is prepared for you,
A marriage better than King Priam himself
In Troy's best days could have obtained for you.
The man who seeks your hand in holy wedlock
Is lord and king over the wide domain
Of Thessaly, the most illustrious hero
Of the Pelasgian race. You shall be called
Child of great Tethys; all sea goddesses,
And Thetis, tranquil queen of Ocean's main,
Will call you theirs; Peleus and Nereus,
Your husband's grandfathers, will welcome you
A daughter to their house, for you will be

The wife of Pyrrhus. Now you must forget
Captivity; take off those ugly clothes
And dress yourself for joy. Smooth that tossed hair
And have it braided neatly by skilled hands.
The fall that you have suffered may yet place you
Upon a higher throne; captives ere now
Have profited from their captivity.
ANDROMACHE: It needed only this! The fallen Trojans'
Last indignity! A time for joy! –
With ruined Pergamum on fire around us.
A time for marriage! Who could look askance
At marriage, under Helen's auspices?
What woman could refuse such happiness? . . .
Bringer of doom, disaster, and destruction
To both our peoples – look upon these graves
Of captains, and the bare unburied bones
That strew the ground! Your marriage brought them
     here.
The blood of Asia and the blood of Europe
Has flowed for your sake, while you sat content
To watch the spectacle of warring husbands,
And knew not which to pray for. Let us have
More marriage, then! Torches and sacred fire –
You need not look for them – Troy will provide
Flames bright enough to celebrate a marriage
Such as was never seen before. Sing, women,
Sing, women of Troy, for the marriage of Pyrrhus,
Due hymns of mourning and of lamentation!
HELEN: Great suffering, I know, can drive the mourner
Beyond the edge of reason; she will hear
No argument, and even hate the friends
Who suffer with her. Yet I have a cause
And will maintain it, even in the face
Of hostile judges; for my suffering

Is worse than yours. Andromache mourns Hector,
Hecuba weeps for Priam – but for Helen
There is no friend to share her grief for Paris,
No one must hear it; she must weep alone.
Is it so hard a thing to be a slave?
I have endured it long, a prisoner
Ten years. You have seen Ilium overthrown,
Her gods cast down? Yes, it is hard to see
One's country lost; harder to be afraid
Of finding it again. You have your friends
For comfort in your ills; I am detested
By conqueror and conquered equally.
What masters you will serve, chance will decide;
There is no chance for me, I am already
My master's prize. You say I was the cause
Of all this war's disaster for the Trojans;
True – if it was a Spartan ship that ventured
Into your seas; but if I was the prize
Of Trojan hands, and given by a goddess[1]
In payment to the judge who favoured her –
Absolve the victim. When I come to trial,
My judge will not be merciful; the verdict
Will rest with Menelaus. Will you now
Withhold your tears awhile, Andromache,
And teach this child . . . alas, I do believe
I must weep too.
ANDROMACHE: Some strange thing it must be
That can make Helen weep! But what? Tell us
Ulysses' whole abominable plot.
Must she be hurled from Ida's highest peak,
Dropped from the summit of the citadel,
Thrown down into the sea over the edge
Of that sheer precipice where high Sigeum

1. By Venus, as a reward to Paris.

Looks out across the bay? Whatever it be,
Tell us the secret that your false face hides.
No outrage could be more intolerable
Than to have Pyrrhus made a son-in-law
To Hecuba and Priam. Speak and declare
What is the penalty you have prepared
For this unhappy girl. Spare us at least
This added insult – to be tricked by lies.
Death, as you see, we are prepared to suffer.

HELEN: If I could have my wish, would I might hear
The word of the interpreter of gods
Commanding me also upon a sword
To end my hated life, or to let Pyrrhus
Roughly dispatch me at Achilles' tomb . . .
To share your fate, my poor Polyxena . . .
You must be given to him, Achilles says,
Given in sacrifice over his ashes,
To be his bride in the Elysian fields.

ANDROMACHE: And look! O the brave spirit, she is happy
To hear the sentence of her death! Eager
To wear the royal ornament, she gladly
Allows the braiding of her hair. Marriage
On earth she would have counted death; this death
She takes for marriage. But alas, the mother . . .
This blow has stunned her, and her senses fail.
Stand up, unhappy Hecuba; take courage
And comfort to your sinking heart. . . . Her life
Hangs on a thread; only a little space
Parts Hecuba from her felicity. . . .
But no, she breathes; she is alive again.
Death has a way to elude the unfortunate.

HECUBA: Still does Achilles live to plague the Phrygians?
Does he fight still? Paris, you struck too lightly.
Can the dead ashes and the tomb still thirst

195

For Trojan blood? A time I can remember
When there were happy faces at my side,
So many children to be mother to,
They tired me out with kissing. Only one
Is left me now – only this one to pray for,
Only this one companion, comfort, rest.
She is all my family, the only voice
To call me mother. O unhappy soul,
O stubborn life, will you not pass away
And spare me this last reckoning with death?
My eyes cannot withhold their tears; the rain
Descends and drowns my cheeks.
ANDROMACHE: Yet are not we,
We, Hecuba, we rather to be mourned?
The fleet will sail and carry us away
Each to some different place. This child will rest
Beneath the soil of her dear native land.
HELEN: And when you know what lot has fallen to you,
You will be still more envious of her fate.
ANDROMACHE: Is there yet more to know?
HELEN: The lots are drawn;
The urn has given each captive to her master.
ANDROMACHE: Whose slave am I to be? Tell me his name.
HELEN: Yours was the first; the prince of Scyros has you.
ANDROMACHE: Lucky Cassandra! – whom Apollo's word
And her crazed soul excluded from the lot.
HELEN: She is the prize of the great king of kings.
HECUBA: You can be glad, my child. You can be happy.
Well might Cassandra, and Andromache,
Envy your fate. Has anyone accepted
The gift of Hecuba?
HELEN: Against his will,
Ulysses has you – for the little time –
HECUBA: What heartless umpire of the lottery,

What blind unfeeling arbiter is he
Who can give royal slaves to royal masters!
Is some malicious god distributing
Us prisoners? Is the decision left
To some malign oppressor of the fallen,
Assigning us without discrimination
To those whom we must serve, with spiteful hand
Apportioning our fates? Is Hector's mother
Included with the armour of Achilles,
To be Ulysses' prize? This, then, is conquest,
This is captivity indeed, the last
Of all indignities. This is my shame –
Not slavery itself, but to be slave
To *him*. Shall he who won Achilles' spoils
Have those of Hector too? Is there a place
In that bleak island amid angry seas
Fit to contain my tomb? Well, I am ready.
Lead on, Ulysses. I will follow you,
And where I go my Fates will follow me.
The sea will have no peace for you; wind, wave,
Tempest, with war and fire and all the ills
That I and Priam have suffered, will destroy you.
Till that day comes, one thing for my revenge
Suffices – that your lot is spent on me;
What better prize you hoped for, you have lost.
    Now here comes Pyrrhus, walking rapidly,
With anger in his looks. . . . What more, then, Pyrrhus?
We are prepared. Plunge in this breast your sword,
And let the parents of your father's bride
Be reunited. Shedder of aged blood,
Strike here! Here's more to suit your liking.
Seize and remove your prisoner. Shame all gods
Of heaven above and all departed souls
With your vile murders. For you Greeks I pray –

What shall I pray? – that on the sea you find
Such fortune as befits this marriage rite.
And may the fate of all your Grecian fleet,
Of all your thousand ships, be like the fate
That shall befall, obedient to my prayers,
The ship that puts to sea with me on board.

CHORUS

Sorrow finds comfort in companionship;
And in the lamentations of great numbers
Is consolation; grief bites not so keenly
When many in the same plight share the mourning.

Jealous, jealous is grief; she likes to see
Many in her distress; she likes to know
That she is not alone condemned to suffer.
All are content to bear what all are bearing.

If none were happy, none would believe himself
Unfortunate, however great his troubles.
Take away wealth, and gold, and thriving lands
With droves of oxen at the plough – how then
The spirits of the down-pressed poor would rise!
What is misfortune but comparison?

Caught in extreme disaster, we are glad
To see no happy faces; he is the one –
The solitary voyager, escaping
Naked from rough seas into harbour – he
Is the one to moan and rail against his fate.
Tempest and shipwreck seem less terrible
To one who sees a thousand vessels sunk
In the same sea and has been swept ashore
On drifting wreckage in the teeth of gales
That fight the billows off the land.

The loss of Helle was great grief to Phrixus.[1]
When the great golden ram bore on his back
Brother and sister, and in ocean's deep
Lost one of them, he wept. Not so Deucalion
And Pyrrha; when those two looked round about them
And saw the sea, nothing but sea, since they
Were the sole human creatures left alive,
They did not weep.

Our sorrowful voices will soon be swept away
Scattered as ships steer off in all directions.
Sails will be spread at the sound of the trumpet; wind
And oar will carry the crews far out to sea,
And the shore will fade from sight.
Then how will we poor women feel – the land
Growing smaller and smaller on every side, the sea
Growing larger and larger, and the heights of Ida
Vanishing far away?

Then son will say to mother, mother to son,
As they show with a pointing finger, far away,
The quarter in which Troy lies: 'There . . . that is Troy,
Where the dreadful cloud of smoke curls into the sky.'
That sight will be the landmark
To show the Trojans where their homeland lies.

1. Phrixus and Helle, children of King Athamas of Thebes; persecuted by their stepmother Ino, they were rescued by the Golden Ram (cf. *Thyestes*, 225) which carried them, not quite successfully, over the Hellespont.

ACT FIVE

Messenger, Hecuba, Andromache

MESSENGER: A cruel fate! A lamentable, vile
And wicked fate! When did the eye of Mars,
In all these ten years past, behold a crime
So horrible, so barbarous? Whose loss
Must I first weep, with what I have to tell –
Yours, aged mother? Or yours?

HECUBA: Choose as you will –
In all you weep for mine. While each of these
Has her one grief to bear, the grief of all
Lies on my heart. Their deaths are all my deaths;
All weeping women are Hecuba's sorrowing daughters.

MESSENGER: The girl is slain; the boy thrown from the
           walls.
Each suffered bravely.

ANDROMACHE: Tell us how they died.
Tell all the circumstances of this act
Of double evil. Sorrow loves to dwell
On every detail of its woe. Tell all –
Leave nothing out.

MESSENGER: All that is left of Troy
Is one great tower, at whose high battlements
Priam was wont to sit, watching his troops
And ordering the conduct of the war.
Here on this tower's top he would embrace
His little grandson in his gentle arms,
And, when great Hector's fire and sword sent Greeks
Flying in panic-stricken rout, would draw
The child's attention to his father's prowess.
This once so famous tower, the masterpiece
Of our defences, now, a dangerous crag,
Stands out alone. Hither from every side

Crowds had assembled; leaders and lower ranks,
The whole Greek multitude had left their ships
And gathered here. Some were on higher ground
Near by, which overlooked the open space;
Some on a spur of rock, pressed close together
And balanced tiptoe on its edge. Tall trees –
Laurel and pine and beech – provided perches,
Till the whole forest swayed with clinging bodies.
One chose a vantage-point on some high hill,
Another on a charred roof-top, or stood
Poised on the leaning cornice of a ruin.
One heartless onlooker was bold enough
To take his seat on Hector's monument.[1]
     At length, across the space between the crowds
The Ithacan advanced, with solemn steps,
Leading the old king's grandson by the hand.
The little boy marched boldly to the tower,
Climbed to its summit, and there stood, his eyes
Glancing this way and that, quite unafraid.
There, in the grip of hostile hands, the boy
Stood, as defiant as a lion's cub
Which, yet unarmed with formidable teeth,
Small and defenceless though it be, shows fight,
Snapping with rage and ineffectual jaws.
The crowd was touched with pity; even the leaders,
Even Ulysses. Tears were in the eyes
Of all, except the one for whom they wept.
Ulysses called on the avenging gods
To accept the sacrifice, but while he prayed
And spoke again the sentence of the prophet,
The boy himself leapt from the tower's height

---

1. The author has forgotten, or never envisaged, the stage setting;
Hector's tomb was presumed visible and accessible in the earlier part
of the play.

To fall, there in the heart of Priam's city.

ANDROMACHE: Ah, when was ever such a sin committed
By any Colchian, any wandering Scythian?
What barbarous people of the Caspian sea
Would dare such wickedness? The fierce Busiris
Would not shed children's blood upon his altars,
Nor Diomede feed his beasts on infants' flesh.[1]
Who will take up my dear son's broken body
And lay it in a tomb?

MESSENGER: From that sheer fall
What body can remain? The bones were smashed
And scattered by the impact; every trace
Of his fair person, every lineament,
The princely likeness of his father, crushed
To nothing by the body's plunge to ground.
His neck was broken as it struck the rock,
The brains spilled from the shattered skull. He lies
A shapeless corpse.

ANDROMACHE: His father's likeness still!

MESSENGER: The boy had fallen from the tower, and now
The assembled Greeks, when they had wept their full
For their own sin, turned to the second outrage
And to Achilles' tomb. Its farther edge
Touches the gentle waters of Rhoeteum;
Its inland side confronts an open space
Encircled by a gently rising slope,
A theatre, to which the crowd converged
Till every place was filled. The thoughts of some
Were with their shore-bound fleet, to be released
By this last execution; some rejoiced
At the destruction of the enemy stock;

1. Two ogres destroyed by Hercules. Busiris, an Egyptian king,
sacrificed immigrants to avert drought. Diomede (not the warrior
of the *Iliad*), a Thracian, fed his horses on human flesh.

Most of the careless multitude remained
Watching, while loathing, the outrageous act.
And Trojans too were gathered here, to mourn
At this, their own last funeral, to tremble
At this last moment of the fall of Troy.
Then suddenly the marriage train appeared,
With torches at the head, Helen herself
Attending on the bride, but bowed with grief.
'Give such a wedding to Hermione!'
The Trojans cry. 'Let Helen for her sins
Be reunited with her husband thus!'
Trojan and Greek alike were held amazed.
The girl came on with humbly lowered face;
But in that face a radiant beauty shone
Even more brightly in its hour of death –
A sun more splendid in its dying fall
Before the stars take up their offices
And night treads on the heels of weakening day.
The multitude was rapt; none could forbear
To admire a sight soon to be lost for ever.
Some marked her beauty, some her innocent youth,
Some thought upon the strange vicissitudes
Of human fate. Not one remained unmoved
By such staunch courage in the face of death.
Behind her Pyrrhus walked. Now every heart
Was struck with terror, wonderment, and pity.
   The young man reached the summit of the mound
And stood on the high platform of the tomb
In which his father lay. The girl, unflinching,
Never withdrew a step, but faced the sword
With grim defiance. Such great courage shocked
Every spectator; and, beyond belief,
Even Pyrrhus paused before the stroke of death.
At last his hand went to his sword and thrust

The blade in to the hilt. Her death was swift;
Blood spurted from the mortal wound; and still,
In the act of death, her courage never left her.
She seemed to fling herself with angry force
Upon the ground, as if to pound the earth
Over Achilles' head. Then, friend or foe,
The people wept; but the lament of Troy
Was timid, while the victors cried aloud.
The sacrifice was done. The pool of blood
Neither stood still nor flowed over the ground;
It quickly sank, drunk by the thirsty soil
Of that inexorable tomb.

HECUBA: Go now,
Go, Greeks! Go home, now all is safe for you.
You have no more to fear. Now let your fleet
Hoist sail and cross the waters that you long for.
A young child and an innocent girl have died;
The war is over. Where shall I now weep?
Where will they let my aged mouth spit out
This lingering taste of death? Daughter, or grandson,
Husband, or country – which desires my tears?
Must I still weep for all, or for myself?
O death, for which alone I pray, can you
So swiftly come to children, and to maidens
So sharply, when you will, yet hold your hand
From me alone? Have I not looked for you
'Mid swords and spears and firebrands in the night?
I have desired you and you have not come.
Enemy, fire, and fall, have not destroyed me;
Was it for this I stood at Priam's side?

MESSENGER: Now, prisoners, you must hurry to the sea.
Sails are unfurled on every ship, the fleet
Is ready to depart.

                    Exeunt

OEDIPUS

WHEN Oedipus, supposedly the son of King Polybus of Corinth, came as a voluntary fugitive from his own country to Thebes, he found that her king Laius had just died in an unpremeditated fight with a traveller on a lonely road. The city was also under the domination of the half-human half-bestial creature, the Sphinx, whose threats were couched in the form of a riddle. Oedipus answered the riddle, destroyed the Sphinx, and was made king in the place of Laius and, as custom required, husband to the widowed queen Jocasta.

Some years later, at the point at which the play begins, the city is in the grip of a pestilence for which neither cause nor remedy can be found. Oedipus determines to use all means to rid the city of this plague, and in so doing uncovers the ugly secrets of his own identity and the acts to which he has been driven by the malignity of fate.

Seneca's drama follows very closely the line of its far superior prototype, the *Oedipus Tyrannus* of Sophocles, though digressing into circumstantial details of the occult rituals conducted by Tiresias, and by compression weakening the suspense and impact of the king's discovery of his past.

DRAMATIS PERSONAE

OEDIPUS, *King of Thebes*
JOCASTA, *his wife*
CREON, *brother to Jocasta*
TIRESIAS, *a blind prophet*
MANTO, *his daughter*
AN OLD MAN, *messenger from Corinth*
PHORBAS, *an old shepherd*
MESSENGER
CHORUS *of Theban elders*

*

Scene: the palace at Thebes

ACT ONE

Oedipus, Jocasta

OEDIPUS: The night is at an end; but dimly yet
The Lord Sun shows his face – a dull glow rising
Out of a dusky cloud. It is a torch
Of evil omen, this pale fire he brings
With which to scan our plague-polluted homes.
Day will reveal the havoc of the night.
What king is happy on his throne? False joy,[1]
How many ills thy smiling face conceals!
As the high peak takes all the winds' assault
And sharp cliffs jutting upon open seas –
Are pounded even by the lightest waves,
So are the heights of royalty exposed
To Fortune's blast. How happy was the day
On which I came, escaped from the domain
Of Polybus my father, free in exile,
A fearless vagabond – so help me, gods! –
To stumble upon a kingdom. Now I fear
A fate unspeakable: to kill my father.
This is the warning of the oracle
In Delphi's laurel grove. And worse, another,
A greater crime is put into my hand.
O filial love, doomed love! I am ashamed
To utter what has been foretold of me.
Apollo bids me fear . . . my mother's bed
(This to her son!), a marriage bed of shame,
Unlawful and incestuous matrimony!
This terror drove me from my father's kingdom;
Not by compulsion banished from the hearth,

---

1. *Quisquamne regno gaudet? O fallax bonum.* The Latin line is quoted, inaccurately, in *The True Tragedy of Richard III* (anon. 1594).

But fearful of myself, I sought to put
The law of nature safe beyond the chance
Of violation. He that goes in dread
Of some great evil, cannot choose but fear
Even what seems impossible. I see
Disaster everywhere. I doubt myself.

   Fate is preparing, even while I speak,
Some blow for me. Why else, when all my people
Suffer this pestilence, when havoc walks
Through all this land, am I alone unscathed?
For what worse punishment am I preserved?
Amid the city's ruin, lamentations
Ever renewed, unceasing funerals,
A massacre of men – I stand untouched . . .
To answer at Apollo's judgement seat;
Why else? Who could expect a sinful man
To be rewarded with a healthy kingdom?
The air of heaven is tainted by my presence.
There is no gentle breeze to cool the breasts
Of fevered sufferers; no kind winds blow here.
The Dog-Star scorches and the Lord Sun's fire
Blows hot upon the Lion's heels. No water
Runs in the rivers, fields are colourless.
Dirce is dry, Ismenus thinly creeps,
A shrunk stream barely moistening the sand.
Apollo's sister, Moon, drifts hardly seen
Across the sky; day, overcast with clouds,
Reveals a pale dull world; the silent night
Is dark, without a star; fog, dense and black,
Broods over all the land; the murk of hell
Has swallowed up the heavenly citadels,
The mansions of the gods on high. The corn,
That should be ripe for harvest, bears no fruit;
The golden ears that sway on springing stalks

Soon wither and the barren crop falls dead.
   No section of the people has escaped
The killing plague; death pays no heed to age
Or sex; young men and old, fathers and sons –
The mortal pestilence makes no distinction.
Husband and wife await one funeral pyre,
And there are no more tears to mourn the dead,
None left to weep; the very magnitude
Of our ordeal has dried up every eye;
As ever in the extreme of misery,
Tears perish at their source. Here you will see
An anguished father bear his burden out
To the consuming fire; a stricken mother there;
And back she hurries for the second victim
Which she must carry to the same death-pyre.
One grief is stricken by a second grief;
Mourners around the dead fall to be mourned.
Some have been known to steal each others' fire,
Fling their own dead upon another's ashes;
Misery knows no shame. There are no tombs
For hallowed bones to rest in; to be burnt
Is boon enough – and few are those that have it.
Now there is no more earth for burial mounds,
No wood for pyres. And for the stricken ones
No art or prayer can find a remedy.
Healers fall sick; the plague defeats all aid.
   Here at the altar bowed, with suppliant hands
I pray, that Fate will quickly come to me,
That I may not outlive my country's death,
Not be the last to fall, not be the last,
Of all the people whom I rule, to die.
O gods too pitiless, O heavy fate!
Can death still be denied, although so near,
To me alone? Then I must turn my back

On this doomed kingdom, which my touch of death
Has blighted – leave these wakes and funerals,
This air polluted with the pestilence,
The curse my own unhappy coming brought –
Leave all behind, begone without delay . . .
Even to my parents' home.

JOCASTA: Why do you choose,
Dear husband, thus to make your misery worse
By lamentation? I believe a king
Should grasp misfortune with a steady hand;
The more unsure his state, more imminent
His fall from sovereignty, so much the more
Should he be resolute to stand upright.
He is no man who turns his back on fate.

OEDIPUS: No man can brand me with the name of coward.
My heart is innocent of craven fears.
Against drawn swords, against the might of Giants,
Against the fiercest rage of Mars himself
I would march boldly forward. Did I run
From the enchantment of the riddling Sphinx?
I faced the damned witch, though her jaws dripped blood
And all the ground beneath was white with bones.
There, as she sat upon her rocky seat,
Waiting to seize her prey, with wings outspread
And lashing tail, a lion in her wrath,
I asked 'What is your riddle?' She replied,
Shrieking above me with a voice of doom,
Snapping her jaws and clawing at the stones,
Impatient to tear out my living heart.
Then came the cryptic words, the baited trap;
The monstrous bird had asked her fatal riddle,
And I had answered it! . . . Fool that I am,
Why should I now be praying for my death? . . .
You could have had it then! And here you have

This crown for your reward; you are well paid
For the destruction of the Sphinx – whose dust,
That subtle creature's dust, now rises up
To fight against you. She, the accursed pest
Whom I destroyed, is now destroying Thebes! . . .
None other but Apollo now can show
If there be any way to our salvation.

CHORUS

Fallen is the noble race of Cadmus, his city utterly
     fallen.
Alas for Thebes, her lands bereft of workers!
Death takes toll of the men of Bacchus,[1] whom he led to
     the farthest Indies;
The men who boldly scoured the eastern plains,
And planted his banners where the world begins.
They saw the Arabs in their lush cinnamon groves,
And the Parthian riders in retreat –
Treacherous retreat, for there was danger in their backs.[2]
They marched to the shores of the ruby sea, the gate
Whence Phoebus rises to bring back the day,
Scorching the naked Indians on whom his fire first falls.

Now the heirs of the undefeated are dying,
Caught in the clutch of a relentless fate.
Hour by hour the procession of death is renewed;
The train of mourners troops to the place of burial,
Or halts, a pitiful throng, where the seven gates
Are not enough for the grave-bound multitude,

1. As the son of Jupiter and Semele, daughter of King Cadmus,
was claimed as a patron god of Thebes. His extensive travels (symbolic of the spread of vine-culture) form the subject of the next
choral ode, following Act II.
2. The celebrated tactic of the Parthian archers, shooting as they
retreated.

Till there stands a mounting pile of death, funeral
   jostling funeral.

The pestilence struck first at the slow-footed sheep;
There was death in the ripe grass on which they grazed.
A priest stood ready to sever a victim's neck;
His hand was raised to strike unerringly,
When the bull, his horns a-glitter with gold, sank limply
   to the ground.
When its throat was opened with a heavy axe, there was
   no blood;
Only a noisome ooze from the black gash left its mark on
   the blade.
A race-horse faltered and fell, in the middle of the course,
Throwing its rider over its bowed shoulders.

Out in the fields the cattle lie abandoned,
A whole herd dying and their bull's strength ebbing
   away.
There is no herdsman to tend what is left of the stock;
He has lain down to die among the sick animals.
Wolves no longer hold any terror for the stags;
The angry lion's roar is no longer heard;
The shaggy bear has no spirit for the fight.
The serpent in the grass is powerless,
His venom lost, dried up in his shrivelled skin.

The woods, whose leafy heads should be throwing deep
   shadows across the hills,
Are gone; gone is the rich green carpet of the country-
   side;
Gone is the vine that was bent with fullness of the gift of
   Bacchus.
There is nothing on which our pestilence has not fallen.

Out of the depths of Erebus their prison
The Furies have rushed upon us with the fire of hell.
Phlegethon, River of Fire, has burst his banks,
The River of Hades is mingled with the River of Cadmus.
Black Death has opened his ravenous mouth to devour
    us;
His mighty wings are spread to cover us.
And the guardian of the angry waters, with his boat that
    takes all in –
Even he, the indefatigable age-old ferryman,
Is almost weary of pulling at his never-resting oar,
For ever carrying fresh multitudes across the river.

Some say the Hound of Hell has broken his iron chains
And is at large in our land; that the earth has roared.
Phantoms, of more than human size, have been seen in
    the woods;
Twice the forest of Thebes has been shaken, its snow
    scattered to the ground;
Twice the River of Dirce has boiled with blood;
The silence of night has been broken by the baying of
    Actaeon's hounds.

Strange and terrible forms of death we have seen,
Symptoms more painful than the death itself.
Slow torpor paralyses the helpless limbs,
The face is flushed, or lightly marked with spots;
A fiery vapour burns in the temple of the body
And causes the cheeks to swell with blood; eyes stare,
And the demon fire eats away the flesh.
There is ringing in the ears, dark blood
Breaking the veins and welling from the pinched nostrils;
Often a strident groan racking the body to its centre.
Sometimes they desperately clutch and embrace cold
    stones;

Yes, and some of you I have seen,
When your guardian himself has collapsed and the house
    is your own,
Rush out to a well to assuage your thirst with draughts of
    water.

Multitudes kneel at the altars, praying for death –
The only prayer the gods are quick to answer.
They crowd to the temples – not to pray for mercy,
But in very haste to offer up their lives
To feed the insatiable gods.

But who comes here, hurrying towards the palace?[1]
Is it the noble and gallant Creon? Or is it
Another delusion of our tormented minds? . . .
It is Creon, returned in answer to all our prayers.

    1. In some texts, Oedipus speaks this and following lines.

ACT TWO

Oedipus, Creon, Tiresias, Manto

OEDIPUS: Fear makes me tremble; to what end does fate
  Now point? Conflicting thoughts divide my heart.
  When good and evil lie so close together,
  The doubting mind must fear the truth it seeks. . . .
    Brother of my wife, if you have help for us
  In our afflictions, speak without delay.
CREON: Dark and uncertain is the oracle.
OEDIPUS: Uncertain help is none, to those in peril.
CREON: It is the custom of the Delphic god
  To wrap his secrets up in dark enigmas.
OEDIPUS: Say what you heard; however dark it be,
  Oedipus is the man for solving riddles.
CREON: The god's instruction is that we avenge
  The murdered king; let banishment atone
  For Laius's death; not until that is done
  Will day once more ride brightly in the sky
  Or the world's air be clean and safe to breathe.
OEDIPUS: Who was he, then? Who killed the noble king?
  Does Phoebus name him? Tell us, and he shall pay.
CREON: God grant it may not be a sin to tell
  What dreadful things I have both seen and heard.
  My blood runs cold; I am still numb with horror. . . .
  Humbly I entered Phoebus' holy shrine;
  And as I raised my hands in the due rite
  Of supplication to the deity,
  The twin peaks of Parnassus, white with snow,
  Gave out an angry roar. The laurel grove
  Rustled its leaves, and swayed above my head;
  The sacred spring Castalia ceased to flow.
  Apollo's priestess shook her flying hair,

Entranced in the possession of the god;
Before she had approached the cave, loud sounds
Had rent the air above us, and a voice,
Louder than any human voice, thus spoke:
  'Kind stars shall shine again on Cadmus's city
  When he that is her guest, the fugitive,
  Is seen no more upon the banks of Dirce;
  King's murderer is he, known to Apollo
  From the hour of his birth. Thy glory, murderer,
  Shall not be long; with thee thou shalt bring war,
  And war shalt leave to thy posterity,
  In sin returning to thy mother's womb.'
OEDIPUS: I am ready to obey the god's command
And do what should already have been done
For the departed king's remains; who knows
What treacherous hands might not have dared to touch
This holy sceptre? Who, if not a king,
Should guard a king? Dead men get no respect
From those who feared them in their lives.
CREON: Worse fears
Made us forget our duty to the dead.
OEDIPUS: What fear could keep you from your pious
    duties?
CREON: Fear of the Sphinx and her dread voice of
    doom.
OEDIPUS: Now for this crime atonement shall be made
As heaven commands. We pray to every god
That looks with favour upon royalty:
Thou, giver of laws to the high heavens, and Thou,
Great glory of the shining universe,
Thou ruler of the twelve signs in their courses,
Whose swiftly moving chariot measures out
The long procession of the centuries;
Thou, sister Phoebe, following by night

Thy brother's footsteps; Thou, lord of the winds,
Driving thy sea-green steeds across the deep;
Thou, governor of the house of darkness – hear us!
Grant that the man whose hand slew Laius
May find no rest, no home, no friendly hearth,
No hospitable land to shield his exile;
Marriage unclean and misbegotten sons
Darken his days; may he with his own hand
Shed his own father's blood; may he commit –
The worst that can be wished for him – the crimes
That I have fled from. He shall find no pardon;
I swear it by the throne to which, a stranger,
I have but now succeeded, and by that
Which I have left behind me; by the gods
With whom I dwelt; by Neptune's parted seas
That lightly wash the two coasts of my country.
Be Thou my witness too, at whose command
The priestess speaks the oracles of Cirrha:[1]
As I for my own father make this prayer,
That peace be with him in his lengthening years,
That he may reign secure on his high throne
Until his life's last day; that Merope
May ever be his wife and his alone;
So do I swear that no reprieve of mine
Shall ever save the culprit from my hands.
But do you know where the foul deed was done?
How was he slain? Was it in open fight
Or by some treacherous plot?

CREON: While on his way
Towards the groves of the Castalian shrine,
He rode along a thickly wooded path
Near to the place at which the road divides
Into three ways across the plain. The first

1. i.e. of Delphi. Cirrha is a village on the coast below Delphi.

Runs into Phocis,[1] land beloved by Bacchus,
From which Parnassus rises from the fields
Into a gentle slope, until it soars
Sky-high with double peak. The second road[2]
Leads to the land of Sisyphus that lies
Between two seas, and on to Olenus.
The third winds through a pass by straggling pools
To ford the cold Ilissos.[3] At this point,
Fearing no danger in a time of peace,
The king was ambushed by a band of thieves
Who did the deed, and left no witness to it. . . .
　Here, opportunely, comes Tiresias,
Moved by the message of the oracle
To make what haste his aged feet can manage.
His daughter Manto guides the blind old man. . . .
OEDIPUS: Servant of gods, Apollo's deputy,
　Expound this oracle, and name the man
　Whose punishment the avenging powers demand.
TIRESIAS: You must not think it strange, most noble king,
　If I am slow to speak, or ask for time.
　More things are true than a blind man can know.
　But where my country, or where Phoebus, calls me,
　There I will follow. Had I youth and strength,
　I would receive the power of the god
　In my own person; we must find a way
　To probe Fate's secrets. Let a snow-white bull
　And heifer not yet broken to the yoke
　Be brought before the altars. You, my child,
　Guide to your sightless father, must report
　The indications of the sacrifice

1. North-west.
2. South-west across the Isthmus and along the northern coast.
3. South of Athens, joining the Cephisus to flow into the Bay of Phalerum.

Which will reveal the future to our eyes.

[*The sacrifice is supposed to proceed*]

MANTO: A perfect victim stands before the altar.

TIRESIAS: Invoke the gods to witness, in due form;
Pour oriental incense on the altar.

MANTO: I have heaped incense on the sacred fire.

TIRESIAS: How is the flame? Does it consume the banquet?

MANTO: It blazed up quickly and as quickly died.

TIRESIAS: Did it stand clear and bright, a single tongue
Rising until its crest dissolved in air?
Or does it curl and waver to one side
Drifting into a scattered cloud of smoke?

MANTO: It was no single kind of flame, but varied,
As when a rainbow, shot with many colours,
Spans with its painted arch a tract of sky
To warn us of the rain. It would be hard
To say what colour is or is not there;
First with a touch of blue, mottled with gold,
Then red as blood; then dying into blackness.
But now I see the flame fighting again,
Dividing into two; one sacrifice
Becomes two warring fires. O horrible!
The wine-libation turning into blood. . . .
Dense clouds of smoke enveloping the king,
Settling around his face . . . the light of day
Lost in black fog. Father, what does it mean?

TIRESIAS: What can I say, so many troubled thoughts
Mazing my mind? I know not which to tell.
Evil is here, but deeply hidden yet.
When gods are angry, they are wont to show it
By no uncertain signs. What can we think
Of something which they wish to show and yet
Wish not to show? When they disguise their anger?
Something is here that shames the gods. Make haste,

Bring up the victims; let the salted meal
Be thrown upon their necks. How do they bear
The touch of hands, the sprinkling of the meal?

MANTO: The bull has raised its head, and when they placed
   it
Facing the east, it seemed to fear the daylight,
And shied at the sun's rays.

TIRESIAS: There – did they fall,
Each at the first stroke, to the ground?

MANTO: The heifer
Breasted the coming stroke; the bull was wounded
Twice, and is staggering this way and that,
Weakened, and loth to lose its struggling life.

TIRESIAS: Does the blood spurt strongly from a little
   wound,
Or well up slowly from the deep-cut flesh?

MANTO: The first is bleeding freely where the wound
Is open at the breast; the other shows
Thin smears of blood around the injured parts.
As if receding from the wounds themselves,
Dark blood is pouring from the eyes and mouth.

TIRESIAS: Such evil portents in the sacrifice
Are greatly to be feared. Tell me what signs
You see in the entrails.

MANTO: Father, what is this?
Instead of gently quivering as they should,
They make my whole hand shake; there is fresh
   blood
Proceeding from the veins. The heart is shrunken,
Withered, and hardly to be seen; the veins
Are livid; part of the lungs is missing,
The liver putrid, oozing with black gall.
And here – always an omen boding ill
For monarchy – two heads of swollen flesh

In equal masses rise, each mass cut off
And covered with a fine transparent membrane,
As if refusing to conceal its secret.
On the ill-omened side the flesh is thick
And firm, with seven veins, whose backward course
Is stopped by an obstruction in their way.
The natural order of the parts is changed,
The organs all awry and out of place.
On the right side there is no breathing lung
Alive with blood, no heart upon the left;
I find no folds of fat gently enclosing
The inner organs; womb and genitals
Are twisted and deformed. And what is this –
This hard protuberance in the belly? Monstrous!
A foetus in a virgin heifer's womb,
And out of place – a swelling in the body
Where none should be. It moves its limbs and whimpers
Twitching convulsively its feeble frame.
The flesh is blackened with the livid gore. . . .
And now the grossly mutilated beasts
Are trying to move; a gaping trunk rears up
As if to attack the servers with its horns. . . .
The entrails seem to run out of my hands.
That sound you hear is not the bellowing
Of cattle, not the cry of frightened beasts;
It is the fire that roars upon the altars,
The hearth itself that quakes.

OEDIPUS: Now, prophet, tell
The meaning of the signs that have appeared
In this most ominous sacrifice; your words
Will have no terror for my ears.
In his worst hour a man can be most calm.

TIRESIAS: You may in time wish to call back again
This evil hour from which you seek escape.

OEDIPUS: Tell me the thing the gods would have me
    know;
  Tell me upon whose hands the king's blood lies.
TIRESIAS: Neither the birds which soar into the sky,
  Nor any entrails plucked from living flesh,
  Can now reveal that name. Another way
  Remains for us to try. The king himself
  Must be evoked from everlasting night;
  He must be summoned up from Erebus
  To name his slayer. Earth must be unlocked,
  The unforgiving ruler of the dead
  Must hear our prayers, the people of the Styx
  Must be fetched hither. You must name a man
  To whom this sacred task can be entrusted;
  That you, holding the office of a king,
  Should look upon the dead, our law forbids.
OEDIPUS: Creon, this task is yours; you are the next,
  After myself, to whom our country turns.
TIRESIAS: Now, while we go to unlock the prison-gates
  Of the infernal Styx, let all the people sing
  Their hymns of praise to Bacchus.

CHORUS

Women, shake loose your hair; let the dangling ivy bind
Your brows; let the wand of Bacchus wave in your
    dancing hands.

  Bacchus, bright star of heaven, come,
  Come to your chosen city Thebes,
  Come to the worshippers
  Who lift their suppliant hands to you.
  Show us the light of your pure face;
  Break with your starbright eyes the clouds
  That cover us; banish grim death

And menacing fate.
We love your hair with spring flowers crowned,
Your head with Tyrian turban bound,
Your smooth brow wreathed with ivy berries,
Loosed be your locks and flying free
Or in a knot confined.
This was the guise in which you grew
To manhood, when you had to hide
From Juno's wrath, with golden hair
And yellow girdle at your waist
In girlish fashion. And you wear it still,
The loose-draped robe and flowing skirt,
The garb of gentleness.

Thus you were known
To all the countries of the farthest East,
To those that drink the waters of the Ganges
And those that break the ice-floes of Araxes,
Upon a golden chariot riding,
Over the lion's back
Your long robes trailing.
And old Silenus on his humble ass
Is there to follow you, with ivy garlands
Crowning his bulging forehead; while a rout
Of ribald merrymakers dance their secret mysteries.

In Thrace your revellers follow you,
Edonian dancers on Pangaeus
And on the heights of Pindus.
In Thebes you are Iacchus of Ogygia,[1]
Your worshippers the Cadmian women,
Wanton maenads, clad in skins,

1. A variant name for Thebes: mythical king Ogyges? (Not the
Homeric Ogygia, home of Calypso.)

Thyrsus in hand, hair flying free,
Possessed with madness at your will.
Pentheus is torn to pieces; then the grip
Of passion is released, the bacchant throng
Regard their horrid handiwork
As if they knew not whose it was.

A sister of the mother of bright Bacchus
Is Theban Ino,[1] mistress of the sea.
The Nereids dance with her; and young Palaemon,[2]
Kinsman of Bacchus and a great god too,
Has joined the company of the divinities
Who rule the waves.
At sea Tyrrhenian pirates made a prize
Of our young Bacchus. Nereus calmed
The angry waves and made the deep blue sea
Become a meadow. Plane trees rose
As green as springtime, and the laurel
Dear to Phoebus; birds sang in the branches.
Round the oars green ivy sprouted,
Vines depended from the yard-arms.
A lion of Ida roared upon the prow,
An Indian tiger at the stern.
The pirates panicked; jumped into the sea;
And as they swam they were transformed;
They lost their arms, their breasts were doubled down
Into their bellies; fins like little hands
Hung from their sides; and through the waves they
    dived,
Round-backed, with crescent tails that flipped the
    water –
A school of graceful dolphins following

1. Sister of Semele, became a sea-goddess.
2. Ino's son Melicertes, drowned and deified as Palaemon.

The flying ship!
In Lydia you would sail
Upon the rich Pactolus, flowing golden
Between its sun-scorched banks;
Where Massagetan warriors, quaffing cups
Of blood and milk, at your command
Unstrung their bows
And laid their barbarous arrows down.
Your power was known
By King Lycurgus,[1] smiter with the axe.
Your power was known by savage Zalaces,
And by the nomad tribes
Who feel the north wind near,
The dwellers on Maeotis' frozen shores,
And those upon whose heads
The Bear and the two Wains look down.

Bacchus subdued the sparse Gelonians.
Bacchus disarmed the women warriors;
The wild hordes of the Amazons
Bowed down their faces to the ground,
Abandoned archery
And joined the Bacchic dance.
Upon Cithaeron's holy mount
The blood of Pentheus flowed.
The daughters of King Proetus ran away
To worship Bacchus in the woods of Argos,
In his stepmother's sight.[2]

In Naxos, the Aegean isle, he found

1. Thracian king, opposed Bacchus, and in madness killed his own
son Dryas with an axe, in the belief that he was cutting down a vine.
2. Like the women of Thebes, the women of Argos, led by their
king's daughters, followed Bacchus, in defiance of Juno.

A bride, deserted by her former lover;
Hers was the gain, far greater than her loss.
And there the juices of the vine,
Beloved of the night-haunting god,
Sprang from the barren rock; new rivulets
Trickled across the fields; the earth drank deeply
Of whitest milk and the thyme-scented wine of Lesbos.
And when the bride was led into high heaven,
Phoebus was there, with radiant hair aflame,
To sing the nuptial song; two Cupids bore aloft
The torches; Jupiter laid down
His fiery darts; he would not touch his thunderbolts
With Bacchus at his side.

As long as the lights of the everlasting heavens run their
    course –
As long as the waves of Ocean wrap the world –
As long as the Moon can wane and wax again to the full –
As long as the Star of Day brings promise of the dawn –
As long as the Great Bear never meets the Lord of the
    deep blue sea –
So long shall we adore the fair face of our lovely
    Bacchus.

ACT THREE

Oedipus, Creon

OEDIPUS: Though there is news of sorrow in your face,
Yet tell it. By whose life must we appease
The jealous gods?
CREON:　　　　You order me to tell
That which my fears would urge me to conceal.
OEDIPUS: Does not the ruin of Thebes urge you to speak?
What of the downfall of the royal house
Of which you are a brother?
CREON:　　　　　　What you seek
So hastily to know, you will soon wish
Not to have known.
OEDIPUS:　　　Evil cannot be cured
By ignorance. To smother every clue
To the solution of our country's plight –
Is that your wish?
CREON:　　　　When medicine is foul,
The cure may be unpleasant.[1]
OEDIPUS:　　　　　　What have you heard?
Tell me, or you shall learn at heavy cost
What force an angered monarch can command.
CREON: What he has ordered to be said, a king
May hate to hear.
OEDIPUS:　　　Your miserable life
Will be the one dispatched to Erebus
For all our sakes, if you refuse to tell
The hidden meaning of our sacrifice.
CREON: Is there no right of silence? Is not that
The smallest privilege a king could grant?

1. *Ubi turpis est medicina, sanari piget.* The Latin line is quoted in
the play *Sir Thomas More* (anon. 1590–1600).

229

OEDIPUS: The right of silence often holds more danger
   To king and kingdom than the right of speech.
CREON: If silence is not free, what freedom is there?
OEDIPUS: He that is silent when required to speak
   Shakes the stability of government.
CREON: What I am forced to say, please hear with patience.
OEDIPUS: There is no penalty for forced disclosure.
CREON: Outside the city, a dark ilex-grove
   Stands near the waters of the Vale of Dirce.
   Above the rest a cypress, evergreen,
   Lifts its tall head and seems to hold the grove
   Sheltered in its embrace; two ancient oaks
   Spread out a tangle of half-rotted boughs,
   One partly crumbled by consuming age,
   The other falling from its withered roots
   And leaning on its neighbour for support.
   The bitter-berried laurel grows there too,
   And Paphian myrtle, and smooth lime, and alder
   (Wood that may soon be speeding under oars
   Across the boundless sea); a lofty pine
   Stands in the eye of the sun, its straight-grained limbs
   Braced firm against the winds. One massive tree
   Stands in the centre, overshadowing
   The lesser trunks, and seems to guard the grove
   With its vast span of spreading foliage.
   Beneath it drips a dark and sombre spring;
   Ice-cold – because it never sees the sun –
   Its sluggish waters creep into a swamp.

   To this place came the aged priest, and soon
   (There was no need to wait for night to fall,
   The darkness of the grove was dark as night)
   A pit was dug and brands from funeral pyres
   Thrown into it. Tiresias put on
   A sable robe, and waved a spray of leaves.

His step was solemn and his aspect grim,
Robed head to foot in the funereal garb,
His white hair wreathed with yew, symbol of death.
Into the pit black oxen and black sheep
Were led; the flames devoured the offering,
A feast of living flesh that leapt in pain
Upon the fire of death. The priest invoked
The souls of the departed, and their king,
And him who guards the gate to Lethe's lake.
In awful tones he spoke the magic words
And incantations, those which can placate
And those which can command the shadowy ghosts.
He poured blood on the hearth, saw that the flames
Consumed the beasts entire, and drenched the pit
With their spilt gore. Libations then, of milk
Snow-white, and wine with his left hand, he poured
Upon the fire, and uttered prayers again.
Then in a louder and more awful voice,
His eyes fixed on the ground, he summoned forth
The spirits of the dead. Loud bayed the hounds
Of Hecate, the valley boomed three times,
A tremor shook the ground beneath our feet.
'They hear me,' said the priest; 'my words had power;
The black void opens and the citizens
Of hell are given a passage to our world.'
The trees bowed down, their foliage bristling;
Trunks split apart and the whole forest quaked.
The earth reeled backwards and groaned inwardly.
Was Acheron enraged at this assault
Upon its secrets – or was this the noise
Of earth bursting its prison gates to give
A passage to the dead? Or Cerberus
The triple-headed hound in anger shaking
His heavy chains? Soon after this, earth gaped

And a vast chasm was revealed. I saw
Down in the darkness the unmoving lake;
I saw the colourless divinities;
I saw the quintessential night. My blood
Froze in my body and my heart stopped beating.
   Out of the pit came forth an angry brood;
They stood before us armed, the viper's brood,
The children of the dragon's teeth, and with them
Plague, the devouring spoiler of our people.
Then came the sound of the grim fiend Erinys,
Of Horror and blind Fury and all things
Created and concealed in the dark womb
Of everlasting night. There Sorrow stood
Clutching her hair, there drooped the heavy head
Of Sickness, Age bowed down with her own burden,
And menacing Fear. No life was left in us;
Manto herself, no stranger to the arts
And rites her father practised, stood amazed.
He showed no fear; his blindness lent him courage;
He called into our sight the lifeless hosts
Of the inexorable king of death,
And there the insubstantial shapes appeared,
Floating like clouds and feeding on the air
Of open sky. Numberless multitudes
Answered the prophet's summons – more than all
The leaves that grow and fall upon Mount Eryx,
The flowers that bloom in the high spring of Hybla
When bees hang in dense swarms, or all the waves
That break across the Ionian sea, the birds
That fleeing winter and the frozen bite
Of Strymon cross the sky from Arctic snows
To the warm valley of the Nile; so, fearful
And shivering, the ghosts came crowding in
To shelter in the grove. First to appear

Was Zethus, wrestling with an angry bull;
Amphion followed, with the tortoise-shell
In his left hand, whose music charmed the stones.
Niobe, reunited with her children,
Held up her head in happy pride, content
With all her dead around her. Next to come
Was a more heartless mother, mad Agave,
Followed by all that company of women
Who tore the body of their king to pieces;
Pentheus was with them too, a mangled wreck,
But arrogant as ever. Last of all,
After the priest had called him many times,
Came one, who seemed ashamed to raise his head,
Tried to remain unseen, and shrank away
From all the other ghosts; the priest insisted,
With oft repeated prayers to the dark powers,
Until he had drawn forth into full view
The hidden face – and there stood Laius!

    How can I tell you – how forlorn he looked
As he stood there, blood streaming down his limbs,
His hair disordered and begrimed. He spoke,
As one deranged, and this is what he said:
'O you wild women of the house of Cadmus,
Lusting for kindred blood, go shake the thyrsus,
But in your orgies let it be your sons
You mutilate; away with mother-love,
It is the cardinal sin of Thebes. O Thebes,
By sin, not by the anger of the gods,
You are destroyed. Your plague has not been brought
By the dry breath of the rain-thirsty earth,
Nor by the south wind's scourge; but by a king
With blood upon his hands, who claimed a throne
As his reward for murder and defiled
His father's marriage-bed: unnatural son,

And yet more infamous a father he,
Who by incestuous rape did violate
The womb which gave him birth, against all law –
A thing scarce any animal will do –
Begat from his own mother sons of shame,
Children to be his brothers! Vile confusion,
Monstrous complexity of sin, more subtle
Than that shrewd Sphinx he boasts of. Murderer!
Whose blood-stained hand now grasps the sceptre, thee
I shall pursue, thy father unavenged;
I and all Thebes shall hunt thee, and shall bring
The Fury who attended on thy marriage
With whips to scourge thy guilt; shall overthrow
Thy house of shame, destroy with civil war
Thy hearth and home. People, expel your king!
Drive him immediately from your land;
Soon as your soil is rid of his curs'd feet,
Its springtime will return, its grass be green,
The beauty of the woods will bloom again,
And pure air fill you with the breath of life.
With him, as his fit company, shall go
Death and Corruption, Sickness, Suffering,
Plague, and Despair. Nay, it shall even be
That he himself would gladly quit our land
As fast as feet can carry him; but I
Shall halt those feet; I shall retard his flight;
He shall go creeping, groping, stick in hand,
Feeling his way like one infirm with age.
While you deprive him of your earth, his father
Will banish him for ever from the sky.'

OEDIPUS: Fear chills my body, every bone and limb.
Of every act that I have feared to do
I am accused. And yet against the charge
Of sinful marriage Merope defends me,

For she is still the wife of Polybus.
And Polybus still lives; my hands are clean
Of that offence. One parent witnesses
My innocence of murder, by the other
I am acquitted of inchastity.
How else can I be guilty? Laius?
His death was mourned at Thebes before I came,
Ay, long before I touched Boeotian soil.
Is the old prophet wrong – or is some god
An enemy of Thebes? . . . Yes, here I have it!
The treacherous conspirators are here!
The priest devised this lie, using the gods
As screen for his deception, and to *you*
He means to give my sceptre.

CREON: Would I want
To see my sister ousted from her throne?
No, if my solemn duty to my house
And to my family were not enough
To keep me in my proper place, the fear
Of greater, and more dangerous, eminence
Would hold me back. Perhaps you would do well
To shed your burden while you safely can,
Rather than wait for it to fall and crush you
When you attempt to shake it off. Step down,
Now, while you can, into a humbler place.

OEDIPUS: Are you advising me to abdicate
My crown and all its cares?

CREON: I *would* advise it
To anyone who had the choice; for you
No choice remains but to endure your fate.

OEDIPUS: There is the power-seeker's surest card!
To cry up moderation, to extol
Peace and contentment! The pretence of peace
Is the sharp practice of the malcontent.

CREON: Does my long loyalty not speak for me?

OEDIPUS: Through loyalty lies the traitor's way to mischief.

CREON: Already I enjoy, without its cares,
All the advantages of royal rank.
My house is blessed with multitudes of friends;
With every day that dawns, remunerations
Of my connexion with the royal house
Flow to my door; rich living, choicest fare,
And the ability to save the lives
Of many men by my good offices.
What more could Fortune give me?

OEDIPUS: That much more
That still you lack. Good fortune knows no limits.

CREON: Am I condemned, found guilty without trial?

OEDIPUS: Have I been given a trial? Has my life
Been put in the balance? Has Tiresias heard me?
Yet I have been condemned already. You
Set the example, I but follow it.

CREON: Is it not possible that I am guiltless?

OEDIPUS: A king must guard against the possible
As against certain danger.

CREON: He that fears
Imaginary dangers should be made
To face the real ones.

OEDIPUS: He that once accused
Escapes conviction, harbours hate thereafter.
Better be rid of doubts.

CREON: Thus hate is bred.

OEDIPUS: No king can rule who is afraid of hatred.
Fear is the sovereign's shield.

CREON: But when men fear,
Then must imperious sovereignty fear them.
Fear must recoil upon its author's head.

OEDIPUS: Arrest this guilty man, and in a dungeon
Keep him confined! I shall return within.

CHORUS

Not yours, not yours the fault that brought such peril
    to us.
Not for that do the Fates bear hard on the house of
    Labdacus.
We are assailed by the ancient anger of the gods.

Castalia's woods gave shelter, long ago, to the wanderer[1]
Who came from Sidon; travellers from Tyre refreshed
    themselves
In Dirce's waters; when Agenor's son paused in these
    forests
After his weary search across the world for her[2] whom
    Jove
Had carried off; he rested here, to worship, while he
    feared,
The ravisher whom he sought. Phoebus commanded
    him to follow
A straying heifer, one whose neck had never felt the
    yoke
Of plough or heavy waggon; so he ceased from wander-
    ing
And gave our people a new name,[3] from that ill-omened
    heifer.

Since then, strange monsters many a time
Have risen from our soil. The serpent
Creeps from the glens to raise its head

    1. Cadmus, son of Agenor.
    2. Europa, daughter of Agenor.
    3. 'Boeotians', after βοῦς.

Hissing above the ancient oaks,
Above the pines; his body's bulk
Sprawls on the ground, his azure head
Tops the Chaonian trees.
Earth has conceived a monstrous brood
Of men in arms; the bent horn shrieked
Its battle-call; the curved bronze trumpet
Sang its shrill song; the tongues of men
That had not learnt the art of speech,
Voices that none had ever heard,
Broke out with cries of battle.
The fields were filled with brother armies;
As was the seed that gave them birth,
Their life was measured in a day;
Born with the Morning Star,
Before the rise of Hesperus they were dead.

Such prodigies appalled the wanderer;
He could not but await in fear
The onslaught of the newborn race.
At last the breed of terror was destroyed,
Their mother Earth received into her lap
Her newborn sons.
So may all civil strife be ended;
So may that fratricidal war
Remain a memory for the land of Thebes,
The land of Hercules.

And still remains to tell the fate of Cadmus' grandson –
The strange growth sprouting from his brow, the wild
    stag's horns,
The hounds that hunted their own master.
Down from the woods and hills Actaeon fled,
Outstripped the pack through glades and stony places,

Shied like a stag at the string of wind-blown feathers,
Drew away from the nets which he himself had set,
Looked in the depth of a still lake, and saw
Horns on his head and his face the face of a beast:
In that same lake the goddess of stern chastity
Had bathed her virgin limbs.

ACT FOUR

Oedipus, Jocasta, Old Man, Phorbas

OEDIPUS: My mind is troubled; all my fears return.
The blood of Laius is upon my hands –
The gods of heaven and hell allege. And yet
My conscience knows no sin; it knows itself
More surely than the gods above can know it,
And it denies the charge. There was a man . . .
As I remember dimly . . . whom I met
Upon a road, and struck down with my staff
And killed. But he began it; I was young
And he was old and arrogant; he leaned
Out of his carriage and commanded me
To stand aside. The place was far from Thebes,
In Phocian land, a place where three roads meet. . . .
O wife, my love, help me resolve my doubts.
Tell me, how old was Laius at his death?
Young, lusty, on the day he died – or ageing?
JOCASTA: Not old, not young; nearer to age than youth.
OEDIPUS: Would he be guarded by a numerous escort?
JOCASTA: The greater part of them had gone astray
Confused by the dividing roads; a few
Still followed faithfully the royal carriage.
OEDIPUS: Did any fall beside their royal master?
JOCASTA: One brave and loyal henchman shared his fate.
OEDIPUS: I know the guilty man. Numbers and place
Confirm it. And the time?
JOCASTA: Ten summers since. . . .
OLD MAN: Sir, you are summoned by the men of Corinth
To take your father's throne. King Polybus
Has entered into everlasting rest.
OEDIPUS: Fortune strikes blows at me from every side.

240

Well, tell me how my father met his end.

OLD MAN: In peaceful sleep the old man passed away.

OEDIPUS: So, my progenitor is in his grave,
And no one killed him. Now, behold, these hands
Are clean and fear no sin; in innocence
I lift them to the sky. Yet still a fate
There is to fear, a fate more terrible.

OLD MAN: No fear will touch you in your father's kingdom.

OEDIPUS: Back to my father's kingdom I would go,
But for one fear – I dare not face my mother.

OLD MAN: Why? Fear your mother? She expects your
coming
And anxiously awaits it.

OEDIPUS: As I love her,
I must avoid her.

OLD MAN: In her widowhood?

OEDIPUS: You say the very word I fear.

OLD MAN: What is it
That weighs upon your soul? This buried fear?
You may confide in me; I am a man
To keep kings' secrets under loyal silence.

OEDIPUS: Delphi has warned me; marriage with my
mother
Fills me with dread.

OLD MAN: Forget that idle fear;
A monstrous fear – have none of it. Our queen
Was not in truth your mother.

OEDIPUS: Not my mother?
What should she want with an adopted child?

OLD MAN: Heirs shield a king in time of disaffection.[1]

OEDIPUS: What gave you access to the chamber secrets?

1. A doubtful line; perhaps 'Heirs bolster up a king's proud confidence.'

OLD MAN: These hands gave you, a baby, to your mother.

OEDIPUS: You gave me to her? Who gave me to you?

OLD MAN: A shepherd, on Cithaeron's snowy slopes.

OEDIPUS: And what chance took you wandering in that
    forest?

OLD MAN: 'Twas on those hills I used to tend my sheep.

OEDIPUS: Did you see any marks upon my body?

OLD MAN: Your feet were pierced with iron pins; those
    ankles,
Maimed and deformed, gave you the name you bear.

OEDIPUS: Who was the man who made a gift to you
Of my poor body? Tell me who he was.

OLD MAN: He was the keeper of the royal flocks,
The chief, with others under his command.

OEDIPUS: Tell me his name.

OLD MAN: An old man's memory
Is not so clear; it rusts with long disuse.

OEDIPUS: You'd know him if you saw him?

OLD MAN: Ay, maybe.
Sometimes a little sign can jog to life
A distant memory long lost and buried.

OEDIPUS: I will have all the shepherds and their flocks
Assembled at the sacred altars. [*To attendants*] Go,
Summon at once all that have charge of them.

OLD MAN: No! Let a secret that has long lain hidden
Whether by chance or by design, remain
Hidden for ever. He that uncovers truth,
Uncovers it, too often, to his harm.

OEDIPUS: What harm, worse than the present, can be
    feared?

OLD MAN: A thing so hard to seek, you may be sure,
Will prove no simple thing when found. Here meet
Two rights, the king's advantage and the state's,
Neither above the other; leave them both

Untouched. Touch nothing; Fate will show her hand.

OEDIPUS: Where all is well, let well alone; no harm
Can come of probing what is desperate.

OLD MAN: Would you seek greater notability
Than royal heritage confers? Beware
Lest you be sorry to have found your father.

OEDIPUS: Yet I must find the truth, though it be shameful,
About my parentage – and search I will. . . .
An aged man approaches; it is Phorbas,
He that was master of the royal shepherds.
Do you recall his name or know his face?

OLD MAN: His looks awake a memory; that face
Is one I know, yet do not know for certain. . . .
When Laius was king, were you a shepherd[1]
Tending his prime flock on Cithaeron's slopes?

PHORBAS: Ay, there was always fine fresh pasturage
In summer on Cithaeron, where I worked.

OLD MAN: Have you seen me before?

PHORBAS: Not to remember –

OEDIPUS: Do you remember giving him a child,
A boy? Speak out. Why does your face turn pale?
You are not sure? You need not choose your words.
Truth won't be hidden by procrastination.

PHORBAS: You delve into the long forgotten past.

OEDIPUS: Speak, or else torture must fetch out the
truth.

PHORBAS: 'Tis true, I gave an infant to this man –
A useless gift, it never could have grown
To enjoy the light of day.

OLD MAN: Say no such thing!
He is alive, and may his life be long.

OEDIPUS: Why do you think the infant must have
died?

1. This question, in some texts, is asked by Oedipus.

PHORBAS: An iron bolt was driven through the feet
   To pin the legs together; swelling sores
   Had festered and inflamed the whole small body.
OEDIPUS: Need you ask more! Fate stands beside you
   now[1] . . .
   Tell me what child it was.
PHORBAS: Duty forbids –
OEDIPUS: Let fire be brought! Hot coals will burn out
   duty!
PHORBAS: Must truth be sought by such inhuman means?
   Have pity!
OEDIPUS: If you think me harsh and ruthless,
   Yours is the power to punish that offence,
   By telling me the truth. Who was the child?
   What father's and what mother's son was he?
PHORBAS: Your wife was that child's mother.
OEDIPUS: Earth, be opened!
   Ruler of darkness, hide in deepest hell
   This monstrous travesty of procreation!
   Thebans, heap stones upon this cursed head,
   Strike me to death with weapons! Let all sons,
   All fathers, draw their swords upon me; husbands,
   Brothers take arms against me; let my people,
   Stricken by pestilence, seize brands from pyres
   To hurl at me! Here walks this age's sin,
   Here walks the abomination of the gods,
   The death of sacred law – from his first day
   Of innocent life deserving only death. . . .
       Now be your courage keen; now dare a deed
   To match your sins! Into the palace, go,
   Go quickly, give your mother joyful greeting,
   Blest in the increase of her happy home! . . .

               1. This line, in some texts, given to Old Man.

CHORUS

Had I the choice, to shape my fate
To my desire, then I would trim my sail
To gentler winds, not fight against the gale
Till timbers trembled at its weight.
Not buffeted from side to side,
But borne by the light breezes' gentle force
On a safe middle course
My ship of life would ride.

There was a youth in Crete, who feared the king
And madly tried to fly towards the stars,
Trusting his life to an untried device,
Hoping to match his skill against the birds
Whom nature made to fly; but those false wings
Betrayed him, and a portion of the sea
Got a new name from him. While Daedalus,
Older and wiser, chose a middle course,
And hovered in the lower air, awaiting
His fledgling son –
Scared like a bird that sees a hawk
And gathers in her frightened young
From every side –
But now, alas, the boy was in the sea,
His hands encumbered with the instruments
Of his too daring flight.
Wherever man exceeds the mean,
He stands upon the brink of danger.

ACT FIVE

Messenger, Oedipus, Jocasta, Chorus

CHORUS: But what is this? The doors are opening ...
One of the king's attendants comes, distraught;
See how he shakes his head. What is your news?
MESSENGER: When Oedipus had understood the fate
Foretold for him and the undoubted truth
Of his disastrous birth; when he had laid
Upon himself the guilt of all the sin
Of which he stood convicted; with swift strides
Into the palace, to the fatal room,
He hurried with grim purpose. Like a lion
Prowling in Libyan fields, with angry face
And tawny tossing mane, so looked the king.
Black rage was in his brow and glaring eyes,
His groaning deep and wild, the cold sweat pouring
From every limb; with foaming lips he cursed
As the great torrent of his passion broke
From deep within his bosom. Who could say
What awful deed, matched to his destiny,
He planned within his own dark soul. 'How long,'
He cried, 'should I delay my punishment?
Where is the sword to strike this guilty breast?
Who will bring fire to burn or stones to crush me?
When will some bird of prey, some hungry tiger
Feed on my flesh? Thou cursed seat of sin,
Cithaeron, send the beasts out of thy forests,
Send thy wild dogs to tear me; send Agave
To do her work again! Dost thou fear death,
My soul? Fear not to die; 'tis death alone
Can steal the innocent from fortune's grasp.'
　　With that he laid his hand, his sinning hand

246

Upon his sword's hilt, and drew out the blade –
But spoke again: 'Stay! Can so great a crime
Be paid for with so brief a penalty?
Will one stroke settle all your debts? To die –
Your father would require no more of you;
What of your mother? And the children born
Of sinful marriage? What will pay your debt
To them, and what, above all else, to her
Whose utter ruin is her chastisement
For your offence, your suffering motherland?
You owe them more than you can ever pay.
Let Nature change – if once she could defy
For one man, Oedipus, her own fixed laws,
When she devised new ways of generation –
Let her be changed again to punish me!
Let there be found a way for me to live
A second life and die a second death,
And live and die again, for every life
To pay with a repeated punishment. . . .
Use all your wits, doomed wretch; devise a way;
Let what can only once be done be done
Slowly; a long slow death. Think of a way,
A way which you must take alone, permitted
Neither to join the number of the dead
Nor dwell among the living. Die, yet die not!
Art thou prepared, my soul?' A flood of tears
Broke forth and poured a torrent down his cheeks.
'What, only tears?' he cried. 'Are drops of water
All that these eyes can spill? Let them be torn
Out of their sockets! O ye marriage-gods,
Will that content you? Let me dig them out!'
     Fury was in his voice and soul, his face
Blazed with a fire of passion, and those eyes
Seemed starting from their sockets of themselves.

Mingled in his wild looks were wrath and madness,
Rage and determination. With a groan,
A terrifying roar, he thrust his fingers
Into his eyes; and those wild orbs stared out
And seemed to rush to meet the hands they knew
And to obey their summons, offering
Themselves to their own fate. The fingers bent
And groped in haste to find the seeing eyes,
Then wrenched them from their roots and tore them out.
And still the fingers probed the open holes,
The nails scratched in the empty cavities
Which now gaped hollow where the eyes had been.
Still in his impotent despair the man
Raged on and on, and would not be content.
He tests his vision, holding up his head
Against the light, scanning the breadth of sky
With eyeless holes, to see if all is dark,
Then tears away the last remaining shreds
Left of the raggedly uprooted eyes.
His victory was won; he cried aloud
To all the gods: 'Now spare my country, gods!
Now justice has been done; my debt is paid.
Here is the darkness that should fitly fall
Upon my marriage-bed.' Once more his face
And wounded brow were bathed, this time with blood
That poured in torrents from the broken veins.

CHORUS: Fate guides us; let Fate have her way.[1]
No anxious thought of ours can change
The pattern of the web of destiny.
All that we do, all that is done to us,
Mortals on earth, comes from a power above.

1. *Fatis agimur; cede fatis.* The line is quoted in Marston's *The Fawn* (1605).

Lachesis measures out the portions
Spun from her distaff, and no other hand
Can turn the spindle back.
All creatures move on their appointed paths;
In their beginning is their end.
God cannot change these things; they must go on,
Cause and effect in one unbroken chain.
For each of us, the order of our life
Goes on; no prayer can alter it.
Fear of his fate is many a man's undoing;
Many a man has come upon his fate
Just where he thought to hide from it.

OEDIPUS: All's done – well done – my father is repaid.
This darkness is my peace. To what god's mercy
Owe I this blackness that enshrouds my head?
By whose decree are all my sins forgiven?
Escaped from your accusing witness, day,
Thank not your own hand, slayer of your father;
Daylight itself has run away from you;
This face is the true face of Oedipus.

CHORUS: Here comes Jocasta, crazed ... on hurrying
    feet ...
Demented ... like Agave in her madness
When she had torn her son's head from his shoulders
And knew what she had done. She hesitates ...
She wants to speak to her afflicted husband,
Yet is afraid to speak. She is appalled
But pity overcomes her shame. ... She speaks,
But haltingly.

JOCASTA: What shall I call you? Son?
You shake your head. Surely you are my son.
Are you ashamed to hear it? Speak, my son.
Will you not speak? Why do you turn away

Your empty eyes?

OEDIPUS: Who is it that forbids me
Darkness, and who would give me eyes again?
That is my mother's voice; it is my mother!
Then we have done our work in vain. We two
Must never meet again; we are accursed.
Let wide seas separate us, let the breadth
Of earth keep us apart; and if there be
Another earth below, where other stars
Look down, under a sun beyond our ken,
Be that the place for one of us.

JOCASTA: Blame Fate;
No man is blamed for what Fate does to him.

OEDIPUS: Peace, mother; spare my ears, I do beseech you
By the last remnant of this ruined body,
By the ill-fated offspring of my blood,
By all that in the union of our names
Was good or evil.

JOCASTA: Art thou dead, my soul?
As thou hast shared the guilt, canst thou not share
The punishment? Unclean, thou hast confounded
All that is noble in the state of man!
Die! Let a sword expel thy impious life!
Never could I, so curs'd in motherhood,
Pay the full forfeit for my sins – not though
The father of the gods who shakes the world
Should strike me with his fiery thunderbolts.
It must be death, and I must find a way. . . .

    Come then, have you a hand to help your mother?
If you could kill your father . . . this remains
For you to do. . . . Then let me take his sword,
The sword that killed my husband – no, not husband,
Father-in-law. . . . Where shall I strike? My breast?
Where plant the weapon – in my naked throat? . . .

You know where you must strike – no need to choose –
Strike here, my hand, strike at this teeming womb
Which gave me sons and husband! . . .

CHORUS: She is dead.
 Her hand dies where it struck, the sword falls out
Expelled by the strong rush of blood.

OEDIPUS: Now hear me,
Guardian and god of truth, Fate's messenger!
One death, my father's, did the fates demand;
But now I have slain twice; I am more guilty
Than I had feared to be; my crimes have brought
My mother to her death. Phoebus, you lied!
I have done more than was set down for me
By evil destiny. . . . Now set your feet
Upon the dark road faltering, step by step,
With cautious fingers feeling through the night.
Onward, away . . . foot after stumbling foot. . . .
Away, begone this instant! . . . But beware –
Not that way, lest you fall upon your mother.
See, I am going, I am leaving you;
Lift up your heads, you that are weak and worn
With sickness and have scarce the heart to live.
There will be brighter skies when I am gone;
All those who on their sickbeds still have life
To cling to, shall have purer air to breathe.
Go, friends, and bring relief to those laid low.
When I go from you, I shall take away
All the infections of mortality
That have consumed this land. Come, deadly Fates,
Come, all grim spectres of Disease, black Plague,
Corruption and intolerable Pain!
Come with me! I could want no better guides.

Exeunt

OCTAVIA

THE action takes place at Rome in the year A.D. 62 and extends over two days, during which the emperor Nero brings to a head his quarrel with his wife Octavia, condemns her to exile and death, and marries his mistress Poppaea. The play contains much retrospective reference to the misfortunes of Octavia's family – she was the daughter of the emperor Claudius and his third wife Messalina – and to the previous crimes of Nero. In A.D. 48 Messalina, divorced, was put to death by the orders of Claudius; in A.D. 54 Claudius was poisoned, reputedly with the complicity of his fourth wife Agrippina, mother of Nero. In A.D. 55 Nero contrived the murder of Britannicus, the brother of Octavia and supplanted heir of Claudius; and in A.D. 59 he devised a plan to murder his mother, the principal obstacle to his divorce, by a prearranged shipwreck; this failing, she was dispatched by the sword of an assassin.

Seneca, who had been recalled from exile to be tutor to the young Nero and was now one of his principal advisers, appears as an ineffective counsellor of moderation; and the Ghost of Agrippina rises to threaten calamity upon the new marriage.

The sympathies of the Chorus lie mainly with Octavia, though a group, perhaps of women attending on Poppaea, at one point expresses admiration for the usurper.

DRAMATIS PERSONAE

OCTAVIA, *wife of Nero*
OCTAVIA'S NURSE
SENECA, *minister to Nero*
NERO, *Emperor of Rome*
A PREFECT
POPPAEA, *mistress and afterwards wife of Nero*
POPPAEA'S NURSE
MESSENGER
CHORUS *of Roman citizens*

★

Scene: Rome, at the palace of Nero

OCTAVIA

OCTAVIA: Resplendent Dawn is driving from the sky
  The wandering stars, the giant Sun
  Lifts up his golden hair to bring
  Bright day back to the universe.
  And what must I do, overcome
  By ills so many and so great,
  But tell again the oft-told tale
  Of my distresses, shed more tears
  Than the sea-haunting Halcyons
  Or the bird-daughters of Pandion?[1]
  Greater than theirs my misery.

  Hear me, my mother, for whose fate
  My tears must ever fall, from whom
  All my afflictions spring.
  O mother, hear your daughter's cry,
  If in the house of death
  Any perception still remains.
  Would that the age-old spinner of my fate
  Had cut my thread before that day
  On which I wept to see
  Your wounded side, your face besmeared with blood.
  How hateful was the light of day,
  Of every day thenceforth to this,
  A light more dreaded than the darkest night;
  While I have had to live
  Under a vile stepmother's rule,

1. Birds mythologically symbolic of lamentation: halcyon, the
metamorphosed Alcyone, wife of Ceyx king of Trachis (Ovid,
Met., XI. 410 ff.); Procne and Philomela (swallow and nightingale,
or vice versa), victims of Tereus (see note on *Thyestes*, 57).

To bear her spiteful enmity
And angry looks.
She was my vengeful Fury, she
Lighted my marriage chamber
With Stygian torches, she destroyed
My hapless father's life;
Whom once the whole world, beyond Ocean's bounds,
Obeyed; whose captains put to rout
The Britons, till that day unknown and free.

And thou art dead, my father,
Struck down by a wife's wickedness,
Thy house and family a tyrant's slaves,
A tyrant's prisoners.

*

NURSE:[1] Does any man in envious amazement
Gape at the specious glories and vain joys
Of hollow monarchy – here let him learn
How Fortune's practised hand, that once upheld
And thrust into success, has now thrown down
The dynasty of Claudius; whose power
Ruled the whole world; at whose command the Ocean
Lost its long freedom and was forced to bear
His ships upon its tide. Here was the man
Who first made British necks to bow; whose fleets
In countless numbers covered unknown seas;
Who lived unharmed among barbaric tribes
And on tempestuous waters; and who died,
Slain by a wicked wife. As she too died
By malice of her son; whose brother[2] died

1. This speech might well be an alternative prologue, since it repeats some of the points introduced by Octavia. In any case, we are to imagine Octavia in an inner room and not yet visible to the Nurse.
2. Britannicus, brother-in-law.

By poison. Here his sister, and his wife –
For she is both – rails at her sorry lot
With rage that cannot let her grief be hid.
Her cruel husband's private company
She loathes and shuns; he burns with equal fire
Of venomous hatred. Little consolation
Can all my duty and devotion bring
To her poor soul; her unremitting grief
Disdains my counsel; her proud indignation,
Beyond control of reason, grows the more
The more she suffers. Ah, what evil deeds
My fear foresees – which may the gods forbid!

OCTAVIA: No other fate can equal mine,
    No other suffering compare,
Not though I should remember thine,
    Ill-starred Electra; thy despair
For father slain was not forbidden;
    Thou hadst a brother, whom thy care
And trustful love had saved and hidden,
    To avenge the crime. I do not dare
To mourn two parents lost, nor pray
    For brother dead; in whom the fair
Hope I might have of brighter day,
    And comfort in my sorrow, were.
Alone I live to weep my heavy fate,
Last lingering shadow of a name so great.

NURSE: It is the voice of my unhappy child
That falls upon my ears.
Can these old feet forbear
To hurry to her room? . . .

OCTAVIA: Ah, let me weep upon your breast,
Dear nurse, my ever faithful confidant in grief.

NURSE: Poor soul, what day will ever bring
An end to so much sorrow?

OCTAVIA: Only the day
 That sends me to the Stygian darkness.
NURSE: Far be that ominous day!
OCTAVIA: Not your desire, dear nurse, but Fate
 Now rules my destiny.
NURSE: Your lot is hard, but God
 In mercy yet will give
 A brighter morrow to your darkness.
 Will you not try to win your husband's love
 By gentleness and service?
OCTAVIA: 'Twere easier to appease
 A lion's wrath, a tiger's rage,
 Than my imperious husband's heart.
 All sons of noble blood
 He hates, all gods and men
 He scorns alike; he knows not how to use
 His own good fortune and the place he won
 By his vile parent's crimes;
 For which – though he repudiate
 The gift of empire so bestowed
 By that fell mother, though he have rewarded
 Her gift with death – yet after death
 That woman till the end of time
 Must bear that epitaph.
NURSE: Nay, check those angry words,
 Speak not so rashly, child.
OCTAVIA: Ah, were these torments such as could be borne,
 And were my patience strong enough to bear them,
 Nothing but death could end my misery.
 My mother and my father vilely slain,
 My brother lost – now bowed beneath this weight
 Of grief and bitterness and woe, I live
 Under my husband's hate, my servant's scorn.
 No day is joy to me, no hour not filled

With terror – not the fear of death alone,
But violent death. O Gods, let me not suffer
A criminal's death, and I will gladly die.
Is it not penance worse than death, to see,
As I must see, the black and angry looks
Of my imperious master, to accept
My enemy's kiss, to fear his lightest nod
Whose kindness would be pain unbearable
After the crime of my dear brother's death,
When he, the perpetrator of that crime,
Now holds the sceptre that was rightly his,
Secure in Fortune's favour? Many a time,
When sleep has come to soothe my weary limbs
And close these ever-weeping eyes, my brother's
Spirit in woeful form has come before me.
Sometimes his helpless hands aim angry blows
With smoking torches at his brother's face;
Sometimes he flees in panic to my chamber,
And while I cling to him, the enemy
Comes on, to thrust his sword through both our sides.
Terror and dread then shake me from my sleep
And start again the miseries and fears
That fill my wretched life. To add to this,
His haughty concubine goes proudly decked
In stolen riches of the royal house;
And for her sake it was that he, my husband,
Sent his own mother on a ship of death
To meet her death; but when she had outlived
The shipwreck and the peril of the sea,
He slew her with a sword – the ocean's waves
Were not so cruel as this murderous son.
If such things can be done, what hope of life
Remains for me? Now in her victory
With hate inflamed my hated rival waits

To dispossess me of my marriage-bed;
And for the price of her adulterous love
Demands the head of Nero's lawful wife.
O Father, hear my prayer! Come back from death
And save thy child! Or let the earth be rent
And Stygian gulfs laid open to receive me
Swiftly in their embrace.

NURSE: That prayer is vain.
In vain you seek your father's spirit; now
In the grave he cares no longer for his own;
Else how could he have let another's son[1]
Usurp his own son's place? How could he stoop
To that unlawful lamentable marriage,
Taking his brother's daughter[2] for his wife?
That was the fount of all this wickedness,
This tale of murder and conspiracy,
Blind lust for power and savage thirst for blood.
When your betrothed Silanus[3] paid the price,
Upon your father's wedding day – struck down,
Lest to be husband of the prince's daughter
Might give him too much power . . . what wickedness!
A young man sacrificed to please a woman!
Falsely condemned, compelled to spill his blood
In his own hearth-gods' sight. Alas the day!
The enemy had gained possession now
And forced his entrance to our house; one stroke
Of your stepmother's guile had made him son
And son-in-law – this infamous young man,

1. Nero, made emperor over the head of Britannicus.
2. Agrippina, daughter of Germanicus, being already the mother
of Nero.
3. L. Silanus Torquatus, betrothed to Octavia, committed suicide
when Claudius married Agrippina and Octavia was given to Nero
(Tacitus, *Annals*, XII. 8).

Master of every evil art, whose mother
Kindled the marriage torch to make you his
Unwilling timorous bride. One victory
Inflamed her lust for more; the holy seat
Of worldwide empire now she dared to covet.
What tongue could tell the many shapes of sin,
The impious hopes, the smooth conspiracies
Conceived in this one woman's breast – a woman
Stepping from crime to crime to gain a throne.
Then pure Fidelity in terror fled
And left this palace empty for the feet
Of vengeful Fury, whose infernal fires
Ravaged this holy hearth, all nature's laws
And human right remorselessly confounding.
A wife compounded poison for her husband,
And died thereafter by her son's foul deed.
And thou, Britannicus, unhappy child,
Art dead and ever to be mourned, bright star
Of all the world, and of the royal house
The one strong pillar; now, alas, pale shadow
And dusty ash. His vile stepmother wept –
Ay, even she – when I gave up his corpse
To the cremating fire and when that face,
The likeness of the winged God himself,
And that fair body perished in the flames.

OCTAVIA: Let him destroy me too – or I shall kill him!
NURSE: You were not born with strength for such a thing.
OCTAVIA: My pain, my rage, my grief, my suffering,
My agony will give me strength enough.
NURSE: Rather, use gentleness to tame your husband.
OCTAVIA: To make him give me back my murdered
brother?
NURSE: No, but to save your life, and to rebuild
With your own blood your father's ruined house.

OCTAVIA: The royal house will soon receive new blood;
    I share in my unhappy brother's doom.

NURSE: Take courage from your faithful people's love.

OCTAVIA: Comfort, not remedy, their love can give me.

NURSE: The people's power is great.

OCTAVIA: The emperor's greater.

NURSE: In time he will respect you as his wife.

OCTAVIA: Not while his mistress lives; she will prevent it.

NURSE: No one respects her.

OCTAVIA: But her husband loves her.

NURSE: He's not her husband, nor is she his wife.

OCTAVIA: She will be soon, and mother of his child.

NURSE: A young man's love is hot in its first flush,
    And cools as quickly; in a lawless amour
    'Tis no more lasting than a puff of smoke;
    His love for a chaste wife will last for ever.
    There was another once[1] who dared to steal
    Your husband from your bed, and, though a slave,
    Long ruled her master's heart; she knew what fall
    She had to fear –

OCTAVIA: The rise of her successor.

NURSE: And she, deposed and humble, left behind
    A monument of stone set up to be
    A witness and confession of her fears.
    This other too will find herself disowned
    By the inconstant winged God of Love.
    For all her eminent beauty, proud position,
    Her triumph will be short.
        The Queen of goddesses herself
        Had the like pains to bear:
        The Lord of Heaven, Father of the Gods
        Would borrow many different shapes –

1. Acte, a Greek freedwoman (Tacitus, *Annals*, XIII. 12; XIV. 2).
According to Suetonius (*Nero*, 50) she assisted at the burial of Nero.

A flying swan, a horn'd Sidonian bull,
A falling shower of gold.
Now Leda has her star in heaven,
Bacchus his seat beside his father's throne,
Alcides lives among the gods
With Hebe for his wife;
The wrath of Juno is appeased
Since he whom once she hated is become
Her son-in-law.[1] That august wife
Could curb her wrath and learn
To conquer by compliance.
Now none but Juno holds
The Thunderer's love, no power
Can move her from her heavenly couch,
No mortal beauty now
Tempts Jupiter to leave his court on high.
You are a Juno upon earth,
Sister and spouse of the August,
And you must conquer grief.

OCTAVIA: Sooner will come the day when raging seas
Are mingled with the stars, when fire drinks water,
When heaven's high pole is sunk in Tartarus,
When kindly light is one with darkness, day
With dewy night – sooner than can my heart,
Which never may forget my brother's death,
Be one with my vile husband's evil soul.
Would that the ruler of the gods in heaven
Might send his fire to strike the sinful head
Of that foul emperor – if he can shake
The earth with horrid thunder and affright

---

1. Thus Juno forgives Jove's infidelities: Leda he courted as a
swan; Bacchus was his son by Semele; Alcides (Hercules) his son by
Alcmena. These instances do not, of course, correspond exactly with
the 'disguises' of Jupiter just mentioned.

Our mortal senses with his sacred fires
And portents strange: comets and shooting stars
Have blazed their fiery trail across the sky
Where cold Boötes stiff with Arctic ice
Wheels his slow wagon through the march of night.
Look, how the air of heaven is diseased
By the infection of this monstrous tyrant's
Destroying breath, when over all the world
Ruled by this evil monarch stars foretell
Renewed calamities. Less dread attended
The giant Typhon whom the angry Earth
Once spawned in spite of mighty Jupiter.
A far more dangerous monster now, the foe
Of gods and men, has driven the holy ones
Out of their temples, banished citizens,
Taken his brother's life, and drained the blood
Of his own mother's body – and still lives,
Still looks upon the light, still draws
His poisonous breath. O Father of mankind!
How can your royal hand so heedlessly,
So indiscriminately, hurl your weapons
Wide of their mark, yet spare a man so guilty?
May the full forfeit of his crimes be paid
By this false Nero, this Domitius' son,
Whose infamous yoke oppresses all the world,
Whose sins besmirch the name he bears, Augustus.

NURSE: I grant he is not fit to be your husband.
Yet let your destiny, your fortune, rule you,
Dear child, I beg. Do not excite his anger,
Which can be terrible. Some god there may be
Who can avenge your wrongs; some day will dawn.

OCTAVIA: Too long the anger of the cruel gods
Has pressed upon my house; Venus at first
Brought ruin on it, through the fatal error

Of my ill-fated mother; married once,
Infatuated by illicit passion,
She made a second marriage,[1] had no thought
For children or for husband, or for law.
On that infernal marriage vengeful Fury,
Her flying locks with serpents bound, attended,
To snatch the torches from the nuptial chamber
And quench their fire in blood; ay, she it was
That spurred the emperor's heart with savage wrath
To impious murder. So my hapless mother
Fell to the sword, and by her death condemned me
To everlasting anguish; husband too,
And son, she took down with her to the grave,
Betrayer and destroyer of our house.

NURSE: Repeat no more your pious lamentations,
No longer call upon your mother's shade;
She has paid heavily for her offences.

*

CHORUS: What new report is this?
Pray God it be but idle talk,
As all too often heard before
And no more worth the hearing.
Our emperor to take another wife?
That must not be; his lawful spouse
Octavia must retain her place
In her own father's house.
And let us pray that she may bear
A child to pledge our peace,
The peace of an untroubled world
In which the honoured name of Rome
May ever live.

1. Messalina went through a form of marriage with Gaius Silius
while still the wife of Claudius.

Queen Juno shares in heaven by right
Her brother's bed; shall our Augustus
Banish from her ancestral house
His sister wife? What then avail
True goodness, fatherhood divine,
Pure virtue and virginity?

We are to blame; we have betrayed,
After his death, our emperor's child,
To sacrifice her to the fears
That threatened us. Yet our forefathers knew
True Roman virtue; they were men
In whom the seed and blood of Mars still lived.
They were the men who drove proud kings
Out of this city. They did well
When they avenged the dying soul
Of a pure maiden whom her father slew
To save her from base servitude,
To rob vile lust of its unlawful triumph.[1]

And, sad Lucretia, for thy sake
Grim war began, when thou wast wronged
By a base tyrant's lust, and died
By thine own hand. The price was paid
Not by Tarquinius alone
For his foul deed, but by his wife[2]

1. The story of the centurion who killed his daughter Virginia, to save her from being claimed as a slave and concubine by Appius Claudius, is told by Livy (III. 44 ff.) – and also in Chaucer's *Physician's Tale*.

2. There is some confusion in the facts and the moral of this instance. Tullia was the wife of Tarquinius Superbus and instigated him to his revolt against the old king Servius Tullius, her father, whom she desecrated as described. This was before the outrage upon Lucretia, which was committed by Sextus the son of Superbus, and which led to the final expulsion of the Tarquins from Rome (*Livy*, I. 46 ff.).

Tullia, who mutilated
Her own dead father's limbs
Under her flying chariot wheels,
Inhuman daughter, and refused his aged corpse
The rite of funeral fire.
We in our time have seen
A son's iniquity:
The emperor's mother lured
Into a ship devised for death
On the Tyrrhenian sea.[1]

The crew obeyed their orders; made all haste
To leave the innocent harbour; plash of oars
Sang on the waves; the ship sped out to sea,
There to collapse, timbers falling apart,
To split, filling with water, and to sink.
Shouts rise up to the heavens, despairing cries
Of weeping women. Spectre of terrible death
Meets every eye; which every man for himself
Seeks to escape. Some on the wrecked ship's planks
Clinging, naked, battle against the waves.
Some make shift to swim to the nearest shore.
Many are doomed to drown.
The emperor's lady rends her clothes,
Plucks at her hair, and tears
Course down her cheeks.
She saw there was no hope;
Helpless in her distress, but loud in wrath
'Is this,' cried she, 'my son's reward
For all that I have given him?
Is this what I have earned? This ship
Is my just punishment

1. The narrative that follows may be compared with the account
in Tacitus, *Annals*, XIV. 1–9, with which it substantially agrees.

For having mothered such a son,
For having given him life. . . . O fool!
For having made him Caesar, Emperor!
Lift up your eyes from Acheron,
My husband, and enjoy the sight
Of my just punishment!
Your death, poor wretch, was of my doing;
Your son's assassination was my work.
Unburied now, as I deserve,
Sunk in the cruel sea,
I come to join your soul in death.'

Upon her speaking lips
The wild waves beat.
She plunged into the sea, sank down,
And rose again above the billows.
Fear forced her hands
To strive against the surging flood,
But soon she tired. Yet in her heart
Remained unspoken hope
And courage to defy death's angry face.
Many there were that rendered gallant aid,
Though with spent strength,
Under the onslaught of the sea.
And while her arms flagged limply
They bore her up and spoke assuringly.

For what then, lady, were you saved
From the destroying sea? You were to die
By your son's sword – a deed
Our sons will shudder to believe
And after ages for all time
Think unbelievable.[1]

1. This thought appears in very similar words in *Thyestes*, 753.

Hearing that she was rescued from the sea
And still alive, this impious son
In rage and desperation planned
A repetition of his villainy.
In haste to seal his mother's fate
He would allow his infamy no pause.
An underling was sent,
And did what he was told to do –
Pierced with a sword his mistress's breast.
Then, dying, the unhappy woman
Implored the murderer to thrust his blade
Into her belly. 'Let the sword
Sink in this womb,' she cried, 'this flesh
That brought so foul a monster forth!'
And with that word,
And a last cry of pain, her stricken soul
From her torn body fled away.

*

SENECA: Almighty Fate, why hast thou smiled on me
With thy deceiving face? Why hast thou raised me
When I was satisfied with what I had,
To this high eminence? That I might see
From this exalted seat how many dangers
Encompassed me, and from this altitude
My fall might be the greater? Happier far
Was my retreat upon the rocky shores
Of Corsica, removed from envy's snares.
My carefree mind, owning no other master,
Was mine to use for my own chosen studies.[1]
My greatest pleasure was to scan the sky,
That noblest work of the great architect

1. Compare this speech with the passage in Appendix II, 2.

Of infinite creation, Mother Nature,
Marking the motions of the universe,
The passage of the chariot of the sun,
The night's recurring phases, and the moon's
Bright orb encircled by the wandering stars,
The vast effulgence of the shining heavens.
Is all this glory doomed to age with time
And perish in blind chaos? Then must come
Once more upon the world a day of death,
When skies must fall and our unworthy race
Be blotted out, until a brighter dawn
Bring in a new and better generation
Like that which walked upon a younger world
When Saturn was the ruler of the sky.[1]
That was the age when the most potent goddess,
Justice, sent down from heaven with Faith divine,
Governed the human race in gentleness.
War was unknown among the nations; arms,
Shrill trumpets, cities guarded by strong walls,
Were things unheard of; roads were free for all,
And all earth's goods were common property.
Nay, Earth herself was happy to extend
Her bounteous fertility to all
Without compulsion, like a joyful parent
Sure in the trust of her devoted sons.
But then a second generation rose
Less gentle than the first; and after that
A third, gifted with skill for new inventions,
Yet still controlled by sanctity of law.
The next, a restless breed, presumed the right
To hunt wild beasts, to drag the sea with nets
For fish that sheltered in its lower depths,
To catch small birds with reed-traps, snare wild game

1. Cf. *Phaedra*, 525 ff.

With cage or noose, and force the savage bull
To bear the yoke; then ploughshares first began
To cleave the yet untroubled earth, which then,
Affronted, hid her fruit more secretly
Within her sacred womb. But those base sons
Spared not to rifle their own mother's body
For gold, and that dread iron whence ere long
They fashioned arms to fit their murderous hands.
This was the generation that set bounds
To establish kingdoms; built new-fashioned cities;
Fought to defend their neighbours' property,
Or marched against it, covetous for spoil.
Then heaven's brightest star, the maid Astraea,
Abandoned earth and fled the wicked ways
And blood-polluted hands of cruel man.
So over all the world the rage for war
And greed for gold increased; and last was born
That most delectable destroyer, Lust,
Whose power grew greater with the growth of time
And fatal Folly. Now upon our heads
The gathered weight of centuries of sin
Falls like a breaking flood. We are crushed down
Under our own intolerable age
When crime is king, impiety let loose,
And lawless love gives reign to Lechery.
All-conquering Lust with hands long used to rapine
Plunders the boundless wealth of all the world
To squander it for nothing.
                              Nero comes,
With agitated steps and angry look.
I dread to think what new intent he brings. . . .

NERO: Obey your orders; tell some of your men
     To bring me the decapitated heads

Of Plautus and of Sulla.[1]

PREFECT: It shall be done
Without delay. I'll to the camp myself. . . .

SENECA: Is that just treatment for those nearest to you?

NERO: Let him be just who has no need to fear.

SENECA: Best antidote to fear is clemency.

NERO: A king's best work is to put enemies down.

SENECA: Good fathers of the state preserve their sons.

NERO: Soft-hearted greybeards should be teaching children.

SENECA: Headstrong young men need to be sent to school.

NERO: Young men are old enough to know their minds.

SENECA: May yours be ever pleasing to the gods.

NERO: I, who make gods, would be a fool to fear them.

SENECA: The more your power, greater your fear should
be.

NERO: I, thanks to Fortune, may do anything.

SENECA: Fortune is fickle; never trust her favours.

NERO: A man's a fool who does not know his strength.

SENECA: Justice, not strength, is what a good man knows.

NERO: Men spurn humility.

SENECA: They stamp on tyrants.

NERO: Steel is the emperor's guard.

SENECA: Trust is a better.

NERO: A Caesar should be feared.

SENECA: Rather be loved.

NERO: Fear is a subject's duty.

---

1. Rubellius Plautus, a great-grandson of Tiberius, and Faustus
Cornelius Sulla Felix, son-in-law of Claudius, had both been suspected
of seditious aims and had been 'advised' to go into retirement,
Plautus to Asia and Sulla to the south of France. They were duly
executed. By Tacitus's account (*Annals*, XIV. 57 ff.) the prefect (Tigellinus) instigated Nero to this decision; and it is to be remarked that
the incident, in Tacitus, immediately follows a touching scene in
which Seneca's retirement from office is offered and accepted with
mutual compliments.

SENECA: Duties irk.
NERO: We order, they obey.
SENECA: Then give just orders –
NERO: I shall decide.
SENECA: – approved by their consent.
NERO: The sword will win consent.
SENECA: May heaven forbid!
NERO: Am I to tolerate conspiracy
  Against my life, and make no retribution?
  To suffer their contempt, and in the end
  Be overthrown? Has banishment put down
  Plautus and Sulla? From remotest exile
  Their unrepentant zeal has furnished arms
  To agents of their plot to murder me.
  If absent outlaws' hopes can be sustained
  By the enduring favour they command
  Here in the city, nothing but the sword
  Can rid me of suspected enemies.
  My wife is one of them, and she must die,
  Like her dear brother. What stands high, must fall.
SENECA: Yet to stand high among the eminent,
  To guard the commonwealth, to show compassion
  To the unfortunate, to sheathe the sword,
  To make an end of strife, bring to an age
  Tranquillity, and peace to all the world –
  Is not this good? It is the highest good.
  It is the way to heaven. By this way
  Augustus, our first *pater patriae*,
  Ascended to the stars, and has his temples
  In which we worship his divinity.
  Yet he had been some time the sport of Fortune
  In many grievous accidents of war
  On land and sea, until he had brought down
  His father's enemies; on you the goddess

Has with a willing and a bloodless hand
Bestowed her sovereignty; placed in your grasp
The reins of government, made earth and sea
Your subjects. Then all jealous rivalry
Ceased, overruled by dutiful accord.
The zeal of senators and knights was kindled
To serve you; common people in their prayers
And senators in proclamations named you
Giver of peace. Of all the human race
Elected arbiter, you rule a world
In peace and hope, the Father of our Country.
That you may ever keep this name, Rome prays,
While she commits her people to your hand.

NERO: 'Tis true I owe it to the bounteous gods,
That Rome and senate are my willing servants;
Also that by the fear they have of me
The tongues of the unwilling can be trained
To humble prayers and speeches of submission.
But to preserve the lives of citizens
Whose birth-proud arrogance is an offence
To state and throne, what madness that would be,
When by a word I can command a death
Wherever I see danger. Did not Brutus
Unsheathe the sword to take his master's life,
To whom he owed his own? And on that day
Caesar, the conqueror of all the world,
Invincible in battle, crowned with honours
Rising from height to height until he stood
Beside the seat of Jupiter, fell dead,
Assassinated by his countrymen.
Then how much Roman blood was Rome to see
Poured out from her so often wounded body!
How many lives did your divine Augustus,
Whose virtues won his way to heaven, destroy!

How many noble Romans young and old,
Sought out in every corner of the world
When fear of slaughter by triumvirate swords
Had driven them from homeland, were proscribed
In lists for death; how many severed heads
Exposed upon the rostra, for the eyes
Of suffering senators to weep at – nay,
Weeping had been proscribed; no man might mourn
The fate of his departed sons; the forum
Stank with corruption and its floor was fouled
With putrid gore that dripped from rotting faces.
Nor was the tale of bloodshed ended there;
Philippi's fatal fields remained long after
A place for birds and beasts to batten on.
Sicilian seas engulfed the wrack of ships
And carcases of men who fought their brothers.
The world was shaken by the embattled powers
Of its two leaders, till the vanquished fled,
In ships provided for his flight, to Egypt,
There soon to die. Thus for the second time[1]
A Roman general's blood watered the soil
Of that lascivious land; where now they lie,
Two unsubstantial ghosts; and there was buried
The long-drawn infamy of civil war.
At last the weary victor sheathed the sword
That battle-blows had blunted; fear sufficed
To hold his power secure; the armed allegiance
Of soldiers was his shield. Divinity
Was given to him by his faithful son;
And when death came, his soul was sanctified
And temples consecrated to his name.
A place in heaven shall await me too,
If I fail not to use a ruthless sword

1. The first, Pompey the Great; the second, Mark Antony.

To rid me of whatever enemies
Stand in my way, and found a royal house
With offspring that are worthy of our line.

SENECA: There is a daughter of the royal blood
Of Claudius the Divine, to fill your house
With heavenly progeny – a second Juno,
Permitted to be consort to her brother.

NERO: Daughter of an adulteress – that blood
Is no more to be trusted; nor was she
Ever a wife to me in heart and soul.

SENECA: Fidelity cannot be judged in youth,
When modesty conceals the flame of love.

NERO: With that fond thought I too deceived myself,
Despite the warning of her loveless face
And unresponsive heart, which plainly told
The measure of her hatred; and at length
My own resentment thirsted for revenge.
Another consort I have found, of breed
And beauty worthier to share my bed,
With whom the wife of Jove cannot compare,
Nor Venus, nor the Goddess armed for war.

SENECA: A wife's fidelity, honour, purity,
And goodness, should be all her husband's joy.
Only the virtues of the mind and heart
Are everlasting, indestructible.
The flower of beauty withers day by day.

NERO: But there is one in whom the gods have joined
All excellent virtues; and for me alone
The Fates have willed that excellence to be.

SENECA: Love must be gently humoured, or you lose him.

NERO: Love? The most potent tyrant in the heavens,
Whose power the Thunderer cannot take away –
Whose presence rules the anger of the sea
And the dark realm of Dis – who can command

The gods above to walk this earth below.

SENECA: It is the error of mankind[1] that makes
The airy sprite of love a ruthless god,
The son of Venus, by the seed of Vulcan,
As they suppose, a god with bow and arrows
Grasped in immortal hands. Love is not that;
It is a powerful motive in the mind,
A pleasant warmth of soul; its seed is youth,
Its nourishment is ease and soft indulgence
Amid the benefits of kindly Fortune.
If once you cease to feed and cherish him,
Love wilts, soon loses all his power, and dies.

NERO: To my mind, Love, which is the cause of pleasure,
Must be the giver of life; he cannot die.
What other force sustains the human race
But the sweet law of love? Wild beasts obey it.
So may the torches of the God of Love
Shine out to lead Poppaea to my bed!

SENECA: The scruples and abhorrence of the people
Will give that marriage bond no countenance;
Nor does the law of sanctity permit it.

NERO: Am I forbidden to do what all may do?

SENECA: From high rank high example is expected.

NERO: Well, we shall see if I have strength enough
To break and crush this reckless partisanship.

SENECA: Better, with grace bow to your subjects' wishes.

NERO: Fine government, when subjects rule their masters!

SENECA: Their rage has cause, if all their prayers are fruit-
less.

NERO: And where prayers fail, are they to win by force?

SENECA: Denial is hard.

NERO: To force a king is sinful.

SENECA: Then let him yield.

1. Cf. a similar thought in *Phaedra*, 195.

NERO: And be reputed beaten?
SENECA: Repute is nothing.
NERO: Yet it often scars.
SENECA: It fears the great.
NERO: But bites them none the less.
SENECA: It is not hard to silence rumour's tongue.
    Let the known virtues of your sainted father
    And your young wife's good name and purity
    Prevail to turn your mind.
NERO: Enough of that;
    You plead beyond my patience. Let me do,
    For once, something which Seneca condemns.
    Indeed, I am too slow in making good
    The event for which my people pray; tomorrow
    I shall be wedded with my bride, whose body
    Already bears the token of our union
    And part of my own blood.

*

GHOST OF AGRIPPINA: Through opened earth from
        Tartarus I come.
    My bleeding hands infernal torches bring
    To greet this impious marriage; by their light
    My son shall wed Poppaea; these bright flames
    The avenging hands of his infuriate mother
    Shall turn to funeral fires. Among the dead
    The memory still lives of my foul murder,
    The infamous offence for which my ghost
    Still cries for vengeance – when a ship of death
    Was my reward for service to my country,
    And for imperial honours I was given
    A night of shipwreck and bereavement; tears
    I would have shed for my companions' deaths,
    My own son's crime; but ere my tears could fall,

He wrought a second and more monstrous crime.
Barely escaped from death by sea, a sword
And hideous mutilation took my life
In my own house, and there I rendered up
My tortured spirit. Yet did not my blood
Suffice to clean the hatred from the heart
Of my inhuman son. His mother's name
Was an abomination to the tyrant;
He would have all my honours blotted out,
All images and records of my acts
Destroyed – such was his fear – throughout the world;
That world which, for my punishment, my hand
And my mistaken love had made his kingdom.
And now my hated husband from the grave
Makes war upon my spirit, brandishing
Torches of vengeance in my guilty face.
With instant threats proclaiming me the cause
Of his own death, he asks me for the life
Of his son's murderer. . . . Be patient, husband,
And you shall have it soon, ay, very soon.
The avenging Fury has a death prepared,
Meet for his crimes, for this obnoxious tyrant;
A scourge will fall upon him, ignominy
Attend his flight, and tortures shall be his
More terrible than the thirst of Tantalus,
The toil of Sisyphus, the agony
Of Tityos devoured by the birds,
The wheel on which Ixion's limbs are racked.
Let his proud majesty build marble halls
And roof his courts with gold, let armed battalions
Stand guard upon his gates, let all the world
Exhaust her infinite wealth to do him service,
Let suppliant Parthians seek his bloody hand
To offer him their treasure and their kingdoms –

The time will come, the day will surely come
When he will pay with his own poisoned life
The forfeit of his crimes; the day when he,
Ruined, abandoned, naked to the world,
Will bow his neck beneath his enemy's sword.
Alas, my labours and my prayers all lost!
Can this extremity, son, to which your fate
And your infatuate folly have condemned you,
Be such that in the face of all this evil
Your stricken mother's anger should be silent,
Whom in your wickedness you killed? Not so.
Would that wild beasts had torn my womb to pieces
Ere I had brought into the light that child
Or held him to my breast! You would have died,
Unknowing, innocent, exempt from sin;
You would have died all mine, flesh of my flesh;
You would have known the everlasting rest
Of those that live no more, you would have found
Your father, and his fathers, all that line
Of noble name; whose portion now remains,
Because of you, base son – because of me,
Mother of such a son – but grief and shame
Until the end of time. Why should I stay,
And not be quick to hide in deepest hell
The face of a stepmother, mother, wife,
Face of calamity for all her kin?

*

OCTAVIA: Weep not, my friends; this day[1]
    Of public gladness and festivity

1. The visit of the Ghost may be supposed to have marked the
passage of a night, and it is now the morning of the wedding-day.
The lapse of time between the episodes which will follow is un-
considered.

Must not be marred by tears.
To show your love
And favour in my cause
So plainly, might enrage our emperor
And bring you sorrow for my sake.
My heart has borne such wounds before;
I have had worse to bear.
This day will see the end,
Be it by death, of my afflictions.
I shall no more be forced to see
My husband's angry frown,
No longer be a slave
In a detested marriage bed.
No more his wife, but still the emperor's sister
I shall be called; and well content,
If I am spared the penalty
And pain of death . . .
Have you such hope . . . fond hope,
Poor fool, when you remember
That evil man's iniquities?
No; for today's glad rite
You are the victim long prepared,
You are its sacrifice.
Look back no longer on your home and gods
With weeping eyes! Away!
Fly from this house, fly from this emperor's
Blood-stricken court! . . .

CHORUS: So dawns the day that we have feared,
The day those many rumours heralded.
Octavia has been set aside,
Banished from the harsh emperor's bed,
And in her place
Victorious Poppaea reigns.

By fear oppressed
Our loyalty must hide its face,
Our grief be dumb.

Where is that Roman people's strength,
The strength that broke ere now
So many great men's power;
That gave, in days gone by, just laws
To our unconquered land, authority
To men of worth;
Voted for war or peace, tamed savage tribes,
Kept captive kings in chains?

Today on every side offends our eyes
The dazzling image of Poppaea
Coupled with Nero.
Let us not spare them!
Tear them down to the ground!
Down with these too true likenesses
Of her imperial highness!
Down with her, too, from her exalted bed!
Then on to the emperor's house
With fire and sword! . . .

*

POPPAEA'S NURSE: Child, why this haste to leave your
        husband's chamber?
    What is the meaning of that anxious look?
    Where are you hurrying to hide yourself?
    Wherefore these tears upon your cheeks? Surely
    This day's bright dawn has answered all our prayers,
    Our vows to the good gods; by marriage rites
    You are united with your Emperor;
    Whose heart your beauty captured; whom great Venus,

Goddess supreme, by holy rites adored,
Mother of Love, has made your prisoner.
Ah, what a picture! When you took your seat
Upon the cushioned divan in the palace!
How the assembled senators were rapt
With wonder at your beauty, as you offered
Incense to the high gods, and poured thank-offering
Of consecrated wine upon their altars!
The golden veil that delicately floated
About your head! And when the Emperor,
Close by your side, his body pressed to yours,
So proudly walked, his happiness proclaimed
In every feature of his face and bearing!
So Peleus must have walked, to meet his bride
Thetis emerging from the frothing sea, –
A wedding celebrated by the gods,
As stories tell, of heaven above and all
The sea's divinities with like acclaim.
And now, what chance has changed those smiles to tears?
Why do you look so pale? Why do you weep?

POPPAEA: The bygone night, dear Nurse, a night of fear
And dreadful visions, has confused my mind
And robbed me of my senses; I am lost.
The pleasant light of day had given place
To starry darkness, night possessed the sky,
And cradled in my Nero's close embrace
I fell asleep. But it was not to be
A long untroubled sleep; soon my whole room
Seemed thronged with a complaining multitude –
Women of Rome, mothers, with hair unbound,
Who wept and beat their breasts in lamentation.
And to a terrible continuing sound
Of trumpets, there my husband's mother stood
Grasping a blood-stained torch, her awful visage

Threatening dire vengeance. In her steps I followed,
By fear compelled, and lo, before my feet
A huge abyss lay opened in the ground,
Where, falling sheer into its depths, I saw,
And was amazed to see, my marriage bed,
On which I sank exhausted. Then appeared
My former husband, with some friends around him,
And his young son. Crispinus hurried forward
As if to take me in his arms and taste
The lips that were no longer his to touch;
But Nero in a frenzy forced his way
Into my room and thrust a deadly sword
Into my husband's throat. By now my terror
Had roused me from my sleep, and trembling seized
Each bone and limb; my heart leapt in my breast;
But silent I concealed my fearful secret,
Which now your faithful love has drawn from me.
What can it mean? What is this punishment
That the dead spirits have prepared for me?
Why was I forced to see my husband's blood?
NURSE: In sleep some power mysterious and divine,
Some swift perception, gives a visible shape
To whatsoever motions in the mind
Its restless energy stirs up. No wonder
You dreamed of husbands and a marriage bed,
While lying in your second husband's arms;
There's nothing strange in that. And were you shocked
By lamentations, beating hands, tossed hair,
Upon a festal day? They were lamenting
The separation of Octavia
From her own brother's house, her father's gods.
The brand which, waved before you by Augusta,
You followed, is a symbol of the name,
The illustrious name which has been won for you

Out of the dark of hate. The infernal powers,
Whose den you saw, promise the permanence
Of your new marriage, and to this your house
Eternal life. The blade buried in blood
By Nero's hand shows he will not unleash
New war, but sheathe the sword in lasting peace.
Take courage then, be comforted, my child;
Have no more fear, and go back to your bed.

POPPAEA: It was my purpose to approach the altars
And holy shrines, and with a sacrifice
Beseech the powers of heaven to avert
The menace of these visions of the night
And turn my fears upon my enemies' heads.
Pray you for me, too, and entreat the gods
That all this present dread may pass away.

*

CHORUS: If all the tales are true
That history so eloquently tells
Of the clandestine loves
Of Jove the Thunderer –
How he became a winged and feathered bird
To lie upon the breast of Leda;
And in the likeness of a savage bull
Carried Europa through the sea –
Once more, for you, Poppaea,
He will desert his kingdom of the stars,
To seek embraces which he must prefer
To those of Leda, or of Danae
Before whose wondering eyes
He fell as a bright shower of gold.

Let Sparta praise her daughter's beauty,
And the young Phrygian shepherd

Boast of his prize; [1]
We have one here, a face
More lovely than the Tyndarid –
That face that launched a lamentable war
And brought the throne of Phrygia to the ground.

But who comes here?
Breathless his haste, and stumbling steps . . .
What news?

MESSENGER:[2] Let every soldier of the royal guard
Defend the safety of the emperor's house
Against the angry mob that threatens it!
Look, where the officers in desperate haste
Are hurrying troops to man the city walls.
This insurrection, born of headstrong folly,
Will not be checked by fear, but grows the stronger.

CHORUS: What stroke of madness has bemused these
people?

MESSENGER: Kindled with zeal upon Octavia's part,
The fury of the mob is bent on mischief.

CHORUS: What is their plan? What have they dared to do?

MESSENGER: They mean to win back for Octavia
Her place, her right to be her brother's consort
And partner of his throne.

CHORUS: Although Poppaea
Is now his lawful and accepted wife?

MESSENGER: That is their desperate policy, which now
Fills them with fire and urges on their haste
To acts of madness. Every graven image,
Each polished bronze or gleaming marble statue

1. Helen and Paris.
2. The events here reported actually occupied several days (cf.
Tacitus, *Annals*, XIV. 60–5). According to Suetonius (*Nero*, 35) Nero
married Poppaea twelve days after the divorce of Octavia.

Bearing the features of Poppaea, lies
Demolished by the mob or overturned
By iron weapons; the dismembered limbs
Are being dragged away with knotted ropes,
Kicked, trampled under foot, and fouled with dirt,
With insults added to these injuries
In words such as I dare not here repeat.
They are about to ring the emperor's house
With fire, unless he will forthwith surrender
His new wife to the angry populace
And own defeat, leaving Octavia
Safe in possession of her house and home.
My orders from the prefect are to bring
These tidings of the popular revolt
To the emperor in person; and this charge
I must with haste deliver. . . .

CHORUS: But what avails the violence of war?
Love's weapons are invincible;
His fires will stifle yours,
His fires have quenched the lightning
And brought Jove captive out of heaven.
You will pay dearly with your blood for this.
Love has no mercy; roused to anger
He is not patient of restraint.
Under his orders bold Achilles
Became a minstrel; to his power
The Greeks and Agamemnon fell.
He broke great Priam's kingdom, overthrew
Many a splendid city; and today
What harm this ruthless god's fierce rage
Will do to us, I dare not guess. . . .

NERO: Too slow, too soft my soldiers' hands! Too weak
My anger at such outrages! Not yet

Drowned in the people's blood those people's torches
Fired to destroy me? Not yet soaked in slaughter
Those cursed streets of Rome, where such men breed?
No! death is far too small a punishment
For such offences; this mob's sacrilege
Deserves far worse. As for that dangerous wife
And sister, whom I long suspect of guilt,
Whom these crazed citizens would have to rule me,
She shall no longer live, but render up
Her spirit to my wrath, and quench my rage
In her own blood. Then, let this city's roofs
Sink in the fires that I shall send upon her!
Let burning ruin, squalor, poverty,
Starvation and bereavement fall upon
Her sinful people's heads. Now in its pride
The monstrous mob, ungrateful, and corrupted
By the good gifts of these beneficent times,
Cannot abide our gentle rule, hates peace,
And ever discontented, now defiant,
Now reckless, rushes onward to its doom.
It must be tamed by suffering, must be held
At all times under an oppressive yoke;
No other way will teach it to beware
Of making any other such attempt,
Nor dare to lift up its rebellious eyes
Against the saintly face of my loved spouse.
The spirit of the people shall be broken
By punishment and fear, that they may learn
To obey their emperor's lightest nod. . . .

                                    Here comes
The captain of my guard, whose loyalty
Well proved, and signal virtue, make him fit
To hold command over my garrison.
PREFECT: I come to tell you, sir, the people's outbreak

  Has, with the death of some few desperate men
  Who made the most resistance, been put down.
NERO: And is that all? Is that a soldier's way
  Of carrying out his lord's commands? Put down?
  Is that to be my only satisfaction?
PREFECT: The guilty ringleaders have lost their lives.
NERO: What of the mob that had the hardihood
  To attack my house with fire, to lay down laws
  For emperors to obey, steal from my bed
  My innocent wife, to desecrate her name
  So far as their foul hands and voices could –
  Are they still wanting their due punishment?
PREFECT: You cry for punishment of your countrymen?
NERO: Of such a kind that time shall ne'er forget.
PREFECT: Your wrath, and not my fears, shall be my law.
NERO: She that first earned it shall first feel my wrath.
PREFECT: Whom does your wrath demand? My hand is
   ready.
NERO: My sister's life – and her detested head.
PREFECT: I am stunned, insensible with fear and horror!
NERO: You hesitate?
PREFECT: You doubt my loyalty?
NERO: If you would spare my foe.
PREFECT: Woman – a foe?
NERO: If charged with crime.
PREFECT: Whose evidence convicts her?
NERO: The mob's revolt.
PREFECT: Hotheads; whose power can rule them?
NERO: His who could stir them up.
PREFECT: Not even he.
NERO: A woman can, by nature taught deceit
  And armed with every artifice of evil,
  But not with strength – so, not invincible,
  Not proof against the breaking power of fear

Or punishment; and punishment, though late,
Shall overtake this too long guilty woman
Whose crime stands plainly proven. Plead no more;
Give me no more advice; obey your orders.
Have her deported to a distant shore
By sea, and executed instantly;
So that the tumult of my wrath may rest.

*

CHORUS: O fatal wind of popularity,
That has destroyed so many!
How propitiously
It breathes to fill the traveller's sails,
And waft him on his way, but all too soon
Drops, and deserts him on the angry sea.

Why was the mother of the Gracchi doomed
To mourn her sons? Because they were destroyed
By too much popularity, too much
Of common love; for they were noble,
Eloquent, upright and true,
Shrewd statesmen, men of courage firm.
And by the same fate fell
Livius, not to be saved
By public rank or sanctity of home.[1]

To tell of more
Our present griefs forbid.
With their own eyes our people now may see

1. 'Whom neither the fasces nor the roof of his own house protected.' Livius Drusus the younger, tribune in 91 B.C., assassinated by
opponents of his project to extend Roman franchise to all Italians.
Velleius Paterculus (11. 14) confirms that he was stabbed in the hall of
his house on returning home, amid a throng, from the forum.

One whom but yesterday they had preferred
To be her brother's consort, queen
Of her late father's court,
A weeping captive dragged away
To punishment and death.

Happy lies poverty, content, unseen
Under her humble roof.
The high house shakes
More often to the winds of heaven
Or falls to Fortune's stroke.

*

OCTAVIA:[1] Where? To what place of banishment
Am I condemned? What is the emperor's will,
Or hers, his queen – if her hard heart
Can soften and be won
By pity for my suffering;
If she will let me live?
Or if she means to crown my misery
With death, is it too little vengeance
To let me die on my own country's soil?
Ah, but I have no hope of life. . . .
I am lost . . . the ship, I see, the ship
My brother has prepared . . . the same
On which his mother sailed . . . for me, his sister,
His banished wife!

Where is the power of piety?
Where are the gods? They are no more.
Fell Fury rules the world.
What eyes have tears enough to weep
For all my ills?

1. Now under arrest.

What nightingale can sing
My song of sorrow?
Ah, would that Fate had given me her wings!
Swift wings would take me far from all my griefs,
Far from the cruel world of man
And his destroying hand.
In some wild wood, alone, I'd sit
Upon a slender branch, to cry
My sorrows in a voice of lamentation.

CHORUS: Fate rules all mortal men; not one of us
Can count his footing firm and permanent
Amid the many accidents that Time,
Our enemy, lays in our way.
Take courage, then,
From the example of the many griefs
Already suffered by the women of your name.
Yours is no harder fate.

Let us remember first
Agrippa's daughter,[1] of Augustus' house,
A Caesar's wife, and mother of nine children.
Her fame was a bright star to all the world;
And though her womb had laboured to bring forth
So many pledges of a peaceful union,
She was to suffer whips,
Chains, banishment, bereavement,
Tortures, and lingering death.

1. Agrippina (mother of Nero's mother), grand-daughter of
Augustus, wife of Tiberius's nephew Germanicus (called Caesar on
his adoption by Tiberius). She enjoyed the prestige of her husband's
brilliant career, but after his death became antagonistic to Tiberius
and suffered banishment and death by hunger-strike.

Livia,[1] wife of Drusus, fortunate
In marriage, fortunate in motherhood,
Fell to a crime and to her punishment.
By the same way went Julia,[2] her daughter;
But not till after many years,
Her guilt unproven, was she slain.
Then your own mother; what a power was hers
When she was mistress of the emperor's house,
Loved by her husband, and in children blest.
She fell to her own servant's mastery,
To die upon a ruthless soldier's sword.
And that great lady, who could once have hoped
To be a queen in heaven, Nero's mother:
Was not she too assaulted
First by a ruffian sailor's hand,
Then mutilated with a sword, condemned
To a slow death by her inhuman son?
OCTAVIA: As that cold-hearted lord is sending me
To outer darkness and the ghostly shades.
What can I hope for from delay?
Take me away to die,
You whom the lot of life
Has made my masters. Gods in heaven!...
O fool! What use to pray
To powers that hate you?... Gods of hell,

1. Also known as Livilla – sister of Claudius, wife of her cousin Drusus (Tiberius's son); was induced by Sejanus, in his intrigues for the succession, to poison her husband; punished in A.D. 23.

2. Married first to Nero Caesar, Germanicus's eldest son and so first heir to Tiberius, she probably aided Sejanus to procure his banishment (Tacitus, *Annals*, IV. 60). By her second marriage she was the mother of Rubellius Plautus. The manner of her death is not known, but Tacitus (XIII. 32) says it was 'by the intrigues of Messalina', so it must have been before A.D. 48, the date of Messalina's death.

To you I pray,
To goddesses of Erebus, whose wrath
Can punish sin. I pray to you, my father,
Who worthily endured such death and pain:[1]
A death I do not shrink from.

Come, hoist sail!
Let us away to sea!
Spread all your canvas to the winds
And, helmsman, steer for Pandataria.

CHORUS: And may the gentle Zephyr's kindly breath
  That bore Iphigenia tenderly,
  Wrapped in a cloak of cloud, unto her death
  At the dread Virgin's altar, carry thee
  To Dian's shrine, beyond all suffering.
  Kinder than ours are those barbarian lands,
  Aulis and Tauris; to their gods they bring
  Tribute of strangers' lives; Rome loves to see
  The blood of her own children on her hands.

Exeunt

1. The sense of this petition is obscure, and the text possibly
corrupt. An interpolation proposed by Leo amends it to: 'Father,
I pray you to destroy the tyrant who deserves such a death and
penalty.'

APPENDIX I

(a) PASSAGES FROM THE ELIZABETHAN TRANSLATIONS

The dates are those of the first publication of each translation, prior to their collection in *The Tenne Tragedies* edited by Thomas Newton in 1581.

1 TROAS, *by Jasper Heywood* (1559), *203–18, with much rearrangement and interpolation:*

> What tyme our sayles we should have spread, uppon Sygeon seas,
> With swift returne from long delay, to seeke our homeward ways.
> Achilles rose whose only hand hath geven Greekes the spoyle
> Of Troia sore annoyde by him, and leveld with the soyle,
> With speede requiting his abode and former long delay,
> At Scyros yle, and Lesbos both amid the Aegean sea.
> Til he came here in doubt it stoode of fall or sure estate,
> Then though ye hast to graunt his wil ye shall it geve to late.
> Now have the other captaynes all the prycc of their manhood
> What els reward for his prowesse then her al onely blood?
> Are his desertes think you but light, that when he might have fled,
> And passing Pelyus yeares in peace, a quiet life have led,
> Detected yet his mother's craftes, forsooke his woman's weede,
> And with his weapons prov'd himselfe a manly man indeed:
> The King of Mysia, Telephos what woulde the Greekes withstand,
> Comming to Troy, forbidding us the passage of his land:
> To late repenting to have felt Achilles heavy stroke,
> Was glad to crave his health agayne where he his hurt had toke:
> For when his sore might not be salv'd as told Apollo playne,
> Except the speare that gave the hurte, restoared help agayne.
> Achilles plasters cur'd his cuttes, and sav'd the King alive:
> His hand both might and mercy knew to slay and then revive.

2 Id. 229–33:

What bootes to blase the brute of him whom trumpe of fame
  doth show,
Through all the coastes where Caicus floud with swelling stream
  doth flow?
The ruthful ruine of these realmes so many townes bet downe,
Another man would glory count and worthy great renowne.
But thus my father made his way and these his journeys are,
And battayles many one he fought whyle warre he doth prepare.

3 Id. 250–91:

The onely fault of youth it is not to refraine his rage
The Fathers bloud already sturres in Pryams[1] wanton age:
Somtime Achilles grievous checkes I bare with pacient hart,
The more thou mayst, the more thou oughtst to suffer in good
  part.
Whereto would yee with slaughtred bloud a noble spirit stayne?
Thinke what is meete the Greekes to do, and Troyans to sus-
  tayne.
The proude estate of tyranny may never long endure.
The King that rules with modest meane of safety may be sure.
The higher step of princely state that fortune hath us signd
The more behov'th a happy man humility of mynd
And dread the chaunge that chaunce may bring, whose gifts so
  soone be lost
And chiefly then to feare the Gods, whyle they thee favour most.
In beating down that warre hath wonne, by proofe I have ben
  taught,
What pompe and pride in twink of eye, may fall and come to
  naught.
Troy made me fierce and proude of mynde, Troy makes me
  frayd withal:
The Greekes now stand wher Troy late fel, ech thing may have
  his fal.

1. An error, for 'Pyrrhus'.

Sometyme I graunt I did myselfe, and Sceptors proudly beare,
The thing that might advaunce my hart makes me the more to
    feare
Thou Priam perfit proofe presentst thou art to mee eftsones:
A cause of pride, a glasse of feare a mirrour for the nones,
Should I accompt the sceptors ought but glorious vanity
Much like the borrowed brayded hayre, the face to beautify.
One sodayne chaunce may turne to naught, and mayme the
    might of men
With fewer than a thousand shippes, and years in lesse then ten.
Not she that guydes the slipper wheele of Fate, doth so delay:
That she to al possession grauntes, of ten yeares settled stay.
With leave of Greece I wil confesse, I would have wonne the
    towne
But not with ruine thus extreme to see it beaten downe.
But loe the battel made by night and rage of fervent mynd,
Could not abide the brydling bitte that reason had assignd.
The happy sword once staind with bloud unsatiable is,
And in the darke the fervent rage doth strike the more amis.
Now we are wreakt on Troy so much let all that may remayne.
A Virgin borne of Princes bloud for offring to be slayne
And geven be to stayne the tombe and ashes of the ded,
And under name of wedlocke see the guiltles bloud be shed,
I wil not graunt for myne should bee thereof both fault and
    blame,
Who when he may, forbiddeth not offence: doth wil the same.

4 Id. 814 ('CHORUS *altered by the translatour'; in fact borrowed, in
    part, from* Hippolytus, 959 ff.):

O Jove that leadst the lampes of fire, and deckst with flaming
    starres the sky,
Why is it ever thy desire to care their course so orderly?
That nowe the frost the leaves hath worne, and now the spring
    doth close the tree.
Now fiery Leo rypes the corne, and stil the soyle should
    chaunged be?

But why art thou that all dost guide, betweene whose hands the
poale doth sway,
And at whose wil the Orbs do slyde, careles of mans estate
alway?
Regarding not the goodmans case, not caryng how to hurt the
yll.
Chaunce beareth rule in every place and turneth mans estate at
will.
She gives the wronge the upper hand, the better part she doth
oppresse,
She makes the highest low to stand, her Kingdom all is order-
lesse.
(and six more lines on the matter of the play)

5 Id. 997 (a mistranslation):

In meane time haps this deepe distress my cares can know no
calme,
I ran the race with Priamus, but he hath won the palme.

6 Id. 1009–23 (the original is repetitive, but the translator expands it
further):

A comfort is to mans calamity
A doleful flocke of felowes in distres.
And sweete to him that mournes in miserie
To here them wayle whom sorowes like oppres
In deepest care his griefe him bites the les,
That his estate bewayles not all alone,
But seeth with him the teares of many one.

For still it is the chief delight in woe,
And joy of them that sonke in sorrowes are,
To see like fates by fall to many moe,
That may take part of all their wofull fare,
And not alone to be opprest with care.
There is no wight of woe that doth complayne,
When all the rest do like mischaunce sustayne.

In all this world if happy man were none,
None (though he were) would thinke himselfe awretch,
Let once the rich with heapes of Gold be gone,
Whose hundred head his pastours overretch,
Then would the poore mans hart begin to stretch.
There is no wretch whose life him doth displease,
But in respect of those that live at ease.

7 Id. 1034 (*Phrixus and Helle translated as Pyrrhus and Helen*):

Ful sore did Pirrhus Helens losse complayne,
What time the leader of his flocke of shepe,
Uppon his backe alone he bare them twayne,
And wet his Golden lockes amid the deepe. . . .

8 OEDIPUS, *by Alexander Nevyle* (1563), 569–81 (*much reconstructed*):

Than out with thundring voyce agayne the Prophet calles and
cryes,
And straight as much with mumbling mouth he champs in
secret wyse.
The trees do turne. The Rivers stand. The ground with roring
shakes.
And all the world as seemes to mee, with fearful trembling
quakes.
I am heard, I am heard, than out aloude the Priest began to cry:
Whan all the dampned soules by heapes abrode outrushing fly.
Then woods with rumbling noyse, doe oft resounding make.
And Heaven, and Earth together goe. And bowes and trees do
crake.
And Thunders roore. And Lightnings flash. And waves aloft do
fly.
And ground retyres: and Dogs doe bawl: and Beastes are heard
to cry.
And whyther long of Acheron, that lothsom flud that flowes
All stinking streames: or of the earth, that out her Bowels
throwes,

Free place to Sprights to geve: or of that fierce infernall Hound,
That at such times doth bustling make with chaynes and ratling
   sound.

9 Id. 596–607:

The Priest himselfe unmoved stoode, and boldly cited out:
Whole Armies of king Ditis men, who clustring in a Rowt:
All flittring thin like Cloudes, disperst abrode in Ayre doe fly.
And bearing sundry shapes and formes doe scud about in Sky,
A thousand woods I think have not so many leaves on trees.
Ten thousand medowes fresh have not so many flowers for bees.
Ten hundred thousand rivers not so many Foule can show:
Nor all the drops and streams, and gulphes that in the Seas do
   flow,
If that they might be wayed, can sure so great a number make
As could those shapes and formes that flew from out of Limbo
   lake.

10 Id. 1009–12:

Fayne would I speake, I am afraide. For what should I thee call
My Son? doubt not. Thou art my Son. My Son thou art for all
These mischiefes great: alas, alas I shame my Son to see.
O cruell Son. Where dost thou turn thy Face? Why dost thou
   flee
From me. From me thy Mother deare? Why dost thou shun my
   sight
And leave me thus in misery, with Cares consumed quight.

11 MEDEA, *by John Studley* (1566), 740–51:

O flittring Flockes of grisly ghostes that sit in silent seat,
O ougsome Bugges, O Goblins grym of Hell I you intreat:
O lowring Chaos dungeon blynde, and dreadful darkened pit,
Where Ditis muffled up in Clowdes of blackest shades doth sit,
O wretched wofull wawling soules your ayde I doe implore,
That linked lye with gingling Chaynes on wayling Limbo shore,
O mossy den where death doth couche his gastly carrayne Face:

Release your pangues, O spryghts, and to this wedding hye
apace.
Cause ye the snaggy wheele to pawse that rentes the Carkas
bound,
Permit Ixions racked Lymmes to rest upon the ground:
Let hungry bitten Tantalus wyth gawnt and pyned panche
Soupe up Pirenes gulped streame his swelling thyrst to staunche.
Let burning Creon byde the brunt and gyrdes of greater payne,
Let payse[1] of slippery slyding stone type over back agayne
His moyling Father Sisyphus, amonges the craggy rockes.
Ye daughters dyre of Danaus whom perced Pychers mockes
So oft with labour lost in vain this day doth long for you
That in your lyfe with bloudy blade at once your husband slewe.
And thou whose aares I honored have, O torch and lampe of
night,
Approche O Lady myne with most deformed vysage dight.

12 HIPPOLYTUS, *by John Studley* (*c.* 1567), 713–18:

Avaunt, avaunt, preserve thy lyfe, at my hand nothing crave,
This filed sword that thou hast toucht no longer will I have.
What bathing lukewarme Tanais may I defilde obtaine,
Whose clensing watry Channell pure may wash me cleane
again?
Or what Maeotis muddy meare, with rough Barbarian wave
That boardes on Pontus roring sea? Not Neptune graundsire
grave
With all his Ocean foulding floud can purge and wash away
This dunghill foule of stane: O woode, O salvage beast I say.

13 Id. 959–88 (*see also* **4**):

O Nature Grandame greate of Heavenly Sprites,
Eake Jove that guides Olimpus mighty sway,
That rakes the race of twinckling heavenly lightes
On spinning Spheare and order dost for aye
The stragling course of roaming planets hie,

1. or *peise*, weight.

And weildes about the whirling Axeltree
The weltring Poales, th' eternal course of Skie
To keepe in frame, what workes such care in thee
That earst the cold which hoary winter makes
Unclothes the naked wood, and now agayne
The shades returne unto the breary brakes.
Now doth the starre of Sommer Lyon raygne,
Whose scalded necke with boyling heate doth frie,
Perbraking flames from fiery foaming jawes:
With scorching heate the parched corne do drie:
Ech season so his kindly course in drawes.
But thou that weildes these thinges of massy might,
By whom the hugy world with egal payse
Even ballanced doth keepe in compasse right,
Each Spheare by measurd weight that justly swaise,
Alas why dost thou beare a retchles breast
Toward mankind? not casting any care
That wicked men with mischiefe be opprest,
And eake to see that good men wel do fare
Dame Fortune topsieturvy turnes at wil
The world, and deales her dole with blinded hand,
And fosters vice mayntayning mischiefe ill.
Fowle lust triumphes on good men brought in band
Deceipt in stately Court the sway doth weild,
In Lordinges lewde the vulgar sort delight,
With glee to such the Mace of might they yeeld,
Some magistrates they do both love and spight,
And pensive vertue brought to bitter bale,
Receyves reward that doth of right aryse,
The continent to Prison neede doth hale,
The Lecher raygnes enhaunced by his vice.
O fruitles shame, O counterfayted port.

14 Id. 1175–83 (*much elaborated*):

Appeare a while, receive my words, for speake I shall none ill:
This hand shal strike the stroake, wherwith thy vengeance quite
I wil.

And sith that I, I Caitiffe, I, abridged have thy life,
Lo here I am content, to yeelde thee mine with bloudy knife.
If ghost may here be given for ghost, and breath may serve for
  breath,
Hippolytus take thou my soule, and come againe from death.
Behold my bowles yet are safe my limms in lusty plight,
Would God that as they serve for me, thy body serve they
  might,
Mine eies to render kindly light unto thy Carkase ded,
Lo for thy use this hand of mine shall pluck them from my hed,
And set them in these empty cells and vacant holes of thine.
Thy weale of me a wicked Wight to win, do not repine.
And if a womans wofull heart in place of thine may rest,
My bosom straight breake up I shall, and teare it from my
  breast.
But courage stout of thine doth loth faint womans heart to have,
Thy Noble mind would rather go with manly heart to grave.
Alas be not so manly now, this manliness forbeare,
And rather choose to live a man with womans sprite and feare,
Then as no man with manly heart in darknesse deepe to sit:
Have thou thy life, give me thy death that more deserveth it.
Can not my profer purchase place? yet vengeance shal thou
  have,
Hell shall not hold me from thy syde nor death of dompish
  grave
Sith fates wil not permit thee life, though I behest thee mine,
My selfe I shall in spite of fate my fatall twist untwine.
This blade shall rive my bloudy breast, my selfe I will dispoile
Of soule, and sinne at once: through floods and Tartar gulphes
  that boyle,
Through Styx and through the burning Lakes I will come after
  thee.

15 Id. 1201–12 (*a fairly close rendering, except for a mistranslation of*
  1210 – incidi in verum scelus):

O wanny jawes of blacke Averne, eake Tartar dungeon grim,
O Lethes Lake of woful Soules the joy that therein swimme,

And eake ye glummy Gulphes destroy, destroy me wicked
   wight
And stil in pit of pangues let me be plunged day and night.
Now, now, come up ye Goblins grim from water creekes alow,
What ever Proteus hugie swolne aloofe doth overflow,
Come dowse me drownd in swallowes depe, that triumphe in
   my sinne:
And father thou that evermore ful ready prest hath binne
To wreake myne yre, adventring I a deede deserving death
With new found slaughter have bereft mine onely Sonne of
   breath.
His tattred lims I scatred have the bloudy field about,
Whyle th' innocent I punish doe, by chaunce I have found out
The truth of al this wickednes: heaven, starres, and sprites of
   hell
I pester with my treachery that me doth overquell.
No mischiefes hap remayneth more: iii kingdoms know mee
   well.

16 Id. 1250-3:

Least that but once, or onely I should be a guilty Wight,
I Sire attempting mischiefe have besought my Fathers might.
Lo I enjoy my fathers gift, O solitarinesse,
A grievous plague when feeble years have brought us to dis-
   tresse.

(b) PASSAGES FROM ENGLISH DRAMATISTS

17 From R. Edwards's *Damon and Pythias* (acted 1564):

DIONYSIUS: A mild prince the people despiseth.
EUBULUS: A cruel king the people hateth.
DION.: Let them hate me, so they fear me.
EUB.: That is not the way to live in safety.
DION.: My sword and my power shall purchase my quietness.
EUB.: That is sooner procured by mercy and gentleness.
DION.: Dionysius ought to be feared.
EUB.: Better for him to be well beloved.

(cf. *Octavia*, 455-7)

APPENDIX I

18 From Greene's (?) *The First Part of the Tragicall Raigne of King Selimus* (published 1594):

AGA.: Do you not feare the people's adverse fame?
ACO.: It is the greatest glory of a king
When, though his subjects hate his wicked deeds,
Yet they are forst to beare them all with praise.
AGA.: Whom fear constraines to praise their princes deeds,
That feare, eternall hatred in them feeds.
ACO.: He knows not how to sway the kingly mace,
That loves to be great in his peoples grace:
The surest ground for kings to build upon
Is to be feared and curst of every one.
What, though the world of nations me hate?
Hate is peculiar to a princes state.
AGA.: Where ther's no shame, no care of holy law,
No faith, no justice, no integritie,
That state is full of mutabilitie.
ACO.: Bare faith, pure vertue, poore integritie,
Are ornaments fit for a private man;
Beseemes a prince for to do all he can.

(cf. Thyestes, 204–18)

19 From Hughes's *The Misfortunes of Arthur* (1587):

Is't meet a plague for such excessive wrong
Should be so short? Should one stroke answer all?
And wouldst thou die? Well, that contents the laws:
What, then, for Arthur's ire? What for thy fame,
Which thou hast stain'd? What for thy stock thou sham'st?
Not death nor life alone can give a full
Revenge: join both in one – die and yet live.
Where pain may not be oft, let it be long.
Seek out some lingering death, whereby thy corpse
May neither touch the dead nor joy the quick.
Die, but no common death: pass nature's bounds.

(cf. Oedipus, 936–51)

20 From the same:

> CONAN: But whoso seeks true praise and just renown,
>   Would rather seek their praising hearts than tongues.
> MORDRED: True praise may happen to the basest groom;
>   A forced praise to none but to a prince.
>   I wish that most, that subjects do repine.
>   (cf. *Thyestes*, 209–12)

21 From the same:

> Even that I hold the kingliest point of all,
> To brook afflictions well; and by how much
> The more his state and tottering empire sags,
> To fix so much the faster foot on ground.
>   (cf. *Oedipus*, 82–5)

22 From the same:

> Thou, Lucius, mak'st me proud, thou heav'st my mind:
> But what? Shall I esteem a crown ought else
> Than as a gorgeous crest of easeless helm,
> Or as some brittle mould of glorious pomp,
> Or glittering glass which, while it shines, it breaks?
> All this a sudden chance may dash, and not
> Perhaps with thirteen kings, or in nine years;
> All may not find so slow and lingering fates.
>   (cf. *Troades*, 271–5)

23 From *Arden of Feversham* (anon. published 1592):

> Well fares the man, howe'er his cates do taste,
> That tables not with foul suspicion;
> And he but pines amongst his delicates,
> Whose troubled mind is stuff'd with discontent.
> My golden time was when I had no gold;
> Though then I wanted, yet I slept secure;
> My daily toil begat me night's repose,
> My night's repose made daylight fresh to me.
> But since I climb'd the top bough of the tree

And sought to build my nest among the clouds,
Each gentle stary gale doth shake my bed,
And makes me dread my downfall to the earth.

(cf. *Thyestes*, 445 ff.)

24 From Marston's *Antonio and Mellida* (1599):

PIERO: 'Tis just that subjects act commands of kings.
PANDULFO: Command then just and honourable things.
PIERO: Where only honest deeds to kings are free,
  It is no empire, but a beggary.

. . .

PIERO: Tush, juiceless graybeard, 'tis immunity
  Proper to princes, that our state exacts;
  Our subjects not alone to bear, but praise our acts.
PANDULFO: O but that prince, that worthful praise aspires,
  From hearts, and not from lips, applause desires.
PIERO: Pish! . . . True praise the boon of common men doth ring,
  False only girts the temple of a king.

(cf. *Thyestes*, 205–18, and *Octavia*, 440–60)

25 From the same:

No matter whither, but from whence, we fall.

(cf. *Thyestes*, 925)

26 From Ben Jonson's *Sejanus* (acted 1603):

Thou lost thyself, child Drusus, when thou thoughtst
Thou couldst outskip my vengeance; or outstand
The power I had to crush thee into air.
Thy follies now shall taste what kind of man
They have provoked, and this thy father's house
Crack in the flame of my incensed rage,
Whose fury shall admit no shame or mean.
Adultery! It is the slightest ill
I will commit. A race of wicked acts
Shall flow out of my anger, and o'erspread

The world's wide face, which no posterity
Shall e'er approve, nor yet keep silent: things
That for their cunning, close, and cruel mark,
Thy father would wish his: and shall, perhaps,
Carry the empty name, but we the prize.

(cf. *Thyestes*, 44–8, 192–5)

27 From the same:

TIBERIUS: Long hate pursues such acts.
SEJANUS: Whom hatred frights,
   Let him not dream of sovereignty.
TIBERIUS: Are rights
   Of faith, love, piety, to be trod down,
   Forgotten, and made vain?
SEJANUS: All for a crown.
   The prince who shames a tyrant's name to bear,
   Shall never dare do anything, but fear;
   All the command of sceptres quite doth perish,
   If it begin religious thoughts to cherish:
   Whole empires fall, sway'd by those nice respects;
   It is the license of dark deeds protects
   Ev'n states most hated, when no laws resist
   The sword, but that it acteth what it list.[1]

28 From the same:

   Still dost thou suffer, heaven! Will no flame,
   No heat of sin, make thy just wrath to boil
   In thy distemper'd bosom, and o'erflow
   The pitchy blazes of impiety,
   Kindled beneath thy throne! Still canst thou sleep,
   Patient, while vice doth make an antick face
   At thy dread power, and blow dust and smoke
   Into thy nostrils! Jove! will nothing wake thee?

(cf. *Phaedra*, 671)

1. Cf. **17**, **18**, **24**, above; with the difference that here it is the emperor's adviser who is urging ruthlessness.

29 From Ben Jonson's *Catiline* (acted 1611):

> GHOST OF SYLLA: Dost thou not feel me, Rome? not yet; is
>   night
>   So heavy on thee, and my weight so light?
>   Can Sylla's ghost arise within thy walls,
>   Less threatening than an earthquake, the quick falls
>   Of thee and thine? . . .
>   What sleep is this doth seize thee so like death,
>   And is not it? Wake, feel her in my breath:
>   Behold, I come, sent from the Stygian sound,
>   As a dire vapour that had cleft the ground,
>   To ingender with the night, and blast the day;
>   Or like a pestilence that should display
>   Infection through the world; which thus I do –
>   [*The curtain draws, and Catiline is discovered in his study*]
>   Pluto be at thy counsels, and into
>   Thy darker bosom enter Sylla's spirit!
>   All that was mine, and bad, thy breast inherit . . .
>   What all the several ills that visit earth,
>   Brought forth by night with a sinister birth,
>   Plagues, famine, fire, could not reach unto,
>   The sword, nor surfeits; let thy fury do;
>   Make all past, present, future ill thine own;
>   And conquer all example in thy one.
>   (cf. *Thyestes*, Act I, and *Oedipus*, 591)

30 From the same:

> Is there a heaven and gods? And can it be
> They should so slowly hear, so slowly see?
> Hath Jove no thunder? . . .
> What will awake thee, heaven? What can excite
> Thine anger, if this practise be too light?
>   (cf. *Phaedra*, 671)

31 From Chapman's *Conspiracy of Byron* (1608):

> LA BROSSE: Forbear to ask me, son;
>   You bid me speak what fear bids me conceal.

BYRON: You have no cause to fear, and therefore speak.

LA B.: You'll rather wish you had been ignorant
Than be instructed in a thing so ill.

BYR.: Ignorance is an idle salve for ill;
And therefore do not urge me to enforce
What I would freely know; for, by the skill
- Shown in thy aged hairs, I'll lay thy brain
Here scatter'd at my feet, and seek in that
What safely thou mayst utter with thy tongue,
If thou deny it.

LA B.:   Will you not allow me
To hold my peace? What less can I desire?
If not, be pleased with my constrained speech.

BYR.: Was ever man yet punish'd for expressing
What he was charged? Be free, and speak the worst.

(cf. *Oedipus*, 509–29)

APPENDIX II

1 *We can carry nothing out* (*Ad Marciam*, x):

All the adventitious ornaments which surround us – our children, high positions, wealth, spacious apartments, corridors thronged with crowds of waiting clients, a distinguished high-born or beautiful wife – all these and other possessions, being dependent on the uncertain and changeable whim of chance, are only so much borrowed furniture. Not one of them has been given us outright. Our stage has been furnished with borrowed properties, due to be returned to their owners; some must go back tomorrow, some the day after, very few will remain in our hands till the end of our time. We are not therefore to regard ourselves as living among our own possessions; we have only been given the loan of them. We have the use of these things, but only for as long as the lender chooses. It is for us to see that we keep them in good order, since they are only ours for a limited time, and to hand them back, when called upon to do so, without complaint. It is only a bad debtor that finds fault with his creditor. It follows that our love for our relatives – both our juniors whom in the course of nature we should wish to survive us, and those who even by their own choice would wish to precede us to the grave – should be tempered by the reflection that we have been given no guarantee of their immortality, or even of their longevity. We need constantly to remind ourselves to bestow on them our love as upon possessions destined to vanish, or indeed already vanishing from our sight. Whatever gifts of Fortune you may be lucky enough to enjoy, you enjoy them only by the permission of their owner. Enjoy by all means the company of your children while you can, and in turn give them the enjoyment of your society; drain every source of pleasure while it lasts, and without procrastination. Tonight is not to be depended on; no, that is too great an allowance – this hour is not to be depended on. Make haste; you are being pursued; this fellowship will soon be broken up; this happy companionship must come to an end, its noisy gaiety be silenced. Destruction is the universal law; do you not know, poor mortals, that life is a race to dissolution?

2 *Consolations in exile* (*Ad Helviam matrem*, VIII):

Against the mere inconvenience of a change of residence – setting aside any other disadvantages of banishment – there is ample compensation (in the opinion of the learned Varro) in the fact that, wherever we go, the same natural world is open for our enjoyment. Marcus Brutus suggests a different consolation: for him it is enough that the exile can always take with him the strength of his own character. Either of these sentiments, taken separately, may seem insufficient consolation for the exile; but the force of both combined must be granted to be considerable. For how little, we should ask ourselves, have we lost, when we may take with us into any new place of residence our two most desirable possessions – our contact with universal nature, and our own character? It was, I am sure, the very intention of the creator of the world, whoever he was – whether the omnipotent God, or an incorporeal reason capable of an immense creative design, or a divine spirit of life breathing its purposes alike into all things great and small, or a blind necessity, an inevitable chain of linked causes and effects – it was the intention of the creator that none but a man's most worthless possessions should ever pass into the control of another man. All that is most valuable to a man lies beyond the reach of other men's power. Such possessions can neither be given nor taken away. The universe around us, that most grand and elaborate work of nature, and the mind which can contemplate and marvel at it (and which is itself a most wonderful part of it), are our own everlasting property and will remain ours as long as we ourselves remain alive. Let us therefore go on our way, wherever it may lead us, fearlessly, with eager and uplifted heart. Let us fare to whatever land we must; no place on the face of the earth can be a place of exile, for there is no place on earth that has nothing to say to man. Stand where we may, and raise our eyes from the ground to the sky, the works of God will always be at the same distance from the works of man, no nearer and no farther. After all, as long as my eyes are not parted from that sight, of which they can never have enough; as long as I may look upon the sun and the moon, may gaze upon the other heavenly constellations, may ponder on their rising and setting and study the causes of their various motions fast or slow – how some are fixed, some not venturing far afield but turning in their own restricted orbits, some newly bursting into light, some drawing a trail of spent fire behind them, as though in a dying fall, or tracing a long arc of light across immense distances; as long as I can have these for my companions and thus share, so far as man may, in the life of the heavenly bodies, and as long as I still have a mind to devote to the contemplation of my fellow-beings on high – how can it matter what ground I tread under my feet?

3 *Early influences* (*Ep.*, 108):

I well remember that when I used to listen to Attalus [*one of his tutors*] inveighing against the follies and misfortunes of life, I would be filled with pity for the whole human race and look upon him as a man standing on a pinnacle of superhuman excellence. He did indeed describe himself as a king, but he seemed more than that to me, if he was able to criticize the conduct of kings. And when he set about commending poverty, and showing that whatever was for all practical purposes superfluous was only so much useless baggage and a burden to the bearer, I was ready to go straight out of the classroom to a life of poverty. If he castigated the pleasures of life, when he advocated bodily purity and simple living, and when he praised the conscience innocent not only of illicit delights but of all superfluous ones – I was at once ready to discipline my appetites. With the result that some of these disciplines remain with me to this day; I adopted all these precepts with great enthusiasm in the first place, and later, when I entered into public life, I retained a certain number of my good intentions. For instance, I have never touched oysters or mushrooms in the whole of my life (and really, these things are not food but just titillations to make people eat when they have already eaten more than enough – beloved by gluttons and over-eaters – something that slips down easily, and as easily comes up again!). From the same source I derived my lifelong abstention from perfumes – the best smell a body can have is no smell; and from bathing – to stew and weaken the body by perspiration always seemed to me a harmful and effete habit. Some other indulgences which I rejected have now returned to me; but I can say that wherever I abandoned an abstinence I have preserved a moderation, almost amounting to abstinence – perhaps more difficult to achieve than abstinence; there are some things which it is easier to give up altogether than to use with moderation. . . .

[*The Pythagorean teaching of Sotion converted him to vegetarianism*] Under this influence I began to abstain from animal food, and after a year's trial I found it not only an easy but an agreeable system. I believed it made my mind more alert – but I wouldn't now take my oath that it actually did. Why did I give it up? Well, my early years coincided with the beginning of Tiberius's reign, and about that time there was some ado about certain religious rites of foreign origin, in which abstinence from some kinds of animal food was involved. So, at my father's request – not so much in fear of scandal as out of his aversion to philosophic theories – I returned to my normal habits. And I can't say he had much difficulty in persuading me to adopt a more satisfying diet! Another thing that Attalus used to recommend was a hard pillow; and that is the kind I still use in my old age – one which doesn't show the slightest depression after use.

4 *Writing in retirement* (*Ep.*, 8):

I have withdrawn not only from company but from business; and especially from my own business. I am now engaged on posterity's business – writing a few things which may possibly be of use to it. I am putting on paper some of the salutary precepts which, like efficacious medical prescriptions, I have found useful in my own disorders and which have, if not entirely cured, at least prevented them from spreading.

5 *Guilty conscience (Ep., 97)*:

On the other hand, even the most depraved characters retain some sense of good, are not blind to their own depravity but prefer to ignore it – as is shown by the fact that they always try to conceal their crimes and even if the crimes are successful will enjoy the fruits while suppressing the facts of their misconduct. A good conscience is ready to come into the open and be seen by all, but wickedness is afraid even of the dark. Epicurus put it very well when he said: a guilty man *may* escape notice, but he cannot *depend on* escaping notice. Or – if you think this expresses his point more clearly – concealment is little comfort to the sinner, because, though concealment may be his luck, it cannot restore his confidence. True enough: crime can be kept hidden, but it cannot be enjoyed without fear. Looked at in this way, I don't think Epicurus's view is at variance with ours; because (as we say) the chief and greatest punishment that sinners suffer is the fact that they have sinned; no crime – no matter how much it is rewarded by the generosity of fortune, no matter if it be protected or even justified – can remain unpunished, because crime is its own punishment. There remain, of course, also the secondary punishments to harry and dog the criminal – his constant fear, anxiety, and feeling of insecurity. . . . Luck frees many a man from the consequences of sin, but from fear never.

6 *'. . . but thinking makes it so' (Ep., 96)*:

Are you going to complain and protest against any misfortune, and not see that the only misfortune lies in your readiness to complain and protest? The way I look at it is that the one and only disastrous thing that can happen to a man is that he should be capable of thinking any occurrence in nature to be a disaster. The day when I find that I cannot endure something, will be the day when I can no longer endure myself.

7 *Never provoke the powerful (Ep., 14)*:

I think one should take care to avoid giving offence. It may be the people, whom we should fear to offend; it may be, in a state so organized as to give power primarily to a senate, the most influential men of that order; it may be an individual, who holds power for the people and over the people. Not that one should be friends with all these people all the time – that would indeed be difficult; but at least one can avoid making enemies of them. A wise man will never provoke the wrath of the power-ful; rather he will keep out of its way – as a sailor tacks before a storm.

8 *'God is within you'* (*Ep.*, 41):

It is not necessary to raise one's hands to heaven; there is no need to request a verger to give us access to the ear of an image, as though that would secure a closer attention to our petitions. God is near you, with you always, within you. There is, I am sure, a divine spirit within us, which keeps watch and ward over all that is good or bad within us. As we treat him, so he will treat us. No man is good without the presence of God; who can rise above the accidents of fate except by his help? From him comes the prompting to high and noble deeds. In every good man there dwells 'what god we know not, but a very god' [*quoting Virgil, Aeneid*, VIII. 352].

9 *Thinking of death* (*Ep.*, 70):

When external circumstances threaten a man with death, should he take his death into his own hands, or wait until it comes to him? One cannot lay down a general rule; there is much to be said on both sides. But if it is a choice between a painful death under torture and a simple easy death, who shall say that a man should not make an end of himself? As I would select a ship on which to make a voyage, or a house to live in, so I would choose the way to end my life. . . . The law of nature never did anything better than when it prescribed one way of entry into life but many ways out of it. Is there any reason why I should wait to suffer the cruelty of illness or of man, when I might make my own escape from the threats that encompass me and cut loose from all adversity?

10 *Everlasting light* (*Ep.*, 102):

Some day nature will reveal to you all her secrets; this darkness will be dispelled and glorious light break in upon you.
Think of the marvel of that light, in which the light of all the
stars is added together – a perfect light, without a shadow of
darkness. The whole expanse of heaven will be one pure radi-
ance; the distinction of day and night is only a property of our
lower atmosphere. When, totally translated, you look upon the
infinite light, which you now perceive only dimly through the
slits of your eyes, you will know that life has been to you but
darkness. Already, even at a distance, that light is something
which you marvel at; what will you think of the divine light
when you are in its very presence? This is a thought to banish
from one's mind all that is sordid, mean, or cruel; to assure us
that the gods watch over everything that happens; to bid us
earn their goodwill, prepare to meet them, and keep the image
of eternity before our eyes.